The

Boundary Waters Canoe Area

Volume 2: The Eastern Region

Robert Beymer

Wilderness Press
BERKELEY

FIRST EDITION July 1979
Second printing January 1982
Third printing January 1984
SECOND EDITION March 1986
Second printing May 1989
THIRD EDITION April 1991
Second printing August 1992
Third printing June 1995

Photos by the author except as noted

Cover photo by Jerry Stebbins
Foldout map by Roger Butler and Chuck Henderson
Inside maps by Larry Van Dyke
Design by Thomas Winnett

Library of Congress Card Catalog Number 85-40197
International Standard Book Number 0-89997-124-5
Printed in the United States of America
Published by **Wilderness Press**
2440 Bancroft Way
Berkeley, CA 94704
Phone (510) 843-8080/FAX (510) 548-1355

Write for free catalog

Library of Congress Cataloging-in-Publication Data
(Revised for vol. 2)

Beymer, Robert.
The Boundary Waters Canoe Area.

(Wilderness Press trail guide series)
Includes indexes.
Contents: v. 1. The western region — v. 2. The eastern region.
1. Canoes and canoeing—Minnesota—Boundary Waters Canoe Area—Guide-books. 2. Boundary Waters Canoe Area (Minn.)—Guide-books.
I. Title. II. Series.
GV776.M62B6815 1985 917.76 85-40197
ISBN 0-89997-053-2 (pbk. : v. 1)
ISBN 0-89997-124-5 (pbk. : v. 2)

Dedication to My Parents

Gerald J. Beymer—Father and Scoutmaster, who introduced me at a very young age to the joys of a camping experience.

Ruth E. Beymer—Mother and Teacher, who always encouraged me to write about those happy experiences.

Acknowledgments

This book could never have been written without the help and encouragement of many people. It would be impossible to mention all of those who had a part in its creation, but it is only fair to at least mention those who offered the greatest contributions.

Rex and Marcia Miller, my expedition companions and very good friends.

A. O. Berglund, Jr., Director of Camp Northland, and Skipper Berglund, founder of Camp Northland.

Herb Evans, former Director of the Voyageur Visitor Center in Ely, who supplied me with the U.S. Forest Service statistical data contained in the original edition of this book.

Jim Higgins, Resource Assistant in the Gunflint Ranger District, Grand Marais.

Wayne A. Smetanka, District Ranger in the Tofte Ranger District.

Earl Fisher, W. A. Fisher Company, who supplied the maps used for research.

Wally Schuette, Low Industries, who supplied the 17-foot Loweline canoe used for research during the summer of 1978.

Richard A. Smith, Chuckwagon Foods, who supplied the trail food at discount for my research trips.

Tom Fay, Outfitting Manager at Gunflint Northwoods Outfitters, Gunflint Lake.

Bill Hanson, Sawbill Canoe Outfitters, Sawbill Lake.

Barb Soderberg, Superior National Forest Headquarters in Duluth, who supplied data for the revisions of this volume.

Mark Janssen, Manager of Sky Blue Water Lodge, Brule Lake.

Jim Leeds and his family, Tuscarora Lodge and Canoe Outfitters, Round Lake.

Dick Rosvall and Scott L. Johnson, Wilderness Retreat Resort, McFarland Lake.

Al Senty and his family, Sawbill Lodge, Sawbill Lake.

Peter Lytle, Assistant Manager of the Minneapolis Eddie Bauer store, whose complete understanding of my need for a compatible work schedule was *most* appreciated.

Eddie Bauer, Inc. and Neal Warner, Manager of the Minneapolis store, who allowed me the time to complete the research for Volume 2.

Paul W. Loaney, who provided the assistance necessary to complete the "Geology" section of Ch. 1.

Greg Hine, of Hine-Snowbridge Co., who allowed me to field-test his Lite-Serex pack.

Bonnie Wilson, Minnesota Historical Society, who assisted me in finding photo illustrations for both Volumes 1 and 2.

Marcia Kull Miller, Tom Zenanko, Steve Nulsen and Jerry Stebbins, who supplied photographs to illustrate my text.

Thomas Winnett, Editor-in-chief of Wilderness Press, for his faith in the success of this guide and his continuing patience in dealing with me.

All of the good people of Cook, Lake and St. Louis counties, with whom I have become acquainted during my research.

A note of special appreciation to Cheryl McFaul Beymer, who shared the miseries as well as the joys, always offering encouragement to complete this project.

Bob Beymer
St. Paul, Minn.
January 1, 1986

Preface

This book is the result of my ten summers of canoeing in the Boundary Waters Canoe Area. I was introduced to the BWCA in June 1967, along with 14 other members of my Explorer Post in Indianola, Iowa. Not a summer since then has gone by without at least one North Woods canoe trip, usually several.

Since my first summer as a guide in the Boundary Waters, I have seen the need for a published trail guide, and as the number of visitors to this aquatic paradise has grown, the need has become even greater.

During the Summer of 1976, the US Forest Service implemented a new Visitor Distribution Program to "protect the water quality and other physical resources of the area and to assure that opportunities for a high-quality wilderness experience are available to its users." Accordingly, from May 1 through September 30, daily limits have been established for the number of overnight permits that may be issued for each of the designated entry points.

With over a million pristine acres of lakes, rivers and forests within its borders, the BWCA is large enough to accommodate the present usage. In 1984 less than ⅓ of the available quotas were actually used. So why do we need a quota system? Because, unfortunately, in 1976 over ⅔ of the visitors to the BWCA used less than 14% of the 75 designated entry points. The result was (and still is) congestion on such popular lakes as Moose, Saganaga, Fall, Trout and Lake One.

It is my firm belief, however, that there would be no need for a quota system if canoeists only knew of the many entry points and routes available to them. Why would anyone want to paddle out of busy, noisy canoe "terminals" when he could be entering the BWCA through the winding wilderness of Hog Creek, or the beautiful Granite River, or isolated Bower Trout Lake?

This book is designed to help you discover a better way into the BWCA. It was written for the canoe camper who is capable of taking care of himself in a wilderness environment. It does not take you by the hand and lead you through the often complicated mazes of lakes and portages that characterize the

Boundary Waters. It does not always tell you when to turn right, when to veer left, or when to stop and take a picture. You should already possess the understanding and the basic skills that are essential for a canoe trip into a wilderness, particularly the ability to guide yourself along the suggested routes without detailed directions. This book does not include such topics as "what equipment you will need," or "how to plan your food," or "how to shoot a rapids," or "how to pack your gear." Many good "how to" books have been written about canoeing and camping. This guide is a "where to" book. If you need information about techniques, I suggest you read several of the "how to" books and pick out what is appropriate to your needs.

American Red Cross, *Canoeing*. Doubleday: Garden City, NY, 1977.

Bearse, Ray, *The Canoe Camper's Handbook*. New York: Winchester Press, 1944.

Bell, Patricia J., *Roughing It Elegantly*. Eden Prairie, MN: Cat's Paw Press, 1987.

Boy Scouts of America, *Canoeing*. Irving, Texas: B.S.A., by Schmidt, Ernest F, 1977 (revised in 1981).

Cary, Bob, *The Big Wilderness Canoe Manual*. New York: David McKay Company, 1978.

Drabik, Harry, *The Spirit of Canoe Camping*. Minneapolis: Nodin Press, 1981.

Furtman, Michael, *A Boundary Waters Fishing Guide*. Minocqua, Wisconsin: NorthWord Press, 1990.

Furtman, Michael, *Canoe Country Camping: Wilderness Skills for the Boundary Waters and Quetico*. Duluth: Pfeifer-Hamilton, 1992.

Jacobson, Cliff, *Wilderness Canoeing and Camping*. New York: E. P. Dutton, 1977.

Mason, Bill, *Path of the Paddle: An Illustrated Guide to the Art of Canoeing*. Toronto and New York: Van Nostrand and Rinehart, 1983.

Riviere, Bill, Pole, *Paddle and Portage: A Complete Guide to Canoeing*. Boston: Little, Brown & Co., 1974.

Sandreuter, William O., *Whitewater Canoeing*. New York: Winchester Press, 1976.

Stensaas, Mark, *A Field Guide to the Boundary Waters and Quetico*. Duluth: Pfeifer-Hamilton, 1993.

For information about canoeing routes in Superior National Forest outside the BWCA Wilderness or in Ontario's adjacent Quetico Provincial Park, read the author's other two guide books:

Beymer, Robert, *Superior National Forest*. Seattle: The Mountaineers, 1989.
Beymer, Robert, *A Paddler's Guide to Quetico Provincial Park*. Virginia, MN: W. A. Fisher Company, 1985.

For a humorous account of one family's explorations, read: Stresau, Marion, *Canoeing the Boundary Waters*, Edmonds, WA: Signpost Books, 1979.

To capture the mood of canoeing in the BWCA, read any of Sigurd F. Olson's vivid accounts: *Reflections from the North Country, The Hidden Forest, Wilderness Days, Open Horizons, Runes of the North, The Lonely Land, Listening Point, The Singing Wilderness*.

This is a *comprehensive* guide, including all entry points that are useful to canoeists in the eastern half of the Boundary Waters Canoe Area, from Sawbill Lake east to John Lake. Volume 1 deals with the entry points in the western half of the BWCA, from Kawishiwi Lake west to Crane Lake.

Preface to the 3rd Edition

Since the first edition of Volume I was published in 1978, more than 30,000 copies of the two volumes have been sold to inquisitive paddlers in search of routes into the BWCA Wilderness. Over the past 12 years, I've received feedback from friends and strangers alike. Most of the comments have been complimentary and quite positive. My work with camping stores in the Twin Cities and in Ely has given me an opportunity to personally encounter many of my readers—a valuable experience that presents itself to few writers. Because of the feedback received, and because of the continuing research I have conducted from my current home on the Kawishiwi River, there have been many changes made to my guidebooks in successive editions. I've tried to make the books interesting and useful, but above all, my #1 goal has been to impart accurate information.

The only major complaints that I have received pertain to my difficulty ratings for the routes and to the lengths of the trips that I have recommended. I stand by my difficulty ratings, arbitrary as they may be. Since they are totally subjective, however, perhaps an explanation is in order. Two major factors contribute to a difficulty rating: 1) average distance paddled per day, and 2) length, frequency and difficulty of portages along the route. I consider an "average" day in the Wilderness to include about 10 miles of paddling, interrupted by 5 or 6 portages, averaging 50–100 rods in length. This should challenge most folks. Anything less is usually rated "easy," while days with a great deal more paddling and/or longer, more frequent portages might be rated "rugged." The ratings are based on my 22 years of BWCA trips and my experience with all age groups and all experience levels.

Apropos the lengths of the recommended routes, people have requested suggestions for shorter routes. It seems that most paddlers simply don't have more than a week to spare. Consequently, in editions since the first, I've added more route suggestions for 2–4 day trips. These cater to people who intend to do a considerable amount of fishing, stretching a 3-day route over a full week, as well as to people who simply don't have more than a long weekend to spend in the Boundary Waters. In this edition, a whole new section has been added, called *Wilderness Weekends*. It consists of brief suggestions for overnight routes from all of the entry points in the eastern part of the BWCA Wilderness.

Both my publisher and I want my guidebooks to serve *you,* the reader. We'll continue to make changes in the future, reflecting new regulations, alterations to existing routes and the wishes of our readers. If you have suggestions, we'd love to hear from you. Thanks! Have a wonderful wilderness experience. . . .

Preface to the 2nd printing of the 3rd Edition

It may seem odd to the casual wilderness observer that frequent changes are necessary to update this guidebook. "How can a wilderness area change?" you might ask. Well, the wilderness itself has changed very little since this book was first published in 1979. Natural changes do occur, however, and readers need to know about these changes, including the effects of destructive forest fires and wind storms, for instance.

More often, the changes that may significantly affect your visit are caused by decisions of Forest Service administrators. These include changes in laws and regulations governing wilderness management, re-designation of entry points, and other administrative decisions. This new edition includes several decisions recently announced by Forest Service officials that could affect your trip plans. Of greatest significance were 1) the decision to restrict parties to using no more than four canoes and 2) the reduction of the maximum party size from 10 to 9 people. Before this announcement, there was no limit to the number of canoes that a group could use (possibly as many as ten, if each was a solo canoe). Other policy changes include a reduction in the use of towboats by canoe-trip outfitters, a reduction in the daily overnight use quotas for canoeists by over 100 permits per day, a 22% reduction in motor use by overnight campers and day visitors, and the elimination of canoe rests on portage trails. Furthermore, visitor use permits will be required year-round for all types of travel, including day-use nonmotor travel. Bear in mind, however, that all of these changes are subject to appeal and litigation (a lawsuit was pending when this edition went to press). So, stay tuned. . . .Even though we try to keep this book as current as possible, it is always wise for you to check before your trip with Forest Service officials about any new or revised regulations affecting the BWCA Wilderness.

Contents

Ch. 1: Introduction to the BWCA 1

History 1

Wildlife.. 2

Fires 3

Bears... 4

Safety 5

Climate... 6

Geology 7

Can the Wilderness Survive You? 11

A True Wilderness? 16

Ch. 2: How To Plan a Trip 18

Maps 21

Obtaining Travel Permits.......................... 22

Heavy Use Periods................................ 24

Rules and Regulations 25

Primitive Management Areas....................... 26

Provisions of the BWCA Wilderness Act 27

A Final Word 29

Ch. 3: Entry from the Sawbill Trail: The Southeastern Area................ 31

#38 Sawbill Lake 31

#39 Baker Lake................................... 38

#40 Homer Lake................................... 45

#41 Brule Lake 51

Ch. 4: Entry from the Gunflint Trail: The Northeastern Area................ 59

#43 Bower Trout Lake 59

#44 Ram Lake 66

#45 Morgan Lake 72
#47 Lizz Lake 74
#48 Meeds Lake 78
#65 Portage Lake 85
#50 Cross Bay Lake 90
#51 Missing Link Lake 96
#52 Brant Lake 103
#54 Seagull Lake 109
#55 Saganaga Lake 115

Ch. 5: Entry from the Gunflint Trail: The Tip of the Arrowhead Area 121
#80 Larch Creek 121
#57 Magnetic Lake 125
#58 South Lake 131
#60 Duncan Lake 136
#61 Daniels Lake 141
#62 Clearwater Lake 144
#64 East Bearskin Lake 148

Ch. 6: Entry from the Arrowhead Trail: The Tip of the Arrowhead Area 153
#68 Pine Lake 153
#69 John Lake 157
#70 North Fowl Lake 160

Ch. 7: Wilderness Weekends 165

Appendix I: Routes Categorized by Difficulty and Duration 173

Appendix II: BWCA Travel Zone Data 175

Appendix III: BWCA Travel Permit Data 176

Appendix IV: Canoe Trip Outfitters 177

Sketch maps 178

Index 181

There is magic in the feel of a paddle and the movement of a canoe,
a magic compounded of distance, adventure, solitude, and peace.
The way of a canoe is the way of the wilderness and of freedom almost forgotten.
It is an antidote to insecurity, the open door to water ways of ages past, and a way of life with profound and abiding satisfactions.
When a man is part of his canoe, he is part of all that canoes have ever known.

——*Sigurd F. Olson*

Ch. 1: Introduction to the BWCA

The Boundary Waters Canoe Area is paradise for the wilderness canoeist. Stretching for nearly 200 miles along the Canadian border of northeastern Minnesota, this magnificent wilderness offers over 1,200 miles of canoe routes through some of the most beautiful country in the world. That's why over 180,000 people visit it each year. At over a million acres, it is the second largest unit of the National Wilderness Preservation system, containing the largest virgin forests remaining east of the Rocky Mountains.

HISTORY

The canoe routes on which you will paddle are the very same ones used for hundreds of years by the Sioux and Chippewa Indians and by the French-Canadian Voyageurs. Jacques de Noyons, in about 1688, was probably the first white man to paddle through the lakes and streams that now compose the BWCA. At that time, the Sioux may have still been the dominant Indians in the area. But by the time of the first fur traders in the 18th Century, the Chippewas had moved into the region from the east and had driven the Sioux farther west onto the plains. From then to about 1800, French-Canadian Voyageurs paddled their birch-bark canoes from the hinterlands of northwestern Canada to the shores of Lake Superior, transporting furs from trappers toward the European markets.

During the latter half of the 19th Century, settlers moved into the area, including farmers, loggers and miners. After the railroad penetrated the area, extensive logging and mining operations threatened to devastate the entire region.

The Superior National Forest was designated in 1909, and within it, in 1926, one thousand acres were set aside as a primitive roadless area. This area was enlarged in the 1930's and in 1939 the wilderness area was redesignated the Superior Roadless Primitive Area, establishing boundaries containing over one million acres. In 1958 the current name was adopted. And the BWCA Wilderness Bill of 1978 established the current boundaries, containing 1,075,000 acres. It also prohibits logging, restricts mining operations and limits the use of motorboats to 33% of the water area in 1979 (24% after 1999). The BWCA is regulated by the U.S. Forest Service.

Thanks to the efforts of conservationists throughout the years, this beautiful regions looks almost the same today as it did when De Noyons first viewed it.

WILDLIFE

Nothing represents the Boundary Waters better than the eerie "laughter" of the loon, the Minnesota State Bird. But many other birds are equally at home here, including the bald eagle, the gull, the great blue heron, and the Canadian jay. In the BWCA you will also find the last substantial population of timber wolves in the "lower forty-eight," as well as a large population of moose, white-tailed deer, black bear, beaver and fox. Other mammals include the lynx, fisher, mink, muskrat, otter, marten, weasel, coyote, and a variety of squirrels.

The predominant game fishes are northern pike, walleye, smallmouth bass and lake trout. Crappies and bluegill are also plentiful in some of the lakes. Even rainbow and brook trout have been stocked in some lakes.

The North Woods are covered largely by a coniferous forest, made up of jack pine, Norway pine, white pine, tamarack, black spruce, white spruce, balsam fir and white cedar. There are also extensive stands of deciduous trees, including paper birch and quaking aspen. Very few land areas in the BWCA are not forested.

FIRES

Under a new Forest Service policy implemented in 1987, lightning-caused fires in the BWCA Wilderness may be allowed to burn without suppression if the fires fall within certain "prescribed" limits regarding location, risks to property and public safety, weather factors and other conditions. Fires that are not within prescribed limits, and all human-caused fires, will be suppressed, as they have been in the past.

For centuries, large areas of the Wilderness burned every decade from lightning-caused fires. Periodic fires were credited with reducing fuel accumulations and creating diverse wildlife habitats. The new fire policy is intended to partly restore fire to its natural role in the wilderness, whenever it can occur within the limits of safety.

Efforts will be made by the Forest Service to inform the public about ongoing fire activity. Notices will be posted at canoe landings, and USFS field crews will notify paddlers within the Wilderness about threatening blazes.

You may encounter natural fires in the BWCA Wilderness. Forest Service personnel may not be present at the site, although all fires will be under some form of surveillance. If you choose to observe the fire, please do so from a safe distance, and consider the following safety tips:

- Fires normally move in the same direction as the wind. Find a safe location away from the fire's path.
- Be careful while visiting a recently burned area. Ashes may remain hot for days, and there is a danger of falling snags and tree limbs.

- Do not attempt to put a prescribed fire out. As a natural fire, it is part of the wilderness. It will cause ecological changes that are consistent with wilderness management.
- Fires may smolder and burn very slowly for days or even weeks without much increase in size. Then weather changes can cause dramatic and dangerous increases in fire size. Respect all fires as potentially dangerous.

Although wilderness fires will bring positive benefits to the forest, fire can also be devastating. Visitors are reminded of their responsibility to prevent human-caused fires. The long-standing Smokey Bear message of fire prevention is still valid. Please be careful!

BEARS

Black bears are common throughout the BWCA. Although they are not considered to be dangerous and are usually quite shy around campers, they may be pests when searching for food—your food. They are becoming more aggressive every year.

Over the years they have learned that canoe campers always travel with food packs. And where campers are most frequently found camping, bears are most frequently a problem. An unpleasant encounter with a bear could bring an abrupt end to your canoe trip. There are no hard and fast rules to insure protection from a bear. Bear behavior differs under different conditions. The bears you may encounter while visiting the BWCA are wild animals, and they *could* be dangerous. Always remember that! Nevertheless, with a few precautions, you will have no problem with these fascinating creatures.

1. Never store food in your tent. If food has been spilled on your clothes, leave the clothes outside your tent at night too.
2. When you are away from your campsite (even just fishing nearby!) and at night, always hang your food pack at least 10 feat above the ground and *away* from tree trunks. Bears are good tree climbers, so the food must be a safe distance (6 feet or more) away from the trunk and from any limbs large enough to support a bear's weight.
3. When you leave your campsite, tie your tent flaps open.

Bears are inquisitive animals, and they may want to tour your shelter. If the tent is closed, they could make a new doorway.

4. Keep a clean campsite. Burn all food scraps and left-over grease. Do not dispose of leftovers in the latrine. Bears will find them and destroy the latrine in the process.
5. Don't let an island campsite lull you into a false sense of security. Bears are very good swimmers.
6. Never get between a mother and her cub(s). If you see a cub, you can be sure the mother is nearby. Female bears are extremely protective of their young.
7. If a bear does wander into your campsite, don't panic! They are usually easily frightened off by loud noises. Try yelling or banging some cooking pots together. Don't charge the bear; it may become defensive.
8. If a bear does not back off or acts strangely, move to another campsite. It's extremely rare for a bear to attack a human being; but it did happen to two campers in separate incidents (same bear) during the summer of 1987. Neither camper was seriously injured, and the bear was later killed by authorities. (Note: this was the *only* such incident during the 22 years that I've been camping in the BWCA Wilderness.)
9. Finally, with all that said, don't lose any sleep worrying about the sounds you hear outside your tent at night. The noisiest critters are also the smallest—mice among the worst! Bears are among the quietest animals in the woods. If you hear rustling leaves at night, chances are good that it's not caused by a bear. Rest assured!

SAFETY

Risk is an integral part of a wilderness trek. Risks associated with isolation, tough physical challenges, adverse weather conditions and lack of rapid communications are inherent in a visit to the BWCA. At all times exercise caution, use common sense, and consider the following tips:

1. Do not take chances to save time.
2. Always wear a life preserver, even if you can swim.

3. Do not attempt canoe travel during a lightning storm or when waves are running.
4. Never stand in a canoe; keep weight low and centered.
5. If you should capsize, stay with the canoe; it won't sink.
6. Use the portages. Do not run rapids unless you are confident you can do it safely, and only after you have scouted them. Remember that water levels change considerably during the summer months. A rapids that may have been perfectly safe to run during your last trip in August could be a dangerous, raging torrent during your next trip in June. Canoeing mishaps occur almost every summer in the Boundary Waters. Some result in drownings. Many result in damaged canoes. Most result in spoiled trips.
7. Carry a good first-aid kit and know how to use it. See to it that *every* member of your group knows CPR.
8. In the event of serious accident, send one canoe for help immediately. Or use a heavy smoke signal to attract a Forest Service patrol plane. Evacuation by plane or other motorized vehicle is approved only when there are no other alternatives available and a person needs the immediate services of a doctor. All emergency searches, rescues and evacuations are authorized by the local county sheriff. If an evacuation is necessary, you will be billed for expenses incurred.
9. Boil or treat water before drinking. Even then, if algae are visible, don't drink the water. Although lake water may *look* pure, drinking it without first filtering, boiling or treating it may cause illness. When using a filter or chemicals, be certain that they are designed to remove or kill *Giardia lamblia*, in particular—a nasty parasite that can cause a harsh intestinal illness.
10. Before setting out on your trip, be sure that someone—Forest Service official, outfitter or friend—knows your itinerary and when you expect to return, with instructions to contact authorities if you are overdue.

CLIMATE

For the canoeist in northern Minnesota, spring, summer and fall are essentially crowded into a span of about five months—May through September. The ice is usually off the lakes by the first week in May, but the trees aren't fully leafed out until at least the middle of the month. That period before the biting insects invade the North Country is an excellent time to explore the tiny creeks that may later be too low for easy navigation. But be prepared for weather cold enough to produce snow. Early June is often a wet, cool and gloomy time of year, usually plagued by hordes of mosquitoes, sand flies and ticks. The fishing is best then. July and early August normally offer the best weather for campers and the worst for anglers (too nice!). As the summer progresses, however, the water levels of some shallow streams may become too low for navigating a loaded canoe, eliminating some excellent route possibilities. From late August through September, after the first hard frost, biting insects have nearly disappeared and so have most visitors. This is a wonderful time to explore the wilderness, but you must be prepared for extended periods of cool and rainy weather, or even snow. After September, contact local authorities for weather updates. It is not unusual to see the lakes ice over in October, and snow may accumulate on the ground.

Temperatures and rainfall vary, of course, throughout the BWCA. The following statistics, recorded in International Falls, represent approximations for the Boundary Waters Canoe Area.

	May	**June**	**July**	**Aug.**	**Sept.**
Average temperature	51°	60°	66°	63°	53°
Average low each day	38°	48°	53°	51°	41°
Average high each day	63°	72°	78°	76°	64°
Precipitation	2.6″	3.9″	3.5″	3.6″	2.9″

Because of its close proximity to Lake Superior, the eastern part of the BWCA sometimes exhibits extremely variable weather. While the lakes in the far eastern region may be blanketed with a cool, misty fog from Lake Superior, nearby lakes to the northwest may be enjoying warm sunshine, thanks to the subtle yet significant effect of the Laurentian Divide. Consequently, no weather data from any one reporting station can accurately represent all of the BWCA's eastern region.

GEOLOGY

It would take another volume to do justice to the geologic history of this incredible country. But it would also be an injustice, perhaps, to not mention it at all.

The rocks in this area are dominantly Precambrian rocks covered by a thin veneer of glacial deposits. For two billion years, during the Precambrian period, vast changes were generated by a large amount of diverse geologic activity that persisted over the area and redefined it many times. Erosion predominated after this until roughly one million years ago, when the great ice sheets of the Pleistocene Epoch began to form. The ice scoured the Precambrian bedrock, gouging out the softer rocks and leaving behind irregular blankets of glacial debris. This created the topography that we see today.

Underneath the Boundary Waters Canoe Area is some of the oldest rock in the world, as old as three billion years. It is part of the vast rock area known as the Canadian Shield, which underlies almost two million square miles of eastern Canada and the Lake Superior region of the United States. In Minnesota this belt of ancient exposed rock extends west from the area of Saganaga Lake on the international border through Ely and International Falls to the northwest part of the state, where the old rocks disappear beneath younger sedimentary deposits. Included in this expanse of ancient rocks are the metavolcanic Ely Greenstone formation, the metasedimentary Knife Lake Group and great granitic *batholiths* like the Vermilion and the Saganaga batholiths. All are known to be older than 2.6 billion years. That date marks the events of the Algoman *orogeny* (mountain-building period), during which the rocks became metamorphosed and strongly deformed, and the granites were intruded from below into the older rocks.

A long period of erosion followed the Algoman orogeny. Rocks that had been formed or altered deep within the earth's crust became exposed at the surface and subjected to erosion. The geologic events that may have been of the most economic significance to the state of Minnesota began with the encroachment of a broad arm of the ocean upon the eroded terrain. Inland seas covered most of what we now call the North Woods. Layers of sedimentary rocks were deposited at the bottom of that enormous sea. Called the Animikie Group, these rocks lie in a belt extending westward along the border lakes from Lake Superior to just south of Saganaga Lake, and then reappearing in the Mesabi Range south of the BWCA. The Animikie rocks include the Pokegama quartzite, the Biwabik iron formation and a sequence of shales and sandstones. Flint, too, is found in abundance in the vicinity of Gunflint Lake. Rich deposits of iron ore are scattered throughout northeastern Minnesota. It is so concentrated in some places that it will cause your compass needle to be deflected from magnetic north. Magnetic Lake, in fact, received its name because of just such a phenomenon.

Around 1.7 to 1.6 billion years ago, another period of mountain building occurred. During the Penokean orogeny the Animikie sedimentary rocks and other existing rocks were folded, faulted, metamorphosed and intruded by granitic *magmas*. Later an outpouring of tens of thousands of feet of lava in and around the area now occupied by Lake Superior created the major rock of the "North Shore." After this volcanic activity subsided, stream erosion and deposition again became the dominant processes in the area.

The inland seas had long since disappeared and new mountains had risen on the continent when the great ice sheet of the Ice Age advanced from the north and began to cover the state of Minnesota. It was the ice sheet that turned this mineral-rich region into the world's best canoe country. During four major periods of glaciation, the glaciers altered the landscape considerably. These periods began perhaps almost one million years ago.

During the last glacial advance and recession (the Wisconsin Glaciation, lasting from about 100,000 to 10,000 years ago), a very distinctive glacial ridge called the Vermilion *moraine* was deposited. The Vermilion Moraine, composed of gray-colored sand and stone, extends from the little town of Isabella to a point southeast of International Falls, bounding lakes Vermilion and Nett. During an earlier advance, the Toimi *drumlins* (isolated oblong hills) were formed in an area south-southeast of the Vermilion moraine and the town of Isabella.

Evidence of the Ice Age is everywhere in the Boundary Waters today. Parallel grooves called *striations* are visible on many rock ledges that were scoured by the ice. Glacial debris unsorted as to size, from small pebbles to huge boulders, is widespread. Here and there one sees large boulders, called *erratics*, which were left "stranded" when the glaciers melted.

Perhaps the greatest distinction of the border lakes area is the domination of exposed bedrock. This region is unlike the rest of the state, which is almost completely covered by glacial deposits, and that explains why there are so many rock-rimmed lakes in the BWCA. The domination of exposed bedrock in the Boundary Waters results in distinctive patterns of lakes and ridges, which reflect the underlying rock structure.

In the eastern third of the area the lakes form a distinctive linear pattern. Long, narrow lakes give the terrain a notable east-west "grain." These lakes are set in two major types of rocks: in the Duluth Gabbro rock, which is a coarse-grained igneous rock, and in the Rove Slate formation, which is a sequence of sedimentary rocks made up mostly of a dark, fine-grained slate.

The lakes on the Duluth Gabbro, which is exposed over an area from Duluth north and east to the Pigeon River, developed their particular pattern because alternating bands of less resistant rock and more resistant rock are oriented east-west. Erosion has removed more of the less resistant rock, creating lake basins. In the area where the Rove Slate formation is exposed—along the international border from Gunflint Lake to Pigeon Point (the Tip of the Arrowhead region)—the east-west linear pattern has a different cause. In this area intervening ridges separate the lakes. These ridges are the exposed edges of south-dipping layers of dark igneous rock that was intruded into the slate after the sedimentary rocks were deposited. The north-facing slopes of the ridges are very steep and form escarpments 200–400 feet high. Huge piles of talus blocks cover the lower parts of many escarpments, the result of erosion by the advancing glaciers as they passed transversely over the ridges. Good examples are found at the northwest end of Brule Lake and at the south end of Gasket Lake.

The lakes set in the Knife Lake group of rocks show a similar linear pattern, but the trend is northeastward. And in the rocks associated with the Ely Greenstone, the pattern is less regular and the depressions in the bedrock are not as deep, resulting in shallower lakes.

In the area underlain by the Saganaga Granite the story is a little different. Here the shapes of the lakes are dictated by cracks in the Precambrian rock. As the cracks were made wider by erosion, they became linear depressions which lakes could occupy. Many of the lakes lie in collections of linear depressions oriented in more than one direction, so that the lakes have zigzag shapes. An overhead view of the area reveals many jagged lakes interconnected by linear channels. Saganaga Lake itself is a good example.

Because of the glaciation of the Ice Age and the characteristic Precambrian rock of northeastern Minnesota, the Boundary Waters Canoe Area has the highest concentation of lakes in the state, which itself has the most lakes of any state.

Thanks largely to the Ice Age, the Boundary Waters Canoe Area, with all its interconnected lakes and streams, is one of the most beautiful and certainly one of the most extraordinary recreational wilderness areas of the world.

CAN THE WILDERNESS SURVIVE YOU?

A wilderness, in contrast with those areas where man and his own works dominate the landscape, is hereby recognized as an area where the earth and its community of life are untrammeled by man, where man himself is a visitor who does not remain.

Using this definition. Congress passed the Wilderness Act of 1964 and created the National Wilderness Preservation System. Included as the only water-based wilderness, and the largest wilderness in the lower 48 states, the BWCA is also the most heavily used wilderness in America, visited by as many as 180,000 people each year. Many of these visitors are not familiar with minimum-impact camping techniques and the need to protect the fragile wilderness resource from damage. Litter strewn along portages and left in fire grates; birch trees stripped of bark; red and white pines carved with initials; and fire-blackened areas resulting from campfires left burning are just some of the signs of abuse seen far too often in the BWCA. Other problems caused by the large number of visitors may be less permanent but still inappropriate in a wilderness setting: large, noisy groups shouting across the lake or singing boisterously around a campfire, and bright-colored equipment easily seen from across a lake—all detract from the feeling of quiet and solitude that wilderness visitors seek.

Wilderness areas are managed to protect and maintain the environment in its natural state for our enjoyment and for the enjoyment of generations to come. The responsibility for protecting these areas lies not only with professional managers, however. As a visitor, *you and your group also share in this responsibility*. You must realize your place within the wilderness not as a conqueror, but as a wise keeper and a good steward of this land and water. By simply utilizing the following suggestions of the United States Forest Service and adhering to the rules and regulations of the BWCA, you will ensure a quality wilderness experience for yourself and others, as well as preserve the area for generations to come.

Pre-Trip Planning

A safe, enjoyable wilderness experience starts at home with careful planning. First, ask yourself and members of your group if you really want a trip into the wilderness—a place where you'll find no piped water, prepared shelters, predictable weather or easy travel. Wilderness travelers cannot count on signs to direct the way; they must know how to read a map and use a compass. In an area which is unfamiliar and sometimes downright hostile, you must be your own doctor, guide and entertainer—prepared for accidents, changes in weather and such obstacles as high winds on large lakes.

Vacationing with a group of people is always challenging, because of variations in skills, interests and physical strength. Get your group together ahead of time to plan your trip. Talk about what each person is looking for and expects on the trip. Decide as a group where to go, when to go, what equipment to take along and what to eat. By looking at these things ahead of time, the group will have a better idea of what to expect from the trip, and there will be fewer "surprises" to dampen spirits. Consider not only the good aspects of BWCA canoe trips—warm sun-drenched afternoons on sky-blue lakes, cooled slightly by a mere whisper of a breeze—but also the dreaded conditions that plague many trips—hordes of hungry flying insects, fish with no appetite at all, long and muddy portage trails, prolonged periods of cold rain, and gale-force winds that make canoe travel extremely difficult or virtually impossible. Both trip scenarios are possible—indeed likely—at one time or another. Be psychologically and physically prepared for the worst.

If at all possible, keep your group size small. Few campsites have tent pads for more than two or three tents. Some are barely large enough for one tent. If your group will be large, plan to split up and travel separately. Better yet, plan completely different routes. You'll have more pictures and experiences to share when you get home. A small group has much less impact on the wilderness and on other visitors.

Equipment: When selecting equipment for your trip, choose environmentally "natural" colored tents, packs and clothing to help you travel and camp inconspicuously. Bright colors contribute to a crowded feeling. Carry a small stove and fuel to use when dry wood is hard to find. Stoves heat more cleanly, quickly and evenly than campfires. Axes and hatchets are not necessary. There is plenty of suitable firewood which can easily be broken or cut with a small camp saw. See that at least one person in each canoe carries a map and a compass, and knows how to use both. Kept in a plastic case and tied to the canoe, the map is readily available for quick and constant reference. Line your packs with large, heavy plastic bags, to keep all the contents dry. And, by all means, practice packing before you leave home. Remember, everything you pack will have to be carried—by *you.*

Clothes: Clothing needs may vary somewhat from season to season, but always plan for all extremes. *Layering* is the most efficient method to stay warm and dry. Lightweight cotton is ideal for warm weather, while wool, even when wet, provides warmth on chilly days and at night. Good raingear is essential, and it can also serve as a great windbreaker on cold, windy days. Bring two pairs of footwear, boots or sturdy walking shoes for portaging, and sneakers or moccasins for walking around the campsite. Wearing the latter at the camp site is not only kind to your feet; it also causes less soil-compaction damage to the site.

Food: Since cans and bottles are not allowed in the BWCA, some foods will have to be repacked in plastic bags or in other plastic containers. If possible, pack each meal's food together in a larger bag to make meal preparation easier.

Travel

When planning your trip route, make sure you aren't overly ambitious. Consider all members of the group, and plan to travel at the speed of the least experienced paddler. It's a good idea to plan for a layover day or two. You'll have more time to fish or relax, and, if you run into rough weather, you won't have to worry about taking unnecessary chances just to stay on schedule.

Respect for other wilderness visitors starts before you ever leave home. Practice picking up a canoe and other canoeing skills before you head out on your trip. The first portage is no place to try to figure out how to get the canoe up on your shoulders.

If a portage is crowded, patiently wait on the water for your turn. Load and unload your canoe as quickly as possible, keeping your gear together off to the side and out of the way of any other people. Avoid dragging your canoe across rocks. Not only does it damage the canoe, but the noise can also be heard a great distance away. Move as quickly as possible across portages; don't stop for rest breaks or for lunch. Know who is responsible for each pack, each canoe and each piece of miscellaneous equipment *before* setting foot on the trail. Accountability reduces the possibility of leaving something behind.

Wildlife Precautions

While traveling throughout the BWCA, always treat the wildlife with respect. Remember, you are a visitor in the wilderness but the wildlife are residents. You can help the wildlife stay wild and healthy by not feeding the creatures and not interfering with their normal routines. Where campsites are kept clean and food packs are suspended between trees properly, bears are generally not a problem. Nor are the smaller pests that might otherwise depend on humans for their sustenance (i.e., chipmunks, mice and their cousins). Seeing a bear on a canoe trip should be a treat, not a tragedy. (See BEARS above.)

If you are fortunate enough to see loons on your wilderness trip, keep your distance. Don't chase them down the lake or holler to them. Should you find yourself near any nesting birds (loons, bald eagles, herons, gulls, etc.), observe the nesting area from a distance. Human disturbance at a nest site may lead to nest abandonment and loss of eggs.

Moose, deer, beavers, otters, mink, owls, hawks and ospreys are just a few of the many kinds of animals that may be seen by peaceful paddlers. The more quietly a group travels, the greater its chances of seeing wildlife.

Dogs: Though dogs are not banned from the wilderness, they are better off left home. Many dogs become real barkers, even if they never bark at home. Other visitors don't want to listen to barking all night long. Other dogs may charge wild animals, including bears. If you choose to bring your dog, it must be kept on a leash at landings and on portages.

Camping

Plan to make camp early enough in the day to assure finding an available campsite. Consider sites that are off the main travel routes and in back bays. They are used less often and offer a better opportunity for privacy.

Most wilderness visitors are there for solitude. . .quiet. . . to seek respite from the hustle and bustle of day- to-day urban living. Each person wants the sensation of being the first and only person in an area. Loud shouting, singing and dogs barking from across the lake are not appreciated.

Tent pads are provided at each developed campsite. Trenching and cutting pine boughs for "mattresses" (once accepted practices) are not only *not* necessary; they are illegal in the BWCA, because of the environmental harm they inflict. If your tent is bright-colored, set it up as far from the shore as possible, so that it cannot be seen by other campers across the lake.

Remember that noise travels a great distance across water. Keep group noise to a minimum, and you'll improve the quality of the wilderness experience for yourself and for others. You will also greatly improve your chance of seeing wildlife.

Dead, downed wood for campfires is abundant in the BWCA—though not always at the campsites. The best place to look is back from the shore, away from campsites. Usually the driest wood is found on fallen trees that are leaning against other windfalls, and not lying directly on the ground. The best wood for campfires comes from dead, dry jack pine, white pine, spruce, tamarack, white cedar, aspen and ash. Paper birch is excellent firewood when cut green, split and dried, but it is usually very poor when found lying on the ground, because it rots quickly. Red pine and balsam fir are also poor firewoods. ***Do not cut live trees!*** Green wood from any tree burns very poorly, if at all. Damage to live trees (cutting, carving or peeling bark) is not only unsightly: it also causes irreparable damage to the forest and it's illegal. Carry some fire ribbon or other starting material to ignite fires in wet weather.

Before heading for the lake to wash dishes, remember: you will get the water for tomorrow morning's coffee from the same place. Soapy water should *never* end up in the lake. Take your dishes and hot water back away from the lake to wash them. Rinse them well and dump all the water at least 150 feet from the lake to avoid polluting it. Likewise, when you feel the urge to wash yourself, jump in the lake to get wet, then soap up and rinse off at least 150 feet from the shore.

Burn all left-over food in a ***hot*** fire. If you must bury left-overs or fish entrails, paddle along the shore away from campsites, go into the woods at least 150 feet from the water and bury it in six to eight inches of soil. *Do not use the latrine as a garbage can,* since bears will tear the toilet box out to get at leftovers.

Put your fire *dead* out anytime you leave it unattended—even if you just go fishing for a while. Pour water over the fire while stirring the ashes. Then, if you feel any warmth in the ashes with your bare hand, douse the ashes again.

Leave No Trace

The general rule for disposal of litter and leftovers is *eat it, burn it or pack it out*. When leaving a campsite, leave no trace of your presence there. After a fire is dead out, sift through the ashes for twist ties, foil and other debris not completely burned. Pack them in your litter bag, along with any cigarette filters or other trash, and carry them out. Add to that any litter found on portages and at canoe landings. Always leave an area cleaner than you found it. Unfortunately, that isn't hard to do.

A TRUE WILDERNESS?

There are those purists who would not classify the BWCA as a true wilderness. In one sense, they are right. Regulations dictate that you must camp only in Forest Service campsites, which are equipped with stationary fire grates and box latrines. There are obvious signs all around you that other people have camped at the very same spot many, many times before.

There are also those who declare that you must paddle for weeks before you can truly feel a sensation of "wilderness." Regarding the BWCA, I must disagree. Seldom are more than one or two long portages necessary for the BWCA visitor to perceive true wilderness around him. The disquieting drone of motors fades into the past, and one enters a new world of only natural sensations. Depending on your point of entry, it could take a day, or maybe two, to find wilderness. On the other hand, it may be waiting only minutes from your launching site, scarcely more than a stone's throw away from the road's end. Wherever you start, a magnificent wilderness is not far away in the BWCA.

Wilderness involves emotions.
A wilderness experience is an emotional experience.
If a person cannot sense deep emotion while camped
on the shores of some placid wilderness lake,
hearing the cry of a loon,
he will never understand the pleas of those who
would save
the Boundary Waters Canoe Area.

——*Charles Ericksen*

Ch. 2: How to Plan a Trip

This guide covers all of the useful entry points in the eastern half of the Boundary Waters, from Sawbill Lake east to McFarland Lake—those accessible from the Sawbill Trail, the Gunflint Trail and the Arrowhead Trail. Volume I covered all the practical entry points in the western half of the BWCA—those accessible from the Echo Trail, the Fernberg Trail and State Highway 1: from Crane Lake east to Kawishiwi Lake. Although each volume suggests entirely different routes, the central part of the BWCA (between the Fernberg Trail and the Gunflint Trail) is included in both volumes.

Each volume is an accumulation of *suggestions*. It does not give all possible routes into the BWCA. Quite the contrary, the routes that you could take are virtually infinite in number. Furthermore, you may wish to follow only a part of one route, or you may wish to combine two or more routes. Nearly all the routes suggested are "round trip"—they begin and end at (or within walking distance of) the same location. For most routes there is no need for a car shuttle between two points.

Any group entering the Boundary Waters must have in its possession a travel permit, granting permission to enter through one of the 83 designated entry points. Since this guide treats only the eastern half of the Boundary Waters, and since not all entry points are well suited for canoeists, only 25 entry points are discussed in this book:

38 Sawbill Lake
39 Baker Lake
40 Homer Lake
41 Brule Lake
43 Bower Trout Lake
44 Ram Lake
45 Morgan Lake
47 Lizz Lake
48 Meeds Lake
50 Cross Bay Lake
51 Missing Link Lake
52 Brant Lake

54	Seagull Lake	62	Clearwater Lake
55	Saganaga Lake	64	East Bearskin Lake
57	Magnetic Lake	65	Portage Lake
80	Larch Creek	68	McFarland Lake
58	South Lake	69	Pine Lake
60	Duncan Lake	70	North Fowl Lake
61	Daniels Lake		

Ten other entry points exist in the eastern half of the Boundary Waters, but they are not included in this guide for the following reasons.

Some are used mostly by hikers:

56	Kekekabic Trail (East)	78, 79	Eagle Mountain Trails
59	South Lake Trail	81, 82, 83	Border Route Trails

Three serve areas that are better served by adjacent entry points:

46 Swamp Lake (Lizz Lake)
49 Skipper Lake (Portage Lake)
66 Crocodile River (East Bearskin Lake)

The routes included in this guide are grouped according to accessibility: 1) those accessible from the Sawbill Trail, 2) those accessible from and *west* of the Gunflint Trail, 3) those accessible from and *east* of the Gunflint Trail, and 4) those accessible from the Arrowhead Trail.

Using statistical data and personal observations, each entry point is briefly discussed. Statistics given pertain to the Summer of 1989, the most recent data available when this book was revised.

1. **Permits:** The estimated number of overnight travel permits issued to groups using the entry point in 1989, using all modes of transportation.
2. **Popularity Rank:** The relative popularity of the entry point, based on total use, compared with all other entry points (total of 77 categories in 1989).
3. **Daily Quota:** The maximum number of overnight travel permits that can be issued each day to groups using the entry point.

Further discussion includes the entry point's location, how to get there, public campgrounds nearby, amount of motorized use through the entry point, and other comments of interest to canoeists.

Following the discussion of an entry point are the suggested routes that use that entry point. Introductory remarks tell you: 1) how many days to allow; 2) the approximate number of miles; 3) the number of different lakes, rivers and creeks to be encountered, as well as the number of portages en route; 4) the difficulty (easy, challenging or rugged), based largely on the frequency, length and difficulty of portages; 5) Fisher maps that cover the route; 6) travel zones through which you will paddle, listed in sequential order (Note: An appendix in the back of this guide provides information about each of the travel zones mentioned in this volume); and 7) general comments, including fishing opportunities. Then each route is broken down into suggested days, giving the sequence of lakes, streams and portages, followed by points of special interest.

> *Example: DAY 2:* **Little Trout Lake,** p. (portage) 376 rods, **Little Indian Sioux River,** p. 40 rods, river, p. 35 rods, river, p. 20 rods, river, p. 120 rods, **Otter Lake,** p. 5 rods, **Cummings Lake.**

Explanation: On the hypothetical second day of this route, you will paddle across Little Trout Lake, and portage 376 rods to the Little Indian Sioux River. You will follow the river to Otter Lake, negotiating four portages along the way. Finally, you will portage 5 rods from Otter Lake to Cummings Lake and make camp there at one of the campsites marked by a red dot on the Fisher map.

A word about travel zones: In the introduction to each canoe route are listed the numbers of the travel zones through which that route passes. In order to acquire statistical data about the travel patterns of canoeists, the Forest Service designated 49 zones in the BWCA. For several years, information was compiled at year's end to statistically summarize the visitation patterns of the previous summer. This has been condensed into Appendix II at the end of this book. It offers you a quick "look" at the regions through which your canoe route will pass. This information, combined with that found in Appendix III (Travel Permit Data), will give you a fairly good idea of just how "busy" your proposed route is. And that might be a factor in determining whether the route is suitable for you.

A word about the use of rods: One rod equals 16½ feet. Since this is roughly the length of most canoes, it is the unit of linear measurement used in canoe country. The Forest Service has posted wood signs indicating the number of rods at the beginnings of some portage trails in the BWCA, and the Fisher maps also use this unit of measurement. However, the indicated number of rods tells little about the difficulty of a portage. Long ones may be quite easy, and short ones may be extremely tough. This guide will warn you about the tough ones.

Of course, any route may be made more difficult by completing it in fewer days than recommended, or made easier by adding days. If you plan to do a great deal of fishing, you should probably add at least one day for each three days suggested. For longer trips, you may also want to add layover days to your schedule, in the event that wind, foul weather, sickness or injury should slow you down. (Always carry an extra day's supply of food too, for just that reason.

In the discussions of routes in this book, reference is often made to the number of canoe rests found along a portage in the BWCA Wilderness. These horizontal-log resting spots were originally built and maintained throughout the Boundary Waters to make portaging a bit easier. This information is included in the route descriptions to help canoeists better gauge their progress across portages. It has been the policy of the Forest Service in recent years, however, not to maintain these canoe rests. You may actually find fewer rests than are mentioned in the various route descriptions.

MAPS

It would be nearly impossible to show detailed maps on the pages of this book. Instead, you will find a foldout map of the entire eastern region inside the back cover. When taking your trip, however, I recommend the waterproof-parchment maps published by the W. A. Fisher Company. Twenty-eight "F series" maps combine to cover all the Boundary Waters Canoe Area and Canada's Quetico Provincial Park. Campsites are updated annually on these maps, which are designed specifically for the canoeist and the fisherman. The campsites are indicated by red dots on the maps.

The discussion of each route tells you which maps cover it. You can order them from:

W. A. Fisher Company
Box 1107
Virginia, MN 55792-1107

Or you can buy your maps from any one of many canoe-trip outfitters when you arrive in northern Minnesota. They are also available at many camping stores in the Twin Cities area, as well as in some other upper-Midwestern cities.

OBTAINING TRAVEL PERMITS

Any overnight visitor in the BWCA Wilderness between May 1 and September 30 must have a BWCA travel permit in possession. It allows a party of up to 9 people to enter the wilderness only on the date and through the entry point specified on the permit. Once in the wilderness, a party is free to travel where it desires, as long as motor-use restrictions are not violated. The permit is free. It may be picked up as early as 24 hours ahead of the scheduled trip at any Superior National Forest office or cooperating business (outfitter, resort, camp, etc.). Permits are also required for daytime visitors using motors (except at the Little Vermilion Lake entry point). Beginning in October 1995, permits will also be required for nonmotorized day uses (including canoeing) and for all winter uses.

Entry quotas have been established for overnight campers in order to reduce competition for the limited number of established campsites and to avoid unauthorized camping on undeveloped sites. The daily limits (which range from only one to as many as 27) are based on the number of campsites on the routes served by each entry point. The quotas do not apply to day users, for which there is no limit established, except for motorists. The quotas are in effect only during the five-month canoeing season. There are no limits on the number of overnight permits issued after September 30 and before May 1.

All permits that are not reserved ahead of time are available on a first-come-first-served basis free of charge on the day of entry or up to 24 hours before the start of your trip.

Reservations

All overnight travel permits are available through advance reservations, for a nonrefundable fee of $9 (in 1995) per reservation. You do not *have* to make a reservation before arriving at the BWCA, but it is advisable, since quotas at many entry points fill up early. There is no charge for the permit—only for the reservation. A reservation simply assures that a permit to enter the wilderness on a specific day and at a certain entry point will be available.

Mailed-in reservations for the following summer are accepted beginning January 1, but are not processed until mid-month. Confirmation letters are not mailed until the last week of January. Phone reservations are accepted starting February 1. Reservations may be made *only* at the central reservation office for the Superior National Forest. Mail your requests to:

BWCAW Reservations
PO Box 450
Cumberland, MD 21501
Or phone: (800) 745-3399; (800) 967-9376 for hearing-impaired.

Phone reservations will be accepted only with the use of a valid Discover, VISA or MasterCard during normal business hours. The office is open from 8:00 A.M. to 4:30 P.M. weekdays. Reservation requests must include the following: 1) the name, address and phone number of the party leader, 2) the desired entry point, 3) the desired entry date, 4) the planned exit point, 5) the planned exit date, 6) the party size, 7) the name of at least one other group member, 8) the method of travel (paddle canoe, motorboat, hiking, etc.), 9) whether or not the trip will be guided and, if so, the guide's name, and 10) payment (check, money order or charge-card number with expiration date). Alternate starting dates and entry points may also be listed on the application in case the first choices are not available.

After calling or writing for a reservation, a trip leader will receive a letter confirming that a reservation has been made. Reservations made within the last seven days before the trip will be processed, but no confirmation letter will be sent to the applicant. The permit must be picked up in person within 24 hours of the trip at a Ranger District Office or at an outfitter or business that is an official issuing station (cooperator). The face-to-face contact is necessary to inform visitors about wilderness ethics and minimum-impact camping techniques. For this reason, permits are not mailed to visitors in advance of their scheduled trips. A permit may be obtained only by the party leader or the alternate whose name appears on the application. Identification is required, and periodic checks may take place in the wilderness.

Information

The Forest Service personnel at the reservation office are available only for reservations. For information about the BWCA contact one of the Forest Service offices listed below. They can answer your questions, but cannot process reservations. Normal business hours are from 8:00 A.M. to 4:30 P.M. weekdays before May 10 and after Labor Day. During the summer, these offices are open daily from 7:00 A.M. to 5:00 P.M.

Entry Points	Closest Ranger Station & Address	Telephone #
38-41	Tofte Ranger Station Tofte, MN 55615	(218) 663-7280
43-70	Gunflint Ranger Station Grand Marais, MN 55604	(218) 387-2451

When you pick up your permit, it is advisable to go to the Ranger Station or cooperating outfitter that is closest to your entry point. Personnel there are likely to be more familiar with your proposed route. They can alert you to high water or low water conditions, bear problems, suitable campsites, road conditions and other particulars.

HEAVY USE PERIODS

When planning your trip, you may increase your chance of obtaining a BWCA permit by considering the following guidelines.

1. The busiest days for entry are Friday, Saturday, Sunday

and Monday. You will have a better chance on one of the other three days of the week.

2. Opening of the fishing season (mid-May), Memorial Day weekend, Labor Day weekend and mid-July through mid-August are the busiest times.

3. Consider using an entry point that has, in the past, ranked low in popularity. A majority of visitors use a very small minority of the entry points.

RULES AND REGULATIONS

The following regulations apply to all users of the BWCA.

1. Travel permits must be obtained before entering the BWCA and must be in your possession while in the BWCA.
2. Party size is limited to 9 people, with a limit of four canoes per party.
3. Camping is permitted only at Forest Service campsites that have steel fire grates and box latrines, or within certain designated "remote areas."
4. Open campfires are permitted only within constructed fireplaces at developed campsites, or as specifically approved on the BWCA permit.
5. Nonburnable, disposable food and beverage containers (i.e., cans and bottles) are not permitted. Containers of fuel, insect repellent, medicines, personal toiletry articles, and other items which are not foods or beverages are permitted.
6. Camping is limited to a maximum of 14 consecutive days at one campsite.
7. Fires must be drowned with water and be dead out before a campsite may be vacated.
8. It is unlawful to cut live trees, shrubs or boughs.
9. Motorized travel and mechanical portaging are permitted only on certain specified routes.
10. No watercraft, motor, mechanical device or equipment not used in connection with the current visit may be stored on or moored to National Forest land and left unattended.

11. No motorized or mechanical equipment of any type is permitted within the BWCA, except as specified above.
12. Trenching is not permitted. It disturbs soil and causes erosion.
13. The use of firearms is discouraged.
14. The use of moss or boughs for a bed is not allowed.
15. Use cord instead of nail and wire.
16. Airplanes must maintain an altitude of 4000 feet above sea level.
17. All state and local laws and regulations must be obeyed.
18. Demonstrate common courtesies. Leave clean campsites for those who follow. Preserve and respect the solitude of the BWCA. Sound carries far across open water—especially on a quiet evening.
19. Use wilderness latrines. If no latrine is available, bury human waste at least 100 feet from shore.
20. Keep soaps, dishwater and grease away from lakes and streams. Use biodegradable soap instead of detergents.
21. Use the bottom of a canoe for a table, rather than constructing one from native materials.
22. The use of metal detectors in the BWCA is allowed *only* when there is specific authorization by the Forest Service. Unauthorized use is strictly forbidden.

PRIMITIVE MANAGEMENT AREAS

For smaller groups of BWCA visitors who desire a more primitive and secluded wilderness experience, there are currently 10 designated areas in the Boundary Waters that are managed similarly to Quetico Provincial Park on the Canadian side of the border. Visitors may camp at any suitable location, as long as standing trees and brush are not cut. Shallow latrines may be dug at sites that do not have box latrines, and campfires are permitted where there are no fire grates, as long as special care is paid to ensure that there are no environmental scars remaining after use of the site.

Primitive Management Areas (PMA's) are located in remote parts of the Wilderness, requiring considerable effort to reach them. Portage trails and campsites are not maintained. To minimize damage to the environment, it is suggested that group size not exceed six.

Access to these areas is very limited, to enhance the opportunities for solitude. After obtaining a travel permit for the desired BWCA entry point, special authorization must be obtained from one of the Forest Service ranger stations where the permit is picked up (see OBTAINING TRAVEL PERMITS earlier in this chapter). No reservations are taken for PMA visits. Authorizations are available only on a first-come-first-served basis. For more information about the locations of these areas, as well as the unique regulations that govern them, contact the Superior National Forest headquarters in Duluth or the USFS ranger station in Tofte or Grand Marais.

PROVISIONS OF THE BWCA WILDERNESS ACT

In the fall of 1978 Congress enacted legislation that drastically altered the regulations governing the BWCA. The Boundary Waters wilderness does not appear any different now than it did before 1979, but it may sound different in places.

Before January 1, 1979, the Boundary Waters was administered in accordance with the 1964 Wilderness Act. Logging was allowed within the Wilderness and motorboats were permitted on 60% of the water surface area.

The BWCA Wilderness Act of 1978 added 20 small additions totalling 45,000 acres to the existing BWCA, and established the current boundaries to include 1,075,000 acres of wilderness. It also prohibited logging anywhere in the BWCA, closed most of the interior motor routes, and restricted motorboats to 33% of the water surface area (24% after 1999)—mostly perimeter lakes served directly by access roads. Some of those lakes will remain open to motorized use indefinitely; others will be phased out over the next 20 years. A few have no horsepower limits, but most are limited to either 10 or 25 horsepower.

The 1978 BWCA Wilderness Act also includes the following provisions.

- Mining is restricted and the Secretary of Agriculture has the authority to acquire mineral rights in the wilderness and along three road corridors in a 222,000-acre Mining Protection Area. No other federal land controls are involved in the MPA.

- Motorboats are prohibited in the wilderness except on the following lakes and rivers:
  a. No horsepower limits, indefinite use: Little Vermilion L., Loon R., Loon L., SW end of Lac LaCroix to Wilkins Bay. (Loon Falls and Beatty Portage trams allowed to remain.)
  b. 25 h.p. limit, indefinite use: Trout, Fall, Moose, Newfound, Sucker, Newton, Basswood (except portion NW of Washington Is. and N. of Jackfish Bay to the Basswood R.), South Farm, Saganaga (except W. of American Pt.), E. Bearskin, and Snowbank lakes.
  c. 10 h.p. limit, indefinite use: Sea Gull E. of Threemile Is., Clearwater, N. Fowl, S. Fowl, Island R., Alder, Canoe.
  d. 10 h.p. limit until 1999: Sea Gull W. of Threemile Is.
- There are no horsepower limits on portions of lakes outside the Wilderness. (parts of Fall, Moose, Snowbank, Sea Gull, Clearwater, E. Bearskin, etc.).
- There are quotas on how many motorboats are allowed on each lake, including day use (average of 1976, '77, '78 use). Resorts, cabin owners and their guests are exempt on their lakes. Overnight camping by motorboat is allowed. Towboats in excess of 25 h.p. may not be used in the BWCA after January 1, 1984.
- Snowmobiles are prohibited in the wilderness except for permanent use of the Crane L.-Little Vermilion winter portage to Canada, and the Saganaga winter route to Canada (access to homes).
- The Secretary of Agriculture is allowed to permit grooming by snowmobile of a limited number of cross-country ski trails near existing resorts.
- Old and deteriorating dams within the Wilderness may be maintained only to protect Wilderness values or public safety.
- The government is given authority to enforce the motorboat and snowmobile regulations of the act on state water. No other federal jurisdiction over state waters is asserted. The state is allowed to impose more stringent regulations.

A FINAL WORD

Believe it or not, these age-old routes *do change*. In fact, they may change several times each year. A rock-strewn rapids that requires a portage in mid-August may be a navigable channel three weeks later, after the autumn rains. A portage indicated as 15 rods on the map may turn out to be 35 rods in reality, when the water level is so low that you must walk an extra 20 rods before the water is deep enough to set your canoe down. When a portage becomes too eroded from over-use, the Forest Service sometimes constructs a new one, which is usually longer than the original. And occasionally an author's memory and notes fail him and a mistake is made. So if you have any comments, suggestions or corrections to make pertaining to this guide, please write the author (in care of the publisher). Thank you.

Entrance to the Sawbill Trail

Ch. 3: Entry from the Sawbill Trail

The Southeastern Area

The southeastern part of the Boundary Waters Canoe Area is served by only four entry points. Two of them, however, are among the 10 most popular entry points in all of the BWCA—Sawbill and Brule lakes. The other two, on the other hand, rank in the bottom half of the popularity scale—Baker and Homer lakes. All four offer quick, easy access to one of the loveliest regions in the Boundary Waters, where scenic hills border crystalline waters and wildlife is abundantly visible. This is one of the best areas in all of the BWCA Wilderness, in fact, to see bald eagles, ospreys and moose.

The Sawbill Trail (Cook County Road 2) originates at the tiny town of Tofte, on the shore of Lake Superior. Like most roads leading inland from the north shore of the lake, it has a hard surface for nearly two miles during its ascent to an elevation high above Lake Superior. When the gradient levels off, the road turns to gravel and continues that way for the remainder of its 22-mile course to Sawbill Lake. Although it has its rough spots, the road is generally in excellent condition, with relatively few sharp curves or steep grades. The only sign of civilization along its entire course is at its end, where Sawbill Outfitters and a Forest Service "encampment" are located along the south shore of Sawbill Lake.

Entry Point 38—Sawbill Lake

Permits: 1888
Popularity Rank: 3
Daily Quota: 14

Location: From US Highway 61 in Tofte drive north on Cook County Road 2 (Sawbill Trail) for 23 miles to its end. Except for a few rough spots, it's a good gravel road all the way.

Description: A very nice, large National Forest campground is located along the southeast shore of Sawbill Lake, adjacent to the public boat access. Fifty campsites accommodate the heavy traffic through this area. With a fee to camp there, it is an excellent place to spend the night before your trip.

Nearby, just inland from the public access, is Sawbill Outfitters, with grocery store, sauna and hot showers—a great place to clean up after the trip. They can outfit you with everything you'll need for your trip into the Boundary Waters.

In spite of its remote location, Sawbill is one of the most popular entry points in the BWCA. And although, prior to 1979, it was part of a designated motor route, less than 13% of the groups that entered here used motorized craft. So, in spite of the fact that Federal legislation in 1978 closed Sawbill to motors, it is still very popular. Today it ranks high among entry points with the highest percent of quotas used each summer. It's a good idea, therefore, to make your reservation early. Yet, with all its popularity, Sawbill Lake is located less than a two-day paddle from several pristine wilderness areas that receive very light use, in travel zones where motors are banned entirely. Moose, mink, beaver and bear are common throughout much of the nearby region.

Route #53: The Louse River Loop

5 Days, 43 Miles, 22 Lakes, 4 Rivers, 1 Creek, 39 Portages.

Difficulty: Challenging

Fisher Maps: F-5, F-11, F-12

Travel Zones: 34, 35, 41

Introduction: This route is for those who like abundant wildlife sightings, a high degree of solitude, small lakes and tiny rivers—and for those who don't mind working hard to find these wilderness qualities.

From Sawbill Lake, you'll paddle west through Alton Lake, down the Grace River to Phoebe Lake, and then down the Phoebe River to Lake Polly. From Polly, you'll turn north and follow the Kawishiwi River system to Malberg Lake. There you will leave this busy part of the loop and follow the Louse River east to Bug Lake and then veer northeast to Mesaba Lake. From Mesaba you'll finally turn south and negotiate the longest portage of the route (1½ miles) before returning to Sawbill Lake.

Fishing is normally excellent throughout the loop. Walleye and northern pike inhabit many of the lakes from Sawbill to Malberg, as do bluegills from Lake Polly to Malberg. Lake trout also may be found in Mesaba and Alton lakes.

If the fish aren't biting, you surely won't starve in midsummer, as blueberries grow thick in this area.

Most of your time will be spent in Zone 36, which ranks relatively low in popularity. But with campsites at a premium, they maintain a 40% occupancy rate. In other words, although there are few other people in this area, find your campsite early or you may be left without one. Portages are frequent and many are difficult, but most are short. Only two are over 200 rods.

This route is most favorable during spring or early summer, when water levels are normally the highest. During late summer or dry years, you may find it to be a drag in places—literally!

DAY 1: **Sawbill Lake,** p. 30 rods, **Alton Lake,** p. 140 rods, **Beth Lake,** p. 285 rods, **Grace Lake,** p. 15 rods, **Grace River,** p. 15 rods, **river,** p. 5 rods, **river,** p. 85 rods, **Phoebe Lake.** The 285-rod portage to Grace Lake looks awesome on the map, but it's not at all difficult—a good, well-worn path with seven canoe rests along the way. (The northern route from Beth through Ella Lake to Grace would seem easier, with two shorter carries of 80 and 130 rods. Both, however, are quite rocky and the landings at both ends of the longer one are poor for put-ins. Nevertheless, you will find lots of blueberries there in season.)

In addition to the three short carries along the Grace River, a beaver dam may be another obstruction near the 5-rod portage.

There are several good campsites near the west end of Phoebe Lake. Since many people visit there, it would be wise to find a site early. Then cast your line for one of the walleye or northern pike lurking in the waters around you.

DAY 2: **Phoebe Lake, Phoebe River, Knight Lake, Phoebe River,** p. 140 rods, **Hazel Lake,** p. 59 rods, **Phoebe River,** p. 24 rods, **river,** p. 92 rods, **river,** p. 15 rods, **river,** p. 97 rods, **Lake Polly.** All six of these portages are basically downhill, as you drop a total of 144 feet from Phoebe to Lake Polly. It's a very scenic part of the route, where moose, beaver and mink abound. You will probably encounter few people between Phoebe and Polly. But on Polly you'll be joined by an influx of paddlers who entered the BWCA at Kawishiwi Lake, the 11th most popular entry point. Do your best to make camp early.

Hang your food pack well this evening. While camping on popular lakes, like Polly, it is not uncommon to encounter bears at campsites. Rather intelligent animals, black bears learn to associate food with campers. And where campsites are plentiful, bears often "make the rounds" in search of food. If you keep a clean campsite and hang your food safely between trees at night and when you are away from the site during the day, however, the chances are slim that you will have any problems.

Watch for moose at dusk. I've seen them four times on my last two trips through this area, including a splendid display by a large bull feeding in a nearby lake.

DAY 3: **Lake Polly,** p. 19 rods, **Kawishiwi River,** p. 48 rods, **river,** p. 127 rods, **river, Koma Lake,** p. 24 rods, **Malberg Lake,** p. 15 rods, **Louse River, Frond Lake, Louse River,** p. 21 rods, **river,** p. 11 rods, **Boze Lake,** p. 36 rods, **Louse River,** p. 59 rods, **river,** p. 20 rods, **river,** p. 41 rods, **river,** p. 56 rods, **river,** p. 21 rods, **Trail Lake.** You'll be hiking downhill again across the portages between Polly and Malberg lakes. But then you will paddle upstream and portage uphill to Trail Lake, a total ascent of 69 feet.

Large boulders may obstruct passage frequently on the lower Louse River during low-water periods. None of the portages is difficult this day, but their frequency will slow travel considerably.

If blueberries are in season, you'll find them in abundance all along the Louse River.

Two nice campsites are on Trail Lake, where good fishing for northern pike awaits you.

DAY 4: **Trail Lake,** p. 130 rods, **Louse River,** p. 50 rods, **river,** p. 115 rods, **Bug Lake,** p. 45 rods, **Dent Lake,** p. 130 rods, **pond,** p. 7 rods, **Chaser Lake,** p. 20 rods, **Mesaba Lake.** The portages this day will be the most difficult so far—uphill from Trail Lake to Dent, then down steeply for 7 rods to Chaser Lake and Mesaba. Your first carry out of Trail Lake is tricky, steep in spots and challenging to even a seasoned tripper. You may find a beaver dam or two and occasional rocky shoals along the Louse River to slow your progress.

Bug Lake is slowly dying and you'll find the build-up of mud and aquatic plants a problem for navigation when the water level is low and the lake is barely deep enough for passage of a loaded canoe. The portage out of Bug maintains the same ugly character—marshy and tricky to negotiate.

DAY 5: **Mesaba Lake,** p. 80 rods, **Hug Lake,** p. 3 rods, **Duck Lake,** p. 80 rods, **Zenith Lake,** p. 480 rods, **Lujenida Lake, Kelso River, Kelso Lake,** p. 13 rods, **Sawbill Lake.** You're in for a rough morning on portages. The two 80-rod carries are uphill, and so is the first 70 rods of the 1½ mile trek to Lujenida. Unless the water level is very low, you can probably by-pass the 3-rod portage from Hug to Duck by pulling your canoe through the shallow creek connecting them. If the water level is so low that you must portage, then you are in for trouble on Duck Lake, which is very shallow, being overcome with mud and aquatic plants.

The long portage to Lujenida begins uphill, crosses over the Laurentian Divide, and then descends much of the rest of the way, following a good, well-traveled path. There are eight canoe rests. You have an opportunity to break up the trek into three segments with brief interludes on ponds adjacent to the trail, but it appears that most people prefer to walk nonstop from Zenith to Lujenida.

Route #54: The Keke-Michi-Saba Route

7 Days, 77 Miles, 41 Lakes, 3 Rivers, 2 Creeks, 56 Portages

Difficulty: Rugged

Fisher Maps: F-5, F-11, F-12

Travel Zones: 41, 35, 34, 33, 29, 32, 27, 36

Introduction: This rugged journey will take you right through the isolated heart of the Boundary Waters Canoe Area. As on Route 53, you will first go west-northwest via the Grace, Phoebe and Kawishiwi rivers to Malberg Lake. From sprawling Malberg, you'll paddle north through Beaver and Adams lakes to Boulder Lake, one of the least visited parts of the BWCA. Then you'll veer west to Fraser and north to Kekekabic Lake, negotiating a series of smaller lakes in between. From big, beautiful "Kek" you will paddle east to Ogishkemuncie and then veer southeast (through one of the most beautiful parts of the BWCA) to Gabimichigami Lake and on to Little Saganaga. After all of this, the toughest part of the trip is yet to come, as you portage your way south to Lujenida Lake and paddle back to your origin at Sawbill Lake.

En route you will encounter some of the most varied, beautiful and fascinating terrain in all of the Boundary Waters. Bountiful wildlife and good fishing, too, will be yours to enjoy.

Nowhere on the route are motors permitted, and a good deal of the loop is only lightly traveled by canoeists. Perhaps the busiest part of the route is from Kekekabic through Ogishkemuncie to Little Saganaga Lake, as well as the immediate vicinity of Sawbill Lake.

Moose, beaver, mink and bear are common in the southern part of the loop. Fishing is usually quite good in many of the lakes. Walleye and northern pike are plentiful in Grace, Phoebe, Polly, Koma and Malberg lakes. Lake trout may also be caught in Alton, Fraser, Kekekabic, Eddy, Gabimichigami, Little Saganaga and Mesaba lakes. If you are an enthusiastic angler, perhaps you should add a day or two to this trip. Seven days allows very little time for casting.

DAY 1: **Sawbill Lake,** p. 30 rods, **Alton Lake,** p. 140 rods, **Beth Lake,** p. 285 rods, **Grace Lake,** p. 15 rods, **Grace River,** p. 15 rods, **river,** 5 rods, **river,** p. 85 rods, **Phoebe Lake.** (See comments for Day 1, Route #53.)

DAY 2: **Phoebe Lake, Phoebe River, Knight Lake, Phoebe River,** p. 140 rods, **Hazel Lake,** p. 59 rods, **Phoebe River,** p. 24 rods, **river,** p. 92 rods, **river,** p. 15 rods, **river,** p. 97 rods, **Lake Polly.** (See comments for Day 2, Route #53.)

DAY 3: **Lake Polly,** p. 19 rods, **Kawishiwi River,** p. 48

rods, **river,** p. 127 rods, **river, Koma Lake,** p. 24 rods, **Malberg Lake,** p. 60 rods, **Kawishiwi River,** p. 15 rods, **Trapline Lake,** p. 30 rods, **Beaver Lake,** p. 90 rods, **Adams Lake, Boulder Creek,** p. 15 rods, **creek,** liftover, **Boulder Lake.** On this day you will penetrate an isolated interior zone of the BWCA. Low water and beaver dams may hinder navigation on Boulder Creek. Under normal water conditions, however, you should be able to paddle all but 15 rods of this half-mile stream. You'll find three campsites on Boulder Lake, and not much competition for them usually.

DAY 4: **Boulder Lake,** p. 220 rods, **Cap Lake,** p. 60 rods, **Roe Lake,** p. 42 rods, **Sagus Lake,** p. 65 rods, **Fraser Lake,** p. 15 rods, **Gerund Lake,** p. 30 rods, **Ahmakose Lake,** p. 90 rods, **Wisini Lake,** p. 10 rods, **Strup Lake,** p. 85 rods, **Kekekabic Lake.** Your first long portage follows a level trail that splits in the middle. The right branch veers northeast to Ledge Lake, so be *sure* to keep left at the junction. Between Fraser and Wisini lakes, you will gain over 100 feet in elevation before dropping back down to Wisini Lake. The final two carries drop steeply to Strup and Kekekabic lakes.

Kekekabic, with hills rising around it as high as 400 feet, is a magnificent lake. Several campsites are located at the southwest end, and you would be wise to take the first one you see, as the lake attracts many visitors.

DAY 5: **Kekekabic Lake,** 5 portages through **Kekekabic Ponds, Eddy Lake,** p 15 rods, **Jean Lake,** p. 15 rods, **Annie Lake,** p. 15 rods, **Ogishkemuncie Lake,** p. 80 rods, **Mueller Lake,** 3 portages, **Agamok Lake,** p. 15 rods, **Gabimichigami Lake.** The five short portages out of Kekekabic Lake connect a series of small ponds. Barely more than "liftovers," they will nevertheless slow your progress.

The 80-rod carry to Mueller looks innocent enough on the map, but it is not. It climbs over a steep hill for a net gain of 52 feet above Ogishkemuncie Lake. Three canoe rests along the way will be a welcome relief if you find that you are not in as good shape as you had thought.

The breath-robbing work is well worth the effort, however, as you will be entering one of the most scenic parts of the BWCA—a favorite of mine. Agamok is more like a river than a lake, connecting big "Gabi" with a series of ponds and rapids that flow into Mueller Lake. Here you have a choice: either three short portages around three sets of rapids, or one continuous carry of 100 rods from Mueller directly to Agamok Lake. If time is of the essence, choose the latter. But you would not regret taking the time for the other alternative. All three portages are rocky and somewhat steep in places, but none exceeds 25 rods. The second portage crosses the famed Kekekabic Trail, which utilizes a wooden bridge to pass over a picturesque waterfall flowing parallel to the portage. Those who bypass the area via the longer portage are missing a real treat.

There are several excellent campsites near the eastern shore of Gabimichigami Lake. Most are large enough for any group, and the view is breathtaking from those that border the main body of this awesome lake.

DAY 6: **Gabimichigami Lake,** p. 25 rods, **Rattle Lake,** p. 30 rods, **Little Saganaga Lake,** p. 45 rods, **Mora Lake,** p. 100 rods, **Whipped Lake,** p. 15 rods, **Fente Lake,** p. 300 rods, **Hub Lake,** p. 105 rods, **Mesaba Lake.** This should be a pleasant day, through scenic lakes connected by easy portages—*until* you leave Fente Lake. Then you will encounter the toughest portage of this trip—nearly a mile-long climb to Hub Lake. The trail ascends steeply for the first 100 rods, gaining nearly 140 feet in elevation, then levels off, and finally slopes gently down to Hub Lake. Only four canoe rests are there to relieve you.

Mesaba is a lovely, isolated lake that attracts relatively few visitors. A very nice campsite is on the south shore of the large peninsula that shapes the lake.

DAY 7: **Mesaba Lake,** p. 80 rods, **Hug Lake,** p. 3 rods, **Duck Lake,** p. 80 rods, **Zenith Lake,** p. 480 rods, **Lujenida Lake, Kelso River, Kelso Lake,** p. 13 rods, **Sawbill Lake.** (See comments for Day 5, Route #53.)

Entry Point 39—Baker Lake

Permits: 244

Popularity Rank: 29

Daily Quota: 3

Location: From US Highway 61 in Tofte, follow the Sawbill Trail north 17 miles to its intersection with Forest Routes 165 and 170. Turn right and follow Forest Route 165 northeast for 5 miles to the junction of Forest Route 1272 (just before the Temperance River bridge). Turn left and drive ½ mile north to the public landing at Baker Lake. You will be on good gravel roads all the way from Tofte.

Description: A small parking lot there will accommodate up to a dozen vehicles. A slightly larger National Forest Campground with four campsites, just east of the boat landing, offers a good place to spend the night before your trip. There is a fee for camping there.

Baker Lake is small, shallow and weedy. It offers easy access to one of the more scenic parts of the BWCA: the Temperance River flowage, where shallow, narrow lakes are surrounded by towering hills and connected by lovely rapids.

Until January 1, 1979, Baker served designated motor routes that led northwest to Sawbill Lake and northeast to Brule Lake. Federal legislation passed in 1978 banned motors in this part of the Boundary Waters. Nevertheless, since only 25% of its permits in 1977 were issued to groups using motors, use patterns have not changed markedly as a result of the Congressional action. In fact, its popularity ranks higher now than in 1977.

Canoeists find that Baker Lake is by far the most peaceful and solitary BWCA entry point in the Sawbill Trail region. Most of the traffic north of it stems from Sawbill Lake, and to a lesser degree from Brule Lake.

Route #55: The Temperance River Route

3 Days, 27 Miles, 14 Lakes, 1 River, 3 Creeks, 18 Portages

Difficulty: Challenging

Fisher maps: F-6, F-5

Travel Zones: 41, 42

Introduction: This lovely loop will take you north, up the Temperance River system of lakes and streams and rapids, to South and North Temperance lakes. Then you will portage northwest to Sitka and Cherokee lakes. From there, you will paddle southwest through a series of small lakes and creeks to Sawbill Lake. From the east shore of that very popular lake, you will portage east to Smoke Lake and continue eastward to Burnt and Kelly lakes. Two short portages and a peaceful paddle south will return you to your origin on the south shore of Baker Lake.

Anglers may find northern pike in several of the lakes along this route. Walleye, smallmouth bass and lake trout are also in some of the lakes.

The northbound part of this loop is through Travel Zone 42, which receives light to moderate use throughout most of the summer. But the southbound part, from Cherokee to Sawbill, is one of the most visited zones in the Boundary Waters, because of heavy canoe traffic from Sawbill Lake. In this zone, you might find campsites at a premium on busy weekends and during peak periods.

DAY 1: **Baker Lake,** p. 10 rods, **Peterson Lake,** p. 3 rods, **Kelly Lake,** p. 65 rods, **Jack Lake,** p. 12 rods, **Weird Lake,** p. 80 rods, **Temperance River,** p. 240 rods, **South Temperance Lake.** You will be traveling uphill, but ascending less than 100 feet all day. Under normal water conditions you may be able to avoid the first two portages by pulling your canoe up the shallow rapids connecting Baker, Peterson and Kelly lakes. When the water level is high enough, you can easily paddle right through the channel connecting Peterson and Kelly lakes. As you should expect, the only real challenge of the day is the final carry to South Temperance Lake—an uphill trek beside the Temperance River. There are 5 canoe rests along the way to facilitate the carry. This is a very scenic part of the BWCA, with hills rising high above your path (as much as 250 feet above Kelly and Jack lakes).

DAY 2: **South Temperance Lake,** p. 55 rods, **North Temperance Lake,** p. 105 rods, **Sitka Lake,** p. 140 rods, **Cherokee Lake, Cherokee Creek,** p. 180 rods, **Skoop Lake,** p. 12 rods, **Skoop Creek, Ada Lake,** p. 80 rods, **Ada Creek,** p. 80 rods, **Sawbill Lake.** Cherokee is a very popular lake, attracting canoeists from Sawbill and Brule lakes. You are likely not to have much time to yourself during your journey southwest. Try to make camp early at the north end of Sawbill Lake.

Portaging will have its ups and downs this day, as you cross the Laurentian Divide twice. Cherokee and Sitka lakes are north of the divide; the rest of the route is south of it. The ½-mile-plus portage to Skoop Lake has 4 portage rests, and it isn't nearly as exhausting as the 140-rod carry to Cherokee Lake which has 5 rests for your convenience.

DAY 3: **Sawbill Lake,** p. 100 rods, **Smoke Lake,** p. 90 rods, **Burnt Lake,** p. 230 rods, **Kelly Lake,** p. 3 rods, **Peterson Lake,** p. 10 rods, **Baker Lake.** You'll escape much of the traffic once you leave Sawbill Lake, and your feeling of isolation will grow stronger the farther east you go. The first portage is nearly level and the others are mostly downhill. The long carry out of Burnt Lake, however, begins with a climb to 70 feet above the lake before leveling off and then dropping down to Kelly. About midway across the trail, you'll cross an old, abandoned logging road immediately before entering a swampy area. There are 4 portage rests along the way.

Route #56: The Five Rivers Route

7 Days, 69 Miles, 38 Lakes, 5 Rivers, 61 Portages

Difficulty: Rugged

Fisher maps: F-6, F-12, F-11, F-5

Travel zones: 42, 41, 36, 37, 34, 35

Introduction: This high-quality wilderness route will first lead you north from Baker to Cherokee Lake, as did Route #55. From there, however, you will continue north to Gordon and then west to Frost Lake. Continuing west, you will paddle down the remote and wild Frost River system of pools, creeks and elongated lakes to Mora Lake. After cruising on to popular Little Saganaga Lake, you will journey southwest through a series of lightly traveled lakes to Malberg Lake. The Kawishiwi River system will carry you farther south, through Koma Lake to Lake Polly. Then you will steer east and paddle up the Phoebe and Grace rivers to Beth and Alton lakes. After crossing busy Sawbill Lake, you will continue east and southeast, across Smoke and Burnt lakes and back to your origin at Baker Lake.

Splendid scenery and bountiful wildlife characterize much of this varied loop. On your third day, in particular, you will be in one of the most pristine and seldom visited parts of the BWCA: the Frost River. In this isolated region moose demonstrate little or no fear of your intrusion.

Motors are not allowed on any part of the route, and most of the zones through which you will be paddling receive light use during all but the peak summer periods. Even then, only in the vicinities of Cherokee, Little Saganaga, Polly and Sawbill lakes are you likely to feel "crowded."

Anglers will have an opportunity to fish for most of the common North Woods species. Walleye and northern pike inhabit many of the lakes. Bluegill are also found in the Malberg-Koma-Polly chain of lakes. Smallmouth bass are caught in Alton and Sawbill lakes. The serious angler will also want to try his luck for the elusive lake trout in Cherokee, Little Saganaga and Alton lakes.

At an average of 9 portages a day, few would argue that this trip deserves a "rugged" rating. Fortunately, though, most of the carries are short. Only 3 are longer than 200 rods; the longest is 285 rods. Nevertheless, unless you are with a strong and experienced crew of Voyageurs, you should consider adding a day's supply of food in case of delays. Basically, if you are willing to *work* for a high-quality wilderness experience, you are bound to enjoy this exceptional route.

DAY 1: **Baker Lake,** p. 10 rods, **Peterson Lake,** p. 3 rods, **Kelly Lake,** p. 65 rods, **Jack Lake,** p. 12 rods, **Weird Lake,** p. 80 rods, **Temperance River,** p. 240 rods, **South Temperance Lake.** (See comments for Day 1, Route #55.)

DAY 2: **South Temperance Lake,** p. 55 rods, **North Temperance Lake,** p. 105 rods, **Sitka Lake,** p. 140 rods, **Cherokee Lake,** p. 13 rods, **Gordon Lake,** p. 140 rods, **Unload Lake,** p. 40 rods, **Frost Lake.** (See comments for Day 2, Route #55.) The 140-rod carry west from Gordon Lake climbs over a fairly steep hill and then levels off and follows a good, smooth path the rest of the way to Unload Lake. Four canoe rests are strategically located beside the trail, if you need them. The final (40-rod) portage to Frost Lake may not be necessary during high-water periods. It's a rough trail and not well-traveled, but it is necessary during late summer or an unusually dry year, when the connecting creek is too shallow for a loaded canoe.

There are two excellent, large Forest Service campsites on the north shore of Frost Lake. Three other sites are also available. Watch for moose along the shoreline during late evening and early morning hours. One August morning, my wife and I saw three moose browsing less than 100 yards from our campsite. A fourth moose was seen sleeping on a sandy beach half a mile away.

DAY 3: **Frost Lake,** p. 130 rods, **Frost River,** p. 10 rods, **Octopus Lake,** p. 15 rods, **Frost River,** p. 25 rods, **river,** p. 5 rods, **river,** p. 30 rods, **Chase Lake,** p. 15 rods, **Pencil Lake,** p. 60 rods, **Frost River,** p. 10 rods, **river,** p. 4 rods, **river,** p. 10 rods, **river,** p. 12 rods, **river, Afton Lake,** p. 20 rods, **Frost River, rapids, Fente Lake,** p. 15 rods, **Whipped Lake,** p. 100 rods, **Mora Lake.** You are in for one long, exhausting day! Area outfitters may suggest that it cannot be done in one day, but my wife and I know for a fact that it can even when the water level is low. One August, we paddled and portaged for over nine hours one hot, sunny day. En route, we saw four moose, two great blue herons, countless aquatic birds and more blueberries than we had ever seen before.

There are no designated Forest Service campsites between Frost and Afton lakes, and the only two official campsites along the entire route are on Afton and Whipped lakes. If you find yourself in a bind, however, there is one site just off the route in Bologna Lake, south of Chase Lake. If sunset is rapidly approaching and you find the campsite at either Afton or Whipped lakes to be vacant, you may want to grab it. You can always make up the "lost time" tomorrow.

Most of the fifteen portages cannot be avoided. The second, however (10 rods to Octopus Lake), can probably be bypassed by walking your canoe down the shallow, rocky river. In addition to the portages mentioned, you may encounter numerous "liftover" obstacles—ones that require stepping out of your canoe—beaver dams, sunken logs, and an assortment of boulders, sand bars and plain old mud. These are particularly a problem in dry periods. In fact, in August you may do more pulling and lifting than paddling, even where there are no portages designated. Watch out, especially, for the stretch from Pencil Lake down-river to the next 10-rod portage and your second portage after Octopus Lake—25 rods along the muddy banks of the Frost River.

You can cut 10 rods off of your portage from Pencil Lake by lifting your canoe over a large beaver dam and paddling on to the top of a small falls where a makeshift campsite is located.

The rapids flowing into Fente Lake may require a liftover, unless the water level is quite high.

Generally, all the portages this day are rocky, not well-marked, and steep in places, and they receive fairly light use. But then, they are also short and not too tiring (except for their frequency). The only dramatically steep and treacherous carry is the 20-rod path between Afton and Fente lakes: very steep up, then very steep down.

Unless you get a very early start and are "psyched up" for a long, hard day, you might consider stretching the Frost River over two days instead of one, in which case you'll need eight days for the entire trip.

DAY 4: **Mora Lake,** p. 45 rods, **Little Saganaga Lake,** p. 19 rods, **pond,** p. 19 rods, **Elton Lake,** p. 45 rods, **Makwa Lake,** p. 65 rods, **pond,** 89 rods, **Panhandle Lake,** p. 55 rods, **Pan Lake.** In contrast to the previous day, on this day none of the portages is difficult, and they are fairly evenly spaced. Little Saganaga is a very popular lake, receiving many visitors from two entry points served by Round Lake, located just off the Gunflint Trail. When you portage west to Elton Lake, however, you will again be entering a part of the BWCA that receives fairly light use most of the summer.

DAY 5: **Pan Lake,** p. 19 rods, **ponds,** p. 25 rods, **Anit Lake,** p. 14–35 rods, **Kivaniva Lake,** p. 40 rods, **Kawishiwi River,** p. 48 rods, **Malberg Lake,** p. 24 rods, **Koma Lake, Kawishiwi River,** p. 127 rods, **river,** p. 48 rods, **river,** p. 19 rods, **Lake Polly.** There is a large moose population in this part of the Boundary Waters, so keep a watchful eye. Fishing for walleye and northern pike is usually very good in Malberg, Koma and Polly lakes. Anglers flock there from Kawishiwi Lake, the 11th most popular entry point and an easy day's travel to the south. So make camp early on Polly.

Hang your food pack well tonight. While camping on popular lakes, like Polly, it is not uncommon to encounter bears at campsites. Rather intelligent animals, black bears learn to associate food with campers. And where campsites are plentiful, bears often "make the rounds" in search of food. If you keep a clean campsite and hang your food safely between trees at night and when you are away from the site during the day, however, the chances are slim that you will have any problems.

DAY 6: **Lake Polly,** p. 97 rods, **Phoebe River,** p. 15 rods, **river,** p. 92 rods, **river,** p. 24 rods, **river,** p. 59 rods, **Hazel Lake,** p. 140 rods, **Phoebe River, Knight Lake, Phoebe River, Phoebe Lake,** p. 85 rods, **Grace River,** p. 5 rods, **river,** p. 15 rods, **river,** p. 15 rods, **Grace Lake.** All 10 of these portages are basically uphill, as you gain a total of 192 feet from Polly to Grace Lake. None of the carries, however, is difficult, and they are in a very scenic part of the route, where moose, beaver and mink abound. You will probably encounter few other people between Polly and Phoebe. East of Phoebe, however, the traffic from Sawbill Lake increases. In addition to the three short carries along the Grace River, a beaver dam may provide another obstruction near the 5-rod portage. Try your luck for the walleyes and northern pike that inhabit Phoebe and Grace lakes.

DAY 7: **Grace Lake,** p. 285 rods, **Beth Lake,** p.140 rods, **Alton Lake,** p. 30 rods, **Sawbill Lake,** p. 100 rods, **Smoke Lake,** p. 90 rods, **Burnt Lake,** p. 230 rods, **Kelly Lake,** p. 3 rods, **Peterson Lake,** p. 10 rods, **Baker Lake.** The 285-rod portage from Grace Lake is not difficult though it does gain 68 feet in elevation. It has a good, well-worn path with seven canoe rests along the way. The northern route through Ella Lake would seem easier, with two shorter portages of 130 rods and 80 rods. Both, however, are quite rocky and the landings at both ends of the longer one are poor for put-ins.

The most exhausting portage of the day is the last long one (230 rods). The trail climbs to nearly 70 feet above Burnt Lake, before leveling off and then dropping 100 feet down to Kelly Lake. About midway across the trail, you will pass over an old, abandoned logging road immediately before entering a swampy area. There are 4 portage rests along the way.

Entry Point 40—Homer Lake

Permits: 197

Popularity Rank: 32

Daily Quota: 2

Location: Homer Lake is 17 miles northeast of the Sawbill Trail via Forest Routes 165 and 326. These are good secondary roads, but there is another route that involves less driving on gravel. The Caribou Trail is a rougher, more winding, hillier road, but it offers a more direct route to Homer Lake from US Highway 61. Designated as County Road 4, the Caribou Trail begins one mile northeast of Lutsen. Follow it 18 miles north to Forest Route 153. Turn left and drive 1½ miles to the junction of Forest Route 326. Turn right and follow the Brule Lake Road 4 miles north to the Homer Lake turnoff (Forest Route 1282) on the left.

Description: Camping is not allowed at the Homer Lake access. A good place to spend the night before your trip, however, is not far away. Crescent Lake Campground is 10 miles by road southwest of Homer (¼ mile south of Forest Route 165, 7 miles northeast of its intersection with the Sawbill Trail). There are 40 campsites, and a fee is charged.

The eastern half of Homer Lake is open to motorized craft. The west end and the interior lakes to which it leads, however, are "paddle only." 36% of the travel permits in 1977, when motors were allowed throughout the lake, were issued to groups using motors. Use of this entry point has dropped considerably (almost 40%) after motors were banned, but it has regained much of its original popularity (up 35% from 1986 to 1990).

Homer Lake now provides easy access to one of the least visited parts of the Boundary Waters—Travel Zone 43—where good fishing for walleyes and northern pike attract weekend anglers but few other people. Bordered by a low ridge covered with spruce and balsam fir, Homer itself is not a particularly attractive lake. There was extensive wind damage to the forest at the west end of the lake, caused by a storm during the fall of 1986. And submerged rocks are a hazard to motorboating anglers using the east part of the shallow lake.

Nevertheless, Homer Lake does provide access to a lovely part of the BWCA, where scenic shorelines of pine and spruce are highlighted by rocky cliffs and surrounded by impressive hills. This is usually a very quiet place to spend a weekend, or a delightful start for a longer itinerary north through beautiful Brule Lake.

In spite of its relatively low ranking in popularity among all entry points, it's a good idea to make a reservation in advance of your arrival. Homer ranks 4th among all entry points with quotas filled the highest percentage of the time, and 7th among entry points most often reserved ahead of time.

Route #57: The Juno Lake Loop

2 Days, 12 Miles, 4 Lakes, 1 river, 4 Portages

Difficulty: Easy

Fisher Map: F-6

Travel Zones: 43, 44

Introduction: This short, peaceful route will take you from the public landing west through Homer Lake and down the Vern River to Vern Lake. You'll then follow this long, narrow lake northwest to Juno Lake, which leads northeast to Brule Lake. The trip will end at the public access on the south shore of Brule Lake, less than 2 miles by road north of your origin.

Motors are allowed only on the east half of Homer Lake. The rest is "paddle only." The region south of Brule Lake is lightly used most of the season, but Brule is one of the more popular lakes in the area.

Anglers will find good populations of walleye and northern pike in all the lakes along this route. Brule Lake, in particular, is famous for its good walleye crop.

Most canoeists could easily complete the trip in one day. But with lovely scenery and bountiful wildlife along the route, it will be more thoroughly appreciated if you allow two full days for completion.

DAY 1: **Homer Lake,** p. 7 rods, **Vern River,** p. 6 rods, **river, rapids, river, Vern Lake,** p. 65 rods, **Juno Lake.** After two short portages along the scenic Vern River, you may have to run, walk or line your canoe through a small, shallow rapids where there is no portage necessary (or available). You could also access Vern Lake by way of a more direct route through Whack Lake, but you would be missing this lovely, short stretch of river connecting Homer and Vern lakes.

With a few rocky outrcroppings along its shoreline, Vern Lake is the most scenic of the three lakes south of Brule. It is bordered by a forest of spruce, fir and birch trees. At the north end of the lake is the most difficult portage of this route. The 65-rod trail has a couple of steep grades, including a steep descent to the west end of Juno Lake.

The forest bordering the west end of Juno was decimated by the same wind storm that damaged the Homer Lake shoreline. If the two campsites near the west end are occupied, keep paddling and you'll find a newer site, large enough for two tents, near the middle of this long lake.

DAY 2: **Juno Lake,** p. 70 rods, **Brule Lake.** Unlike the preceding portage, the 70-rod trail follows an excellent path to the south shore of Brule Lake. On windy days, use caution while crossing large Brule Lake. Treacherous waves can make navigation quite difficult, if not impossible, at times. Don't take any unnecessary risks!

If you have not made arrangements to have your car waiting at the Brule Lake landing, you will have to walk 1.9 miles south to the Homer Lake parking lot at the end of your excursion.

Route #58: The Jack-Frost Loop

6 Days, 60 Miles, 32 Lakes, 4 Rivers, 40 Portages

Difficulty: Rugged

Fisher Maps: F-6, F-12, F-5

Travel Zones: 43, 44, 42, 41, 36

Introduction: This high-quality wilderness route will lead you into one of the most isolated and pristine regions of the Boundary Waters Canoe Area. From Homer you will loop north through Vern and Juno Lakes to Brule Lake. You'll portage from the northwest end of Brule to Cam Lake and proceed north through a series of small, scenic lakes to Town Lake. After Cherokee and Gordon lakes, you will then portage west to Frost Lake. Draining the southwest end of Frost Lake, the Frost River will lead you west through one of the wildest parts of the BWCA. From Fente Lake, then, you will steer south through Hub and Mesaba lakes and on to Kelso Lake. Turning east, you'll cross busy Sawbill Lake to Smoke, Burnt and Kelly lakes. Then you'll paddle northeast up the Temperance River flowage to South Temperance Lake, from which you will steer east and end your trip at the Brule Lake landing.

Most of this route is lightly traveled. Only on Brule, Cherokee and Sawbill lakes may you feel crowded. Wildlife is abundant and scenery is outstanding. The quiet observer is bound to view moose, beaver and otter. And in the right season, fresh blueberries will be a part of your diet.

Portages, however, are all too frequent. Several are quite difficult. In dry periods the going may be even slower and tougher, as parts of the Frost and Vern rivers may be too low for navigation of a loaded canoe. The entire loop most certainly deserves a "rugged" rating.

DAY 1: **Homer Lake,** p. 7 rods, **Vern River,** p. 6 rods, **river, rapids, river, Vern Lake,** p. 65 rods, **Juno Lake,** p. 70 rods, **Brule Lake.** (See comments for Days 1 and 2, Route #57.) Three campsites are located near the west end of Brule Lake.

DAY 2: **Brule Lake,** p. 100 rods, **Cam Lake,** p. 45 rods, **Gasket Lake,** p. 75 rods, **Vesper Lake,** p. 110 rods, **Town Lake,** p. 10 rods, **Cherokee Lake,** p. 13 rods, **Gordon Lake,** p. 140 rods, **Unload Lake,** p. 40 rods, **Frost Lake.** Though not long, the portages in store for you today are *not* easy. All four carries between Brule and Town lakes are very rocky, being strewn with boulders that make walking treacherous. The first portage (100 rods) gradually ascends a hill for 80 rods, then drops 20 rods to Cam Lake. The 75-rod trail from Gasket to Vesper Lake climbs steeply to cross over the Laurentian Divide. From that point on to Fente Lake, the portages are generally downhill, as the waters flow north to Hudson Bay. The 140-rod path from Gordon Lake to Unload surmounts a fairly steep hill at its east end, then levels off and follows a good, smooth trail the rest of the way. Four canoe rests are strategically situated beside the trail. The final portage to Frost Lake may not be necessary during high-water periods. It's a rough path and not well-traveled, but you will probably find it necessary during late summer or an unusually dry year.

The scenery in this lightly traveled area is stunning, enhanced by large "fields" of boulders on the west shores of Gasket and Brule lakes. Five campsites await you on the tranquil shores of Frost Lake. Moose abound in this area, so keep a watchful eye at dusk and dawn. During one visit my wife and I saw four moose along the lake's north shore.

DAY 3: **Frost Lake,** p. 130 rods, **Frost River,** p. 10 rods, **Octopus Lake,** p. 15 rods, **Frost River,** p. 25 rods, **river,** p. 5 rods, **river,** p. 30 rods, **Chase Lake,** p. 15 rods, **Pencil Lake,** p. 60 rods, **Frost River,** p. 10 rods, **river,** p. 4 rods, **river,** p. 10 rods, **river,** p. 12 rods, **river, Afton Lake,** p. 20 rods, **Frost River, rapids, Fente Lake,** p. 300 rods, **Hub Lake.** (See comments for Day 3, Route #56.) Your last portage, the toughest of the whole trip, is hard to take after an already long day. The trail gains nearly 140 feet in elevation during the first 100 rods, then levels off, and finally slopes gently down to Hub Lake. Only four canoe rests are there to relieve you.

DAY 4: **Hub Lake,** p. 105 rods, **Mesaba Lake,** p. 80 rods, **Hug Lake,** p. 3 rods, **Duck Lake,** p. 80 rods, **Zenith Lake,** p. 480 rods, **Lujenida Lake, Kelso River, Kelso Lake.** (See comments for Day 5, Route #53.)

DAY 5: **Kelso Lake,** p. 13 rods, **Sawbill Lake,** p. 100 rods, **Smoke Lake,** p. 90 rods, **Burnt Lake,** p. 230 rods, **Kelly Lake,** p. 65 rods, **Jack Lake.** You are likely to encounter a good deal of canoe traffic on Sawbill Lake, which has an outfitter at its southern end. You'll regain a sense of isolation, however, as you paddle farther east. The only challenging portage connects Burnt and Kelly lakes. It begins with a climb to 70 feet above Burnt Lake, then levels off, and finally drops 100 feet to Kelly Lake. About midway across the trail, you will cross an old, abandoned logging road immediately before entering a swampy area. There are 4 portage rests along the way.

You'll camp on one of the more scenic lakes in the BWCA, with hills rising around you as much as 250 feet above the lakes.

DAY 6: **Jack Lake,** p. 12 rods, **Weird Lake,** p. 80 rods, **Temperance River,** p. 240 rods, **South Temperance Lake,** p. 10 rods, **Brule Lake.** Unless the wind objects to your crossing of Brule Lake, this final day should be fairly easy. The only challenge is the ¾-mile carry to South Temperance Lake, which climbs 60 feet along the banks of the Temperance River. The portage has 5 canoe rests along its course. Like Route #57, this loop ends at the public access for Brule Lake, about two miles by road north of the Homer Lake landing.

There is a more direct canoe route to Homer Lake for those who dare: From Weird Lake paddle east, up the Vern River to Vern Lake, portage 15 rods to Whack Lake and another 16 rods to Homer Lake. The Vern River is not maintained by the Forest Service as a canoe route, and very few people use this primitive, difficult route. The river is very rocky and shallow, and there is considerable brush hanging into it. You are likely to spend much of your time pulling your canoe over rocks.

Entry Point 41—Brule Lake

Permits: 1055

Popularity Rank: 10

Daily Quota: 16

Location: Brule Lake is 19 miles northeast of the Sawbill Trail via Forest Routes 165 and 326. The Caribou Trail (County Road 4), however, offers a more direct route from US Highway 61. One mile northeast of Lutsen, turn off of Highway 61 and drive north on County Road 4 for 18 miles. Then turn left on Forest Route 153 and drive 1½ miles to the junction of Forest Route 326. Turn right and follow the Brule Lake Road 6 miles north to the public landing on the left side of the road, at the west end of the large parking lot. The Caribou Trail is rougher, more winding and hillier than the Sawbill Trail, but it requires fewer miles of driving on gravel.

Description: Since camping is not allowed near the Brule Lake access, the best place to camp the night before your trip is at Crescent Lake Campground. Located 12 miles by road southwest of Brule Lake (¼ mile south of Forest Route 165), this National Forest campground has 40 campsites, and there is a fee to camp there. If you prefer all the amenities that civilization can offer, perhaps your last night should be spent at Sky Blue Water Lodge, a lovely resort at the southern tip of the lake, 1 mile south of the landing.

Brule is one of the largest lakes in the eastern region of the Boundary Waters. Brule rests in the shadow of Eagle Mountain, the highest point in Minnesota. A trail to its summit leaves Forest Route 153 at the junction with Forest Route 158. The panoramic view at 2301 feet above sea level is breathtaking. Dotted with 67 picturesque islands, Brule is one of the more beautiful sights around.

Prior to 1986, Brule Lake was designated for 10-horsepower motors. Much of its popularity was attributed to motorboating fishermen in search of the fine walleye population in the lake. In 1984 nearly ⅓ of the permits went to motorists; yet barely more than ¼ of the available permits were used. In accordance with the BWCA Wilder ness Act of 1978, motors were banned from the lake after Sky Blue Waters Lodge ceased operations.

Since then, use of this entry point has increased considerably by canoeists. Brule has always been a beautiful lake. Now it is even more desirable for canoeists who seek a quick escape into wilderness solitude.

Although its quota is seldom filled, Brule Lake is large enough to accommodate an influx of canoes. But its vastness is also something to beware. Strong winds can whip up large waves on the open expanse. The islands and peninsulas at the east end of the lake afford some protection from gales, but there is no protection in the west-central part of the lake. Be alert to wind direction and use caution!

Route #59: The Winchell Lake Loop

2 Days, 14 Miles, 10 Lakes, 1 Creek, 11 Portages

Difficulty: Challenging

Fisher Maps: F-6, F-13

Travel Zones: 44, 46

Introduction: This lovely, short route will take you north from Brule Lake through a chain of small, slender lakes to beautiful Winchell Lake. The next day, then, you'll return to Brule via a slightly longer route through a chain of somewhat larger lakes and their interconnecting creeks. It's an ideal weekend loop. Or, for avid anglers, it might be stretched over three or even four days.

Once part of a motor route between Brule and Poplar lakes, the entire route is now reserved strictly for paddlers. But you can still see underwater remnants of old docks that once protruded from the ends of most of the portages.

The forest north of Brule Lake creates a boreal scene, consisting almost entirely of conifers—spruce, fir, pine and cedar. Unlike in most of the BWCA Wilderness, where aspens and birch are common, deciduous trees are few and far between in this region.

Anglers will have plenty of opportunity to wet their lines. Walleyes, northern pike and smallmouth bass occupy Brule and the Cone lakes. Winchell also harbors some large lake trout, while brook and rainbow trout have been stocked in Mulligan Lake. With any luck at all, your fry pan should be sizzling.

DAY 1: **Brule Lake,** p. 37 rods, **Lily Lake,** p. 32 rods,

Mulligan Lake, p. 40 rods, **Grassy Lake,** p. 200 rods, **Wanihigan Lake,** p. 14 rods, **Winchell Lake.** The first three portages are short, but they climb a total of nearly 100 feet. Most of that climb (60 feet) is on the 32-rod trail from Lily to Mulligan Lake, where there is a lovely path through tall pines. Mulligan is a state-designated trout lake, named after the Tofte District's first ranger, John E. Mulligan. Grassy is a very shallow lake—barely deep enough for passage of a loaded canoe. Watch carefully for the beginning of the 200-rod portage along the grassy east shore of the lake. It follows a nearly level course with an excellent path to the south end of Wanihigan Lake.

There are several nice campsites on the north shore of Winchell Lake, including five within a mile of the Wanihigan Lake portage. From all of them, you will be able to enjoy the lovely view across Winchell toward the steep and rocky ridge along the south shore of the lake.

DAY 2: **Winchell Lake,** p. 14 rods, **Wanihigan Lake,** p. 14 rods, **Cliff Lake,** p. 160 rods, **North Cone Lake,** p. 2 rods, **Cone Creek, Middle Cone Lake,** p. 25 rods, **Cone Creek, South Cone Lake, Cone Creek,** p. 15 rods, **creek, Brule Lake.** All the portages between Winchell and Brule lakes have rocky paths that necessitate careful steps. The half-mile trail climbs for about 25 rods up from Cliff Lake and then descends more than 100 feet to the shore of North Cone Lake. The 2-rod path between North Cone and Middle Cone lakes is little more than a liftover around a small rapids. You can avoid a carry by walking, lining or running your canoe through the narrow channel. When the water level is high enough, the final 15-rod portage between South Cone and Brule lakes may not be necessary. Cone Creek is usually deep enough to accommodate canoe traffic.

Cliff is an especially scenic lake, bordered by a steep, pine-covered ridge along the north shore and rocky cliffs near the east end of the lake. The hills on both sides of this slender lake tower 250 feet above the water.

On a windy day, use caution when crossing Brule Lake's open expanse. If necessary, rest during the windiest part of the afternoon at one of the campsites near the last portage and wait for the evening calm. No need to fight the lake. Lean back and enjoy its beauty!

Route #60: The Omega-Long Island Lakes Loop

3 Days, 29 Miles, 16 Lakes, 1 River, 1 Creek, 18 Portages

Difficulty: Challenging

Fisher Maps: F-6, F-13, F-12

Travel Zones: 44, 45, 36, 41, 42

Introduction: This scenic route will take you through a moderately used part of the BWCA. From the public landing you will paddle to the north shore of Brule Lake and then continue north through a chain of small, scenic lakes and interesting portages to Winchell Lake. From Winchell, then, you'll continue northbound to Omega Lake. From this point, you will steer west through Kiskadinna and Muskeg lakes to Long Island Lake. You will exit that busy lake via the Long Island River and paddle south through Gordon Lake to another popular lake—Cherokee. After portaging southeast to Sitka Lake, you will return to Brule by way of the Temperance lakes. A long eastward paddle across Brule will take you back to your origin.

Brule, Long Island and Cherokee lakes receive many visitors during the busier summer periods. But the rest of the route receives light-to-moderate use most of the season. Anglers will find lake trout, walleye and northern pike in lakes along this wilderness loop, and photographers will see plenty at which to point their cameras. The Laurentian Divide passes through the middle of the route, from just east of Sitka Lake northeast to just west of Omega Lake. The beautiful Misquah Hills lie southeast of the Divide. But to the northwest, the landscape is much flatter and generally not as impressive.

DAY 1: **Brule Lake,** p. 37 rods, **Lily Lake,** p. 32 rods, **Mulligan Lake,** p. 40 rods, **Grassy Lake,** p. 200 rods, **Wanihigan Lake,** p. 14 rods, **Winchell Lake,** p. 44 rods, **Omega Lake.** (See comments for Day 1, Route #59).

DAY 2: **Omega Lake,** p. 35 rods, **Kiskadinna Lake,** p. 185 rods, **Muskeg Lake, Muskeg Creek,** p. 4 rods, **creek,** p. 20 rods, **Long Island Lake, Long Island River,** p. 5 rods, **river,** p. 25 rods, **Gordon Lake,** p. 13 rods, **Cherokee Lake.** The first two portages are both steep and rocky. The 185-rod trail climbs slightly at the beginning and then follows a fairly level ridge that affords a north view through the forest. It then descends abruptly to cross a small stream on a log bridge. Beyond the stream, the well-traveled path descends more gradually to the shore of Muskeg Lake—a total drop of more than 170 feet. Employ caution on this steep portage. Though not as exhausting as hiking uphill, steep descents are often more diffucult and more treacherous, especially when wet. The first short portage on Muskeg Creek may not be necessary, if the water level is high enough for you to paddle through the creek. During late July and August you will probably see many other people on Long Island and Cherokee lakes, two points of convergence for trips beginning at popular Sawbill and Ham lakes. Find your campsite early, and then take time to fish for the nearby lake trout and northern pike.

DAY 3: **Cherokee Lake,** p. 10 rods, **Town Lake,** p. 110 rods, **Vesper Lake,** p. 75 rods, **Gasket Lake,** p. 45 rods, **Cam Lake,** p. 100 rods, **Brule Lake.** Although the portages are relatively short, they are certainly not easy. All four, from Town Lake south to Brule, are very rocky, strewn with boulders that make walking treacherous. The carry from Vesper to Gasket Lake is particularly rough, as the path climbs steeply over the Laurentian Divide. From then on, however, you'll be walking mostly downhill. The scenery in this lightly traveled area is stunning, enhanced by large boulder fields on the west shores of Gasket and Brule lakes.

Route #61: The Cherokee-Vista Lakes Loop

5 Days, 50 Miles, 26 Lakes, 2 Rivers, 1 Creek, 30 Portages

Difficulty: Challenging

Fisher Maps: F-6, F-12, F-13

Travel Zones: 44, 42, 41, 36, 45, 46, 47

Introduction: This route will first take you west through the Temperance lakes to popular Cherokee Lake. Then you'll paddle north through Gordon to Long Island Lake. From there you'll steer east, cross Muskeg Lake and navigate a chain of long, slender lakes to Horseshoe Lake, scarcely more than a stone's throw from the Gunflint Trail. From Vista Lake you will paddle southeast to Ram Lake and portage over a mile farther south to Bower Trout Lake. Your final day will be in the most scenic part of this route, as you paddle up the South Brule River flowage, straight west to Brule Lake.

Fishing is usually quite good in many of the lakes en route. Walleye, northern pike and small mouth bass inhabit many of them. Anglers will also have an opportunity to catch tasty lake trout in Cherokee and Long Island lakes. Brule, Horseshoe and Vista lakes are particularly well-known for the large walleye they produce.

After your first day, you will be paddling in parts of the BWCA that receive light use throughout most of the season. And your last two nights will find you camped in a travel zone that ranks near the bottom in popularity, despite the outstanding scenery that it contains.

Portages are generally easy. Two, however, are quite long, and two more are very difficult. Nevertheless, a group of good trippers should have no problem completing this loop in five days. Less experienced paddlers and serious anglers should probably allow six or seven days for completion.

None of the lakes on this route is open to motorboats. But your portage from Ram to Bower Trout Lake will take you briefly out of the BWCA, following Forest Route 152 most of the way.

DAY 1: **Brule Lake,** p. 10 rods, **South Temperance Lake,** p. 55 rods, **North Temperance Lake,** p. 105 rods, **Sitka Lake,** p. 140 rods, **Cherokee Lake.** None of the portages this day is difficult, but a westerly wind could be a drag, if not a hazard, to your paddling progress. You'll portage over the Laurentian Divide between North Temperance and Sitka lakes. Cherokee is a very popular lake, attracting many paddlers from Sawbill Lake. There are many good campsites, however, to accommodate the heavy traffic.

DAY 2: **Cherokee Lake,** p. 13 rods, **Gordon Lake,** p. 25 rods, **Long Island River,** p. 5 rods, **river, Long Island Lake,** p. 20 rods, **Muskeg Creek,** p. 4 rods, **creek, Muskeg Lake,** p. 185 rods, **Kiskadinna Lake,** p. 35 rods, **Omega Lake.** Long Island is another busy lake, attracting visitors from both Ham Lake, to the north, and Sawbill Lake, to the south. But few of them, if any, will join you en route to Omega Lake. Your second portage (4 rods) along Muskeg Creek may not be necessary if the water level is high enough. You will need every ounce of energy on the next portage, to Kiskadinna Lake. During the first 100 rods of this steep trail, you'll climb 170 feet above Muskeg Lake; then the path is rather level the rest of the way to Kiskadinna. You will find several nice campsites scattered around Omega Lake.

DAY 3: **Omega Lake,** p. 20 rods, **Hensen Lake,** p. 58 rods, **Pillsbery Lake,** p. 95 rods, **Allen Lake,** p. 50 rods, **Horseshoe Lake,** p. 21 rods, **Vista Lake.** This will be by far your easiest day of the whole trip, so enjoy it! Portage trails are well-worn, but traffic is usually not heavy. The terrain is low and the shores are forested with cedar and spruce—not too exciting. But fishing for walleye is normally very good, especially in Horseshoe and Vista lakes. Northern pike and smallmouth bass are also present.

DAY 4: **Vista Lake,** p. 50 rods, **Misquah Lake,** p. 190 rods, **Little Trout Lake,** p. 60 rods, **Rum Lake,** p. 55 rods, **Kroft Lake,** p. 80 rods, **Ram Lake,** p. 480 rods, **South Brule River, rapids, river,** p. 72 rods, **Bower Trout Lake.** You won't be far into the morning when you encounter a very rough portage, between Misquah and Little Trout lakes. With 5 canoe rests along the way, the path is fairly level but rocky and sometimes hard to see to the second canoe rest. You'll then climb steeply uphill to the third rest, drop steeply to the fourth and climb steeply again to the fifth before dropping steeply to Little Trout Lake. The next (80-rod) portage is equally steep over another hill. But the long one from Ram Lake to the road is mostly downhill—and sometimes quite steep at that.

The portage trails from the road into Little Trout Lake appear well-used, but not between Little Trout and Vista lakes. Ram and Kroft lakes are quite murky and have no campsites on them.

The last 20 rods of the ½-mile trail from Ram Lake to the road is a primitive one-lane road itself. At the Forest Route, turn right and portage one mile gently downhill to the South Brule River bridge. Just past it, on the right (west) is the access to the river.

You'll encounter a small rapids eight rods upstream from the put-in, which can be easily walked up or vigorously paddled. The portage to Bower Trout Lake is another eight rods upstream.

The two campsites are rather hard to see until you're right on them—one on the north shore and one on the south.

DAY 5: **Bower Trout Lake,** p. 90 rods, **Marshall Lake,** p. 30 rods, **Dugout Lake, South Brule River, Skidway Lake,** p. 35 rods, **South Brule River,** p. 40 rods, **river,** p. 40 rods, **Swan Lake, South Brule River,** p. 292 rods, **Vernon Lake,** p. 49 rods, **Brule Bay, Brule Lake.** This is one of the lovelier days of the whole route—scenic lakes and a crystalline river, surrounded by high hills and connected by relatively pleasant portages. All day will be spent paddling and portaging up the S. Brule River system, but seldom are the pathways steep, except for the final carry from Vernon Lake to Brule Bay. There you'll climb steeply for about 35 of the 49 rods before dropping to Brule Lake.

Even the 292-rod trail to Vernon Lake is surprisingly pleasant. It climbs gently to a ridge above the river and follows a good, smooth path most of the way, with six canoe rests along the trail. Then it drops down from the sixth rest to Vernon Lake. You'll pass the dilapidated remains of an old logging camp near the east end of the portage.

Some maps show a 29-rod portage between Dugout and Skidway lakes, but you should not need it. The river here is deeper than the east end of Dugout Lake where a small rapids straddles the narrow channel.

You'll surely find this to be a very scenic part of the Boundary Waters.

Ch. 4: Entry from the Gunflint Trail (West)

The Northeastern Area

The northeastern part of the Boundary Waters Canoe Area contains most of the entry points included in this guide. It includes the 11 entry points that are accessible from, and to the *west* of, the Gunflint Trail (Cook County Road 12).

The Gunflint Trail begins in the center of Grand Marais, on the shore of Lake Superior. It heads north for 25 miles, then veers west for another 25 miles, and then again leads north to its end at Gull Lake, 57 miles northwest of Grand Marais. All of the road is hard-surfaced and usually in good condition.

Resorts, outfitters and public campgrounds are located intermittently along the road's entire course. Traffic is fairly heavy during the summer months. And that stands to reason, since the northernmost entry point (Saganaga Lake) is the most popular entry point in the eastern half of the BWCA.

Grand Marais is a small but bustling town that is supported almost entirely by tourism. For canoe trippers in need of refuge before or after their trip, a municipal campground is located near the center of the village. Adjacent to the campground is a municipal indoor swimming pool where the grimy tourist may purchase an inexpensive shower or sauna.

Entry Point 43—Bower Trout Lake

Permits: 100

Popularity Rank: 41

Quota: 1

Location: Follow the Gunflint Trail north from US Highway 61 in Grand Marais for 17 miles to its junction with

Forest Route 325. You'll find it on the left side of the Gunflint Trail, *one* mile past the Greenwood Road. A sign there points left to "Twin Lakes." Turn left and follow this narrow, winding, gravel road west 6 miles to a T-intersection with Forest Route 152. Turn left and drive ½ mile southeast on Forest Route 152 to the South Brule River bridge. You may put in at the base of the bridge and follow the river west to a (72-rod) portage leading to Bower Trout Lake.

Description: There is a small parking area, large enough for four or five vehicles, on the east side of the road, about 50 yards north of the bridge. Or, if you would rather portage directly from your car to the lake, without a short paddle on the South Brule River, you may park at a different location. A primitive one-lane road leads west from Forest Route 152 about midway between its junction with Forest Route 325 and the bridge. It leads 0.4 mile west, past a large gravel pit, to a small parking area on the left, large enough for three or four vehicles. A short distance beyond the parking spot, the old road becomes impassable, due to mud and water. But a 67-rod portage trail continues on down the same old, overgrown road. After the muddy section, the level path has a good, dry surface on the final 40-rod stretch to Bower Trout, where there is a good boat access on the north shore of the lake.

There are no campgrounds in the vicinity of the access. A large National Forest campground at East Bearskin Lake, 26 miles up the Gunflint Trail from Grand Marais, however, is a good place to spend the night before your trip. A fee is charged to use one of the 43 campsites.

Along with Ram Lake and Morgan Lake, its neighbors to the north, Bower Trout is one of the least accessible entry points served by the Gunflint Trail. But its popularity has grown during the past few years—up 75% from 1977 to 1989 (while use of the BWCA as a whole declined). With a quota of only one group per day, Bower Trout ranks third among all entry points with quotas filled the highest percent of the time. A reservation is advised. Canoeists may be discovering that it is one of the most scenic entry points in this part of the Boundary Waters. In fact, the region between Bower Trout and Brule ranks as one of my favorites! And with but a few notable exceptions, travel here is fairly easy.

The BWCA Wilderness Act of 1978 prohibited motorboats and motorized canoes on Bower Trout Lake. The only motors you'll hear are in vehicles using the nearby roads. Beyond Bower Trout the beautiful lakes and rivers are also reserved for paddlers only.

Route #62: The South Brule-Vista Route

4 Days, 28 Miles, 20 Lakes, 1 River, 22 Portages

Difficulty: Challenging

Fisher Maps: F-13

Travel zones: 44, 46, 47

Introduction: This scenic route will lead you first through the lakes, ponds and creeks that compose the upper reaches of the South Brule River and then northeast to the headwaters of the North Brule River. From Bower Trout Lake you'll paddle west through Marshall, Swan and Vernon lakes to Brule Lake. From the north shore of this awesome lake, you will portage north through a series of small lakes to Winchell Lake and follow a popular route eastward through Winchell, Gaskin and Horseshoe lakes to the source of the North Brule River. Then you'll turn south to Vista Lake and continue southeastward to Forest Route 152, leaving the BWCA at Ram Lake.

Your trip will begin and end on the highest notes, perhaps, as this corner of the BWCA offers more outstanding scenery and fewer people than the region northeast of Brule Lake. This corner is Zone 47 and it ranks near the bottom in popularity (45th of 49). Only 12% of those entering this zone do so from Bower Trout Lake. Though campsites are few and far between, they are seldom occupied.

Anglers will find excellent fishing along this route for walleye, smallmouth bass and northern pike.

Portages are generally short and quite easy, but there are just enough long ones to warrant a "challenging" rating.

DAY 1: **South Brule River, rapids, river,** p. 72 rods, **Bower Trout Lake,** p. 90 rods, **Marshall Lake,** p. 30 rods, **Dugout Lake, South Brule River, Skidway Lake,** p. 35 rods, **South Brule River,** p. 40 rods, **river,** p. 40 rods, **Swan Lake.** The first day of this route is one of the lovelier first days you can have anywhere in the Boundary Waters—scenic lakes and a crystalline river surrounded by high hills and connected by relatively pleasant portages. You will encounter a small but swift rapids 8 rods upstream from your put-in below Forest Route 152. It can be easily walked or vigorously paddled, but there is no portage around it. The trail to Bower Trout Lake is another 8 rods upstream.

Your map may indicate a 29-rod portage between Dugout and Skidway lakes, but you should not find it necessary (or even in existence). If the water level is so low as to necessitate a carry there, you will certainly have trouble all the way across Dugout Lake.

Swan is a beautiful lake. There are three campsites from which to choose, the northernmost at a location where a logging camp once thrived.

DAY 2: **Swan Lake, South Brule River,** p. 292 rods, **Vernon Lake,** p. 49 rods, **Brule Bay, Brule Lake,** p. 37 rods, **Lily Lake,** p. 32 rods, **Mulligan Lake,** p. 40 rods, **Grassy Lake,** p. 200 rods, **Wanihigan Lake,** p. 14 rods, **Winchell Lake.** This day will rate as the roughest of the trip, though it is not really as bad as it may appear on the map.

Perhaps the toughest carry is one of the shorter ones—the path between Vernon and Brule lakes. There you will climb steeply for 35 of the 49 rods, before dropping to Brule Lake, 83 feet above Vernon Lake. The long trail leading to Vernon Lake (292 rods) is surprisingly easy. It climbs gently to a ridge above the South Brule River and follows a good, smooth path most of the way. There are six canoe rests. After the last canoe rest, the trail descends to Vernon Lake. You will pass the dilapidated remains of the Alger Smith lumbering camp, in operation from 1920–1923, near the east end of the portage.

Like the 49-rod trail to Brule Bay, the 32-rod portage north from Lily Lake also climbs steeply to Mulligan Lake—a 60-foot gain in elevation. But it follows such a lovely path through tall pines, you probably won't even notice the effort required. Mulligan is a state-designated trout lake (rainbows and brookies) that was named after the Tofte District's first ranger, John E. Mulligan. Grassy is a very shallow lake, barely deep enough for passage of a loaded canoe. Watch carefully for the beginning of the 200-rod portage along the grassy east shore of the lake. It follows a nearly level course with an excellent path to the south end of Wanihigan Lake.

Winchell is a beautiful lake, with rock cliffs bordering its southern shoreline and nearby hills towering nearly 350 feet above the water. It's also a popular lake, receiving visitors from both the Lizz Lake and Brule Lake entry points. Find your campsite on the north shore of the lake as early as possible. There are five lovely sites within a mile of the Wanihigan Lake portage from which to choose. Winchell is a popular lake, receiving visitors from both the Lizz Lake and Brule Lake entry points.

DAY 3: **Winchell Lake,** p. 60 rods, **Gaskin Lake,** p. 102 rods, **Horseshoe Lake,** p. 21 rods, **Vista Lake.** This day will be the easiest of your trip. The scenery after Winchell Lake, however, is nothing to point a camera at—lakes surrounded by a low terrain, shoreline forested with cedar and spruce. There are very few deciduous trees in this region to enhance the scenic appeal of the forest. You may encounter more people on Winchell, Gaskin and Horseshoe lakes than on all of the other lakes combined. But Vista Lake is a pleasant exception—off the "beaten path" and scenic. And if you came here to fish, you're camped in the right spot. Vista and Horseshoe lakes are teeming with large walleye, northern pike and smallmouth bass.

DAY 4: **Vista Lake,** p. 50 rods, **Misquah Lake,** p. 190 rods, **Little Trout Lake,** p. 60 rods, **Rum Lake,** p. 55 rods, **Kroft Lake,** p. 80 rods, **Ram Lake,** p. 110 rods, Forest Route 152. You haven't far to go this day, but you're in for a *bad* portage en route. The worst carry of the entire trip, in fact, connects Misquah and Little Trout lakes. With five canoe rests along the 190 rods, it first follows a level but rocky path that is sometimes hard to see. Then it abruptly surmounts two *steep* hills before reaching Little Trout Lake. The next 60-rod trail is equally steep over yet another hill. But the long one from Ram Lake to the road is mostly downhill—and sometimes quite steep at that. The last 20 rods of it are on a primitive one-lane road.

Rum and Kroft lakes may be very murky. Get your drinking water from Little Trout Lake.

If you didn't make arrangements to have a car waiting at the Ram Lake portage, you'll have to walk a mile downhill (right) to the South Brule River.

Route #63: The Swan-Cherokee-Banadad Route

6 Days, 50 Miles, 30 Lakes, 2 Rivers, 33 Portages

Difficulty: Challenging

Fisher Maps: F-13, F-12

Travel zones: 47, 44, 42, 41, 36, 45, 46

Introduction: Like Route #62, this fascinating loop will first take you up the South Brule River flowage to Brule Lake. But you will continue paddling west this time, through the Temperance lakes to Cherokee Lake. Then you will steer north to Long Island Lake. From there, you'll portage into a seldom visited chain of lakes that lead northeast through Banadad and Rush lakes to Poplar. From the south shore of that busy, populated lake, you will portage to Lizz Lake and head southeast through Caribou, Horseshoe and Vista lakes to Misquah Lake. Then you'll steer east to Ram Lake and end your expedition by portaging out of the BWCA to Forest Route 152.

Most of this route is very lightly traveled, and three of the five nights will be spent in extremely isolated parts of the BWCA. Motors are allowed only on Poplar Lake, where resorts are also located.

Like Route #62, this loop begins and ends in one of the prettiest parts of the entire BWCA. And during your swing through Travel Zone 45, between Long Island Lake and Poplar Lake, you will have an excellent opportunity to view moose.

DAY 1: **South Brule River,** rapids, **river,** p. 72 rods, **Bower Trout Lake,** p. 90 rods, **Marshall Lake,** p. 30 rods, **Dugout Lake, South Brule River, Skidway Lake,** p. 35 rods, **South Brule River,** p. 40 rods, **river,** p. 40 rods, **Swan Lake** (See comments for Day 1, Route #62.)

DAY 2: **Swan Lake, South Brule River,** p. 292 rods, **Vernon Lake,** p. 49 rods, **Brule Bay, Brule Lake,** p. 10 rods, **South Temperance Lake.** (See comments for part of Day 2, Route #62.) Watch overhead for soaring bald eagles. A nest is located near the north shore of Brule Lake, and this area, in general, is one of the best parts of the BWCA in which to see bald eagles and ospreys. Beware of strong winds, as they may whip up treacherous waves with little warning on big Brule Lake.

DAY 3: **South Temperance Lake,** p. 55 rods, **North Temperance Lake,** p. 105 rods, **Sitka Lake,** p. 140 rods, **Cherokee Lake,** p. 13 rods, **Gordon Lake,** p. 25 rods, **Long Island River,** p. 5 rods, **river, Long Island Lake.** You'll cross over the Laurentian Divide on your portage between North Temperance and Sitka lakes. From that point on, it's all downhill to Long Island Lake. During the busiest part of the summer, from late July through August, campsites may be at a premium on Long Island Lake. It's a popular destination for canoeists originating their trips from Ham Lake and from busy Sawbill Lake. Grab the first site you see!

DAY 4: **Long Island Lake,** p. 109 rods, **Cave Lake,** p. 195 rods, **Ross Lake,** p. 180 rods, **Sebeka Lake,** p. 95 rods, **Banadad Lake,** p. 10 rods, **Rush Lake.** This will be the roughest day, so far, through one of the least used regions in the BWCA. Though within hearing range of the Gunflint Trail, it is evident from the portage trails and campsites that few canoeists venture this way. Even when all of the campsites on Long Island Lake are occupied, you are likely not to see any other visitors en route to Rush.

All four portages from Long Island to Banadad are TOUGH—uphill, rocky, rooty and with marshy stretches where log "bridges" have been laid. The paths are very slippery when wet. There is only one portage rest on each of the first two portages, but two rests on each of the last two. The 180-rod carry seems twice that long, because it is uphill nearly all the way.

Camped on Rush Lake, you will feel as if you were 1000 miles from any semblance of civilization—until you hear trucks roaring along the not-so-distant Gunflint Trail.

DAY 5: **Rush Lake,** p. 50 rods, **Little Rush Lake,** p. 21 rods, **Skipper Lake,** p. 320 rods, **Poplar Lake,** p. 51 rods, **Lizz Lake,** p. 73 rods, **Caribou Lake,** p. 20 rods, **Horseshoe Lake,** p. 21 rods, **Vista Lake.** You'll pass quickly from a feeling of utmost isolation to one of chaotic civilization and back to tranquil isolation this day. Poplar Lake, located just outside the Boundary Waters, is bustling with the business of several resorts and a canoe outfitter. The 21-rod portage connecting Little Rush and Skipper lakes is not easy to locate and appears to be seldom used. You'll find the portage originating in the small bay just north of the bay into which the creek flows.

Under normal water conditions, however, you should have no problem paddling or walking your canoe through the shallow creek, eliminating the need for a portage.

The long carry to Poplar Lake is not difficult, but it's bound to provide you with a good workout. It is mostly level or gently downhill, follows a good path, and has seven rests along the way.

South of Poplar Lake, the portage trails are incredibly easy—wide, smooth, sandy paths that are heavily traveled. But fortunately, most of the traffic steers west from Horseshoe Lake, rather than south to Vista Lake.

DAY 6: **Vista Lake,** p. 50 rods, **Misquah Lake,** p. 190 rods, **Little Trout Lake,** p. 60 rods, **Rum Lake,** p. 55 rods, **Kroft Lake,** p. 80 rods, **Ram Lake,** p. 110 rods, Forest Route 152. (See comments for Day 4, Route #62.)

Entry Point 44—Ram Lake

Permits: 112

Popularity Rank: 39

Quota: 1

Location: Follow the Gunflint Trail north from US Highway 61 in Grand Marais 17 miles to the junction with Forest Route 325, one mile past the Greenwood Road. A sign there points left to "Twin Lakes." Turn left and follow this narrow, winding, secondary road 6 miles west to the **T**-intersection with Forest Route 152. Turn right and drive ½ mile north to where you see a portage sign indicating "Ram Lake 160 rods" to the west.

Description: Although there are no designated campsites here, it appears that the parking spaces at the beginning of the portage have been used for camping. The closest public campground at which to spend the night before your trip is at East Bearskin Lake, 1¼ miles east of the Gunflint Trail, 26 miles north of Grand Marais. There are 43 campsites available, and a fee is charged.

Ram is a crystal-clear, state-designated trout lake that is stocked with rainbow and lake trout. The portage to Ram Lake begins as a primitive, one-lane road for 20 rods. On both sides of this road are several open spaces where a dozen cars may park. As the trail narrows, it slopes downhill slightly for a few rods. But from then on, it is all uphill—quite steep at times. Although the sign at the beginning of the trail reads "160 rods," the portage actually measures only 110 rods. Nevertheless, it may *seem* like 210 rods, because of the incline! The well-traveled path is narrow and cluttered with rocks, boulders and roots that make walking hazardous, especially when the trail is wet. Be very careful at the end, in particular, where the trail drops steeply over the final three rods to the shore of Ram Lake.

Because Ram Lake is not easily accessible from the Gunflint Trail (and, perhaps, because of the long uphill portage leading to it) this entry point is generally overlooked by visitors to the BWCA. Less than ⅓ of its available permits were used in 1984. But that doesn't mean it's not worth visiting. On the contrary, Ram Lake offers the wilderness canoeist a quick escape into relative isolation, where motors are prohibited and the setting is quite lovely.

Route #64: The Misquah Hills Loop

2 Days, 9 Miles, 8 Lakes, 9 Portages

Difficulty: Rugged

Fisher Maps: F-13

Travel Zone: 47

Introduction: This loop is short but rugged, and visited by only a few canoeists. The fishing is excellent, the scenery nice, and the immediate solitude refreshing.

From Ram Lake you will paddle and portage northwest through Kroft, Rum and Little Trout lakes to Misquah and Vista lakes. The next morning you will turn east and paddle through Jake and Morgan lakes to the Morgan Lake Trail, which exits the Boundary Waters and leads to Forest Route 315, 4 miles north of your origin.

All of the route is contained in Travel Zone #47—one of the prettiest yet least visited parts of the BWCA. Nevertheless, on a busy summer weekend, the five campsites from Ram Lake to Little Trout may all be occupied. Very few travelers, however, continue on to Misquah Lake.

If you don't mind starting your trip with a 400-rod portage, this route could just as well be taken in reverse, ending at the Ram Lake portage (see Entry Point 45). Either way, you stand a good chance of viewing moose and beaver en route. And anglers will have an outstanding opportunity to catch large walleye, northern pike, smallmouth bass and stream trout.

DAY 1: p. 110 rods, **Ram Lake,** p. 80 rods, **Kroft Lake,** p. 55 rods, **Rum Lake,** p. 60 rods, **Little Trout Lake,** p. 190 rods, **Misquah Lake,** p. 50 rods, **Vista Lake.** You'll soon learn why this short loop is called "rugged." Nearly all of the half-mile portage to Ram Lake is uphill. The next two aren't bad, but the 60-rod carry to Little Trout Lake surmounts a steep hill—and the worst is yet to come! The 190-rod trail from Little Trout to Misquah Lake ranks among the meanest of portages in this part of the BWCA. You'll climb over two steep hills during the first 100 rods, before the rough, rocky path levels. Five canoe rests are strategically located along the way.

Vista Lake produces large walleye, smallmouth bass and northern pike. So does Horseshoe Lake, to the north, if you feel like a side trip this evening. En route, lake trout occupy the depths of Ram and Little Trout lakes.

DAY 2: **Vista Lake,** p. 35 rods, **Jake Lake,** p. 55 rods, **Morgan Lake,** p. 400 rods, Forest Route 315. All three of these portages appear to be used more by moose than by men. In spite of light use, however, they follow good paths.

The Morgan Lake Trail (400-rod portage) is long, but mostly downhill after the first ¼ mile, with a smooth path much of the way. Only three canoe rests have been constructed along the trail. A picturesque beaver pond marks the halfway point. It's a good site for lunch—for both you and the resident moose! The worst part of the trail is the last 7 rods, through a swampy area next to the road.

If you haven't left a car here, you'll have to end this trip with a 4-mile hike south on Forest Routes 315 and 152, to your origin at the Ram Lake portage.

Route #65: The Vista-Mesaba Loop

8 Days, 70 Miles, 42 Lakes, 4 Rivers, 4 Creeks, 54 Portages

Difficulty: Rugged

Fisher Maps: F-13, F-12, F-5, F-6

Travel Zones: 47, 46, 45, 36, 41, 42, 44

Introduction: This high-quality wilderness route will take you through some of the loveliest, most animal-populated, yet least visited parts of the Boundary Waters Canoe Area. From Ram Lake you will first head northwest through Little Trout and Vista lakes to Horseshoe Lake. Then you will paddle west via a chain of long slender lakes to popular Long Island Lake. Continuing west, you'll enter the winding wilderness of the Frost River, where moose are far more abundant than paddlers. From Fente Lake you will portage south to Hub Lake and continue southeastward through Mesaba Lake to Kelso and Sawbill lakes. Then, you'll paddle northeast to Cherokee Lake and east to big Brule Lake. From the east end of Brule Bay you'll follow the lovely lakes, pools and rapids that compose the upper reaches of the scenic South Brule River system all the way back to Forest Route 152, just one mile south of your origin.

The only lakes on the route that receive moderate-to-heavy use are Horseshoe to Gaskin, Long Island, Sawbill to Cherokee, and Brule. Elsewhere you should have no difficulty finding solitude.

DAY 1: P. 110 rods, **Ram Lake,** p. 80 rods, **Kroft Lake,** p. 55 rods, **Rum Lake,** p. 60 rods, **Little Trout Lake,** p. 190 rods, **Misquah Lake,** p. 50 rods, **Vista Lake.** (See comments for Day 1, Route #64.)

DAY 2: **Vista Lake,** p. 21 rods, **Horseshoe Lake,** p. 102 rods, **Gaskin Lake,** p. 80 rods, **Hensen Lake,** p. 20 rods, **Omega Lake,** p. 35 rods, **Kiskadinna Lake.** Horseshoe and Gaskin lakes are part of a popular canoe route from Lizz Lake that receives fairly heavy use at times. Portages are not long enough to be much of a problem. The second, third and fifth, however, surmount fairly steep hills, with one or two canoe rests per carry. This will be your easiest day of the trip, so enjoy it.

DAY 3: **Kiskadinna Lake,** p. 185 rods, **Muskeg Lake, Muskeg Creek,** p. 4 rods, **creek,** p. 20 rods, **Long Island Lake, Long Island River,** p. 5 rods, **river,** p. 25 rods, **Gordon Lake,** p. 140 rods, **Unload Lake,** p. 40 rods, **Frost Lake.** Eat a good breakfast, because you'll need all the energy you can muster up on that first portage. The trail first gradually ascends, but then drops 170 feet to Muskeg Lake. With most of the drop occurring in the final 100 rods, it is quite steep in places. The first short portage along Muskeg Creek may not be necessary, if the water level is high enough to paddle through the creek.

You are likely to see many other people on Long Island Lake during the busy summer periods. The 140-rod path from Gordon Lake to Unload goes over a fairly steep hill at its east end, then levels off and follows a good, smooth trail the rest of the way. The final carry to Frost Lake may not be necessary during the high-water periods. It is a rough path that receives little use, but it is necessary during late summer or an unusually dry year.

There are two beautiful campsites on the north shore of Frost Lake, as well as three other sites. Moose inhabit the surrounding area, so keep a watchful eye at dusk and dawn. During a visit my wife and I saw four moose along the lake's north shore.

DAY 4: **Frost Lake,** p. 130 rods, **Frost River** p. 10 rods, **Octopus Lake,** p. 15 rods, **Frost River,** p. 25 rods, **river,** p. 5 rods, **river,** p. 30 rods, **Chase Lake,** p. 15 rods, **Pencil Lake,** p. 60 rods, **Frost River,** p. 10 rods, **river,** p. 4 rods, **river,** p. 10 rods, **river,** p. 12 rods, **river, Afton Lake,** p. 20 rods, **Frost River,** rapids, **Fente Lake,** p. 300 rods, **Hub Lake.** (See comments for Day 3, Route #56.) Your last portage, the toughest one of the whole trip, is hard to take after an already long day. The trail gains nearly 140 feet in elevation during the first 100 rods, then levels off, and finally slopes gently down to Hub Lake. Only four canoe rests are there to relieve you.

DAY 5: **Hub Lake,** p. 105 rods, **Mesaba Lake,** p. 80 rods, **Hug Lake,** p. 3 rods, **Duck Lake,** p. 80 rods, **Zenith Lake,** p. 480 rods, **Lujenida Lake, Kelso River, Kelso Lake,** p. 13 rods, **Sawbill Lake.** (See comments for Day 5, Route #53.) There are several nice campsites at the north end of Sawbill Lake. Canoe traffic is heavy there, however, as Sawbill is the third most popular entry point in the BWCA. If you arrive at Kelso Lake late in the afternoon, perhaps you should stop there for the night.

DAY 6: **Sawbill Lake,** p. 80 rods, **Ada Creek,** p. 80 rods, **Ada Lake, Skoop Creek,** p. 12 rods, **Skoop Lake,** p. 180 rods, **Cherokee Creek, Cherokee Lake,** p. 140 rods, **Sitka Lake,** p. 105 rods, **North Temperance Lake,** p. 55 rods, **South Temperance Lake.** Portaging will have its ups and downs today, as you will cross the Laurentian Divide twice, on the portages to Cherokee and North Temperance lakes. A quick liftover may be necessary at Ada Lake, before the 12-rod portage to Skoop Lake. The 180-rod carry climbs over the Divide and then drops down to Cherokee Creek, a rather marshy stream that leads to one of the more popular lakes in this part of the BWCA. It has 4 portage rests, but it isn't nearly as exhausting as the 140-rod portage to Sitka Lake, which has 5 canoe rests along the way.

DAY 7: **South Temperance Lake,** p. 10 rods, **Brule Lake,** p. 49 rods, **Vernon Lake,** p. 292 rods, **South Brule River, Swan Lake.** Brule is a mighty big lake where strong winds may pose a threat to canoeists. Should you become wind-bound there, you could shorten this route by ending your trip at the public landing on its shore. Brule is well-known for its good walleye fishing, and anglers will also find lake trout and northern pike there. (See comments for Entry Point 41.)

The portage to Vernon Lake follows a very steep path that drops 83 feet from Brule Bay. Your final carry of the day is one of the longest of the entire trip, but not at all difficult. After you climb for the first 40 rods to a ridge above the South Brule River, the rest of the trail is level or gently downhill. It is a good, smooth path, with six canoe rests along the way. Near the end, you will pass the dilapidated remains of the Alger Smith lumbering camp, which operated from 1920–1923.

Swan is a lovely lake with three nice campsites. Walleye and northern pike live beneath its surface.

DAY 8: **Swan Lake,** p. 40 rods, **South Brule River,** p. 40 rods, **river,** p. 35 rods, **Skidway Lake, South Brule River, Dugout Lake,** p. 30 rods, **Marshall Lake,** p. 90 rods, **Bower Trout Lake,** p. 72 rods, **South Brule River,** rapids, **river,** Forest Route 152. This will be an easy and very scenic final day. Steep hills surround crystalline lakes and pools that receive few visitors.

Your map may indicate a 29-rod portage between Skidway and Dugout lakes, but you should not find it necessary, or even in existence. If the water is so low as to necessitate a carry there, you will surely have trouble all the way across Dugout.

Unless you have made other arrangements, you will have to walk the final mile of this round trip. The Ram Lake portage is north of the South Brule River, via Forest Route 152.

Entry Point 45—Morgan Lake

Permits: 41

Popularity Rank: 55

Daily Quota: 1

Location: From Highway 61 in Grand Marais, drive 21½ miles north via the Gunflint Trail to Lima Mountain Road (Forest Route 152). Turn left there and proceed 2.3 miles west on this fair gravel road to an unmarked Y-intersection. Bear right for another 1/10 mile to the junction of Forest Route 315. Turn right and proceed 1.9 miles north to the Morgan Lake portage on the left side of the road. There is a small parking space, large enough for only one vehicle.

Description: There are no campgrounds in the vicinity of this entry point. The large national-forest camppground at East Bearskin Lake, 26 miles up the Gunflint Trail from Grand Marais, is a good place to spend the night before your trip. A fee is charged there to use one of the 43 campsites.

Access to Morgan Lake is by way of a 400-rod trail that begins at the parking spot. A 1¼-mile portage is a rugged way to begin *any* canoe trip, but the portage essentially follows a good path that's fairly easy to negotiate—*after* the first eight rods, that is! The only bad part is the beginning, where you'll have to wade through a wet, muddy alder swamp. Plan on wet feet for the remainder of the hike! Most of the trail, however, is on dry, level to gently rolling terrain, through a lovely upland forest of aspen and birch, mixed with pine, fir and spruce. The only steep part is where the trail abruptly drops to cross a small creek draining a large bog. Just before reaching the creek, you'll pass an opening that affords a nice view of the bog—a good place to watch for moose. Beyond the creek, then, is the only significant climb, back up to high ground, before you gradually descend to the lake. There are six canoe rests to assist you along the way.

Along with its neighboring entry points to the south (#43 and #44), Morgan Lake is one of the least accessible and most overlooked BWCA entries along the Gunflint Trail. But unlike entry through Bower Trout Lake, you should seldom have difficulty getting a permit for Morgan Lake. Only 27% of its annual quota is used each summer. Few people avail themselves of this good, quick way to escape into wilderness.

In addition to the short loop described below, you can also use the Morgan Lake entry point to reverse Route #64, by ending, rather than starting, at Ram Lake. You can also "plug into" Routes #62, 63, and 65, safely adding *at least* one full day to each of those suggested trips.

Route #66: The Trout Lakes Loop

2 Days, 9 Miles, 5 Lakes, 8 Portages

Difficulty: Challenging

Fisher Maps: F-13

Travel Zone: 47

Introduction: This short loop will take you through a small chain of lakes that entertains few visitors. From the end of the long portage, you'll paddle straight west through Morgan and Jake lakes to Vista Lake. Then after a peaceful night's rest on Vista Lake, you'll return to Morgan Lake by way of Jake, Lux and Carl lakes. After that first long portage, the route is actually quite easy. And even with the long hikes at the beginning and the end, strong paddlers, traveling light, could easily complete the loop in just one day.

For the anglers in your group, the destination (Vista Lake) is a good source for northern pike and walleyes. The other four lakes were reclaimed a few years ago and stocked with stream trout.

For anyone who seeks solitude and a good opportunity to view moose and other wildlife, but who doesn't have a great deal of time for the search, this route is a good choice. Even on the busiest weekends and holiday periods of summer, you're not likely to feel crowded anywhere on this loop.

DAY 1: P. 400 rods, **Morgan Lake,** p. 55 rods, **Jake Lake,** p. 35 rods, **Vista Lake.** After the first portage, unless there is a strong west wind, you're in for an easy day of paddling and portaging to one of the three campsites on Vista Lake. Although yours is the only permit issued for the Morgan Lake entry point this day, bear in mind that there may be other visitors on Vista Lake who started at one of the Poplar Lake entry points. So, in spite of the relative isolation of Vista Lake, it might be a good idea to stake your claim at a campsite as soon as possible. There aren't many other choices if your favorite destination is already taken.

DAY 2: **Vista Lake,** p. 35 rods, **Jake Lake,** p. 20 rods, **Lux Lake,** p. 15 rods, **Carl Lake,** p. 5 rods, **Morgan Lake,** p. 400 rods. Of course, if you don't mind backtracking, you can replace three short portages with the same 55-rod trail you took yesterday between Jake and Morgan lakes. Lux and Carl lakes are recommended simply for a little diversion.

Entry Point 47—Lizz Lake

Permits: 359

Popularity Rank: 20

Daily Quota: 7 (including Swamp and Meeds lakes)

Location: From US Highway 61 in Grand Marais, follow the Gunflint Trail northwest for 31 miles to Poplar Lake, on the left side of the road. Lizz Lake is 51 rods south of Poplar.

Description: Public access to Poplar is at the western tip of the lake. As you drive up the Gunflint Trail, watch carefully for the Forest Service access sign on the left side of the road 1.8 miles beyond Windigo Lodge. Turn left there and follow this rough, primitive road ½ mile west to an intersection. Turn left again and follow this even rougher road south to the 80-rod portage trail leading to Poplar Lake. The Forest Service recommends this road only for high-clearance vehicles. It is not suitable for passenger cars.

If you don't have a 4WD vehicle, you may prefer to use a private landing at Poplar Lake Lodge, Windigo Lodge or Rockwood Lodge. All charge fees for parking and boat launching, but those fees are likely to be much less than the towing fee you may have to pay if you get stuck on the primitive forest road.

A National Forest Campground at Flour Lake is the closest place to camp the night before your trip. It is located 2 miles up the Clearwater Road, which leads northeast from the Gunflint Trail 27 miles up this road from Grand Marais. It's a large campground, with 34 sites. A fee is assessed.

In addition to Lizz Lake, Swamp Lake (#46), Meeds Lake (#48) and Skipper Lake (#49) are BWCA entry points accessible from Poplar Lake. Only Lizz Lake, however, ranks high in popularity, as it offers the easiest entry into the Boundary Waters. While 359 groups passed through Lizz Lake in 1989, only 294 groups used the other three entry points, combined.

Because of their close proximity, and because they serve essentially the same part of the BWCA Wilderness, Lizz, Swamp and Meeds lakes are grouped together under just one quota for all three entry points combined.

If your heart is set on an easy entry through Lizz Lake, make your reservation early. Lizz is one of the most difficult entry points for which to get a permit. Since 80% of its quota was used in 1989 during the entire 5-month canoeing season, reservations are a must for this popular entry point.

Until 1979, Lizz Lake was part of an extensive motor route from Poplar Lake all the way through Brule Lake to Sawbill Lake, 22 miles southwest. Federal legislation in 1978 banned motors in this part of the BWCA. Since only 21% of the permits in 1977 were issued to groups using motors, however, use patterns have not changed drastically since the motor restrictions were imposed, although 35% fewer groups entered the Wilderness here in 1989.

Travel in this area is generally easy. Portage trails are well-worn. Campsites are plentiful. Fishing is usually quite good. But the scenery is not outstanding. This is a unique area with a boreal forest of spruce, fir, cedar and pine. You'll see few of the aspens and birch that characterize most of the BWCA Wilderness. Nevertheless, for a weekend away from the city, it's lovely. There are many places in the BWCA much prettier—and not far away, either.

Route #67: The Winchell-Hensen Loop

3 Days, 20 Miles, 10 Lakes, 13 Portages

Difficulty: Easy

Fisher Maps: F-13

Travel Zones: 46, 45

Introduction: This route will take you south from Poplar Lake, through Lizz and Caribou lakes to Horseshoe Lake. You will portage from the west end of Horseshoe to Gaskin Lake and continue paddling west through the prettiest part of this loop, Winchell Lake. You'll then portage north to Omega Lake and, from there, begin your eastward journey back to Horseshoe, by way of a series of long, narrow lakes. Finally, you will retrace your strokes north to Poplar Lake.

There is probably no place along this route where you will feel isolated. But you will encounter fewer people after you portage from the west end of Winchell Lake. And you'll notice that the portage trails are less worn in that northwestern part of the loop than along the southern part.

DAY 1: **Poplar Lake,** p. 51 rods, **Lizz Lake,** p. 73 rods, **Caribou Lake,** p. 20 rods, **Horseshoe Lake,** p. 102 rods, **Gaskin Lake.** You'll follow a well-traveled route all day. Portage trails are wide and smooth. Only the last one presents any challenge, as it climbs rather steeply over a hill, with two rests en route. It provides the only real challenge of the whole route. Anglers will find walleye and northern pike inhabiting these waters.

DAY 2: **Gaskin Lake,** p. 60 rods, **Winchell Lake,** p. 45 rods, **Omega Lake,** p. 20 rods, **Hensen Lake.** You may find Winchell Lake, with rock cliffs bordering its southern shoreline, to be the most scenic part of the route, but it may also be the windiest. When a strong westerly wind prevails, travel is quite slow across this long lake. You'll find that Omega and Hensen receive less use than Gaskin and Winchell lakes.

DAY 3: **Hensen Lake,** p. 58 rods, **Pillsbery Lake,** p. 95 rods, **Allen Lake,** p. 50 rods, **Horseshoe Lake,** p. 20 rods, **Caribou Lake,** p. 73 rods, **Lizz Lake,** p. 51 rods, **Poplar Lake.** You are likely to encounter more and more people as you paddle farther and farther east. Most of these long, narrow lakes receive moderately light use, however, throughout most of the summer.

Route #68: The Wanihigan-Kiskadinna Loop

5 Days, 47 Miles, 24 Lakes, 1 River, 1 Creek, 29 Portages

Difficulty: Challenging

Fisher Maps: F-13, F-12

Travel Zones: 46, 44, 42, 41, 36, 45

Introduction: This busy route will lead you through some of the most popular lakes southwest of the Gunflint Trail. From Poplar you'll first head south to Horseshoe Lake. Then you will veer southwest through Gaskin, Winchell and the Cone chain of lakes to beautiful Brule Lake. From the west end of Brule, you'll steer northeast through the Temperance lakes to Cherokee Lake and then straight north to Long Island Lake.

With an eastward heading, you'll finally negotiate a series of long, slender lakes that lead back to your origin at Poplar Lake.

Most of this route is fairly well-used during the busier summer periods. The parts from Poplar to Winchell, on Brule Lake, and from Cherokee to Long Island Lake, in particular, receive the most use. Until 1979, all of the route from Poplar to Cherokee was designated for motorized craft. Now, however, motors are not allowed on any part of the route within the BWCA.

Portages are relatively short (only two are more than 140 rods) and generally easy, with one dramatic exception. Most groups will have no trouble completing the loop in five days. Avid anglers, however, may wish to add a day to ensure plenty of time to avail themselves of the many fishing opportunities.

DAY 1: **Poplar Lake,** p. 51 rods, **Lizz Lake,** p. 73 rods, **Caribou Lake,** p. 20 rods, **Horseshoe Lake,** p. 102 rods, **Gaskin Lake,** p. 60 rods, **Winchell Lake.** Portage trails are wide and smooth on this well-traveled part of the route. But the last two surmount steep hills, each with two canoe rests along the way. Anglers should take their time and cast their lines for the walleye and northern pike that inhabit these waters. Winchell is a scenic lake, with the impressive Misquah Hills towering nearly 350 feet above its southern shore. Several good campsites are located along the opposite shoreline.

DAY 2: **Winchell Lake,** p. 14 rods, **Wanihigan Lake,** p. 14 rods, **Cliff Lake,** p. 160 rods, **North Cone Lake,** p. 2 rods, **Middle Cone Lake,** p. 25 rods, **South Cone Lake,** p. 15 rods, **Brule Lake.** In keeping with your stay on Winchell Lake, this day's journey will continue through scenic terrain, with the Misquah Hills rising over 100 yards above the northeast shore of Wanihigan Lake and a steep pine-covered ridge bordering the north shore of Cliff Lake. The only challenging portage is the half-mile trail connecting Cliff and North Cone lakes. Fortunately, though, it follows a good downhill path, descending 80 feet to North Cone. If the water level is not too low, you may be able to eliminate the final carry to Brule Lake by paddling through the connecting stream.

There are several campsites near your entrance to Brule Lake. Make camp early and cast a line for the plentiful walleye, northern pike and lake trout that inhabit the lake. Island-studded Brule is one of the loveliest lakes around!

DAY 3: **Brule Lake,** p. 10 rods, **South Temperance Lake,** p. 55 rods, **North Temperance Lake,** p. 105 rods, **Sitka Lake,** p. 140 rods, **Cherokee Lake,** p. 13 rods, **Gordon Lake.** This part of the route is fairly well-traveled. Cherokee Lake, in particular, ranks as one of the most popular lakes in this part of the Boundary Waters, receiving many visitors from nearby Sawbill Lake (the BWCA's third-busiest entry point). Many canoeists paddle through Gordon Lake, but with only two campsites there—one at each end—your third night should be spent in solitude.

DAY 4: **Gordon Lake,** p. 25 rods, **Long Island River,** p. 5 rods, river, **Long Island Lake,** p. 20 rods, **Muskeg Creek,** p. 4 rods, creek, **Muskeg Lake,** p. 185 rods, **Kiskadinna Lake,** p. 35 rods, **Omega Lake**. Long Island is another very popular lake, receiving numerous visitors both from Sawbill Lake and from Ham Lake (to the north). Once you leave Long Island, however, you may not have to share "your" wilderness with many other people.

There is a good reason why few people head east from Long Island Lake. The portage connecting Muskeg and Kiskadinna lakes is one of the toughest to be found. It steeply climbs to 170 feet above Muskeg Lake before leveling off and then gently descending to Kiskadinna.

If the water level is not too low, the preceding 4-rod carry may not be necessary to bypass that part of Muskeg Creek.

DAY 5: **Omega Lake,** p. 20 rods, **Hensen Lake,** p. 58 rods, **Pillsbery Lake,** p. 95 rods, **Allen Lake,** p. 50 rods, **Horseshoe Lake,** p. 20 rods, **Caribou Lake,** p. 73 rods, **Lizz Lake,** p. 51 rods, **Poplar Lake**. Your final day will be the easiest, with relatively short portages connecting long, narrow lakes that receive moderately light use throughout most of the summer. Nevertheless, you are likely to encounter more and more people as you paddle farther and farther east.

Entry Point 48—Meeds Lake

Permits: 165

Popularity Rank: 35

Daily Quota: 7 (including Lizz and Swamps lakes)

Location: Meeds Lake is 220 rods southwest of Poplar Lake, which is 31 miles up the Gunflint Trail from Grand Marais (see Entry Point 47—Lizz Lake).

Description: Of the four BWCA entry points accessible from Poplar Lake, Meeds is the second most popular—but a far distant second, receiving less than half the number of visitors that paddle through Lizz Lake. Why? Because Meeds offers a much rougher entry to the Boundary Waters Canoe Area. Because of their close proximity, however, and because they serve essentially the same part of the BWCA Wilderness, Meeds Lake is grouped together with Lizz and Swamp lakes under just one quota for all three entry points combined.

The 220-rod portage from Poplar Lake climbs steeply for 30 rods, and then surmounts several small hills en route to Meeds Lake. The path is rough in places, marshy in others, and is enveloped in dense foliage over much of its course. The worst will be over when you cross an old, overgrown logging road. Seven canoe rests are located along the trail for your convenience, and you'll find them a welcome sight.

Yes, it's work. But wilderness canoeists may consider it well worth the effort. You'll sense the feeling of isolation—the essence of true wilderness—much quicker here than by entering the BWCA through Lizz Lake. People are far more scarce, and motorboats are not permitted.

Route #69: The Gaskin-Horseshoe Loop

2 Days, 12 Miles, 9 Lakes, 9 Portages

Difficulty: Challenging

Fisher Maps: F-13

Travel Zones: 45, 46

Introduction: This weekend route will take you southwest from Poplar Lake to the west end of Meeds Lake. Then you'll portage and paddle south across several small, narrow lakes to Gaskin Lake. Heading east, you'll then follow a more popular route to Horseshoe Lake and then veer north through Caribou and Lizz Lakes to your origin on Poplar Lake.

Except for the very first portage, this is an easy route. An ambitious group of paddlers could easily complete the loop in a day. But, then, an avid angler may want to stretch it over three days to take advantage of the walleye, northern pike and smallmouth bass that inhabit some of the waters.

Your southwest-bound paddling will be in Travel Zone #45, which receives moderately light use most of the time. But your northeast-bound return will be in Zone #46, all of which was once part of a motor route that extended all the way from Poplar Lake southwest to Sawbill Lake. This area receives moderate use, approaching heavy use at times in the vicinity of Horseshoe, Caribou and Lizz lakes. Campsites are plentiful, and in spite of the sometimes heavy traffic, it is unusual for all the sites to be occupied. On the other hand, you are not likely to find yourself alone at night.

DAY 1: **Poplar Lake,** p. 220 rods, **Meeds Lake,** p. 110 rods, **Swallow Lake,** p. 93 rods, **Pillsbery Lake,** p. 58 rods, **Hensen Lake,** p. 80 rods, **Gaskin Lake.** Your first portage is downright rugged, but the rest aren't bad (unless you're an "armchair canoeist" who hasn't been on the water since last year's weekend extravaganza). All but one offer uphill challenges, each with two canoe rests along the way, but none is long enough to worry about.

DAY 2: **Gaskin Lake,** p. 102 rods, **Horseshoe Lake,** p. 20 rods, **Caribou Lake,** p. 73 rods, **Lizz Lake,** p. 51 rods, **Poplar Lake.** After your first portage, which surmounts a large hill separating Gaskin and Horseshoe lakes, you'll find the going quite easy all the way back to Poplar Lake.

Route #70: The Wild Rivers Route

10 Days, 95 Miles, 52 Lakes, 7 Rivers, 1 Creek, 81 Portages

Difficulty: Rugged

Fisher Maps: F-13, F-12, F-11, F-5, F-6

Travel Zones: 45, 36, 34, 35, 41, 42, 44

Introduction: This high-quality wilderness route will take you through several of the most isolated and least traveled river systems in the BWCA. From Meeds Lake you will paddle in a westward direction through a chain of long, slender lakes to Long Island Lake. From that popular lake you will first veer south to Gordon Lake and then continue westward into the winding wilderness of the Frost River. From Fente Lake you will again steer south to Hub and Mesaba lakes. Then you'll continue west, down the Louse River to Malberg Lake. The Kawishiwi River will carry you south to Lake Polly, and then you'll paddle up the Phoebe River, southeast to Phoebe Lake. Past Beth and Alton lakes, you will continue eastward through Sawbill, Smoke and Burnt lakes, to Kelly Lake. Then you will paddle up the beautiful Temperance River system to South Temperance Lake. Halfway across Brule Lake, you'll turn north and follow the Cone chain of lakes northeast to Winchell Lake. One last day of northeastward paddling will bring you back to your origin at Poplar Lake, exiting the Boundary Waters via Lizz Lake.

With only a few exceptions, most of your time should be spent in isolation, as you'll be traveling through the most remote interior part of the BWCA. Only in the vicinities of Long Island, Koma, Sawbill, Brule and Gaskin lakes are you likely to encounter many other canoeists. Poplar is the only lake on the route where motors are permitted.

Fishing for walleye and northern pike is good in many of the lakes. Smallmouth bass, bluegill and lake trout are also present in several places.

It is largely because of the great number of portages that this route rates as "rugged." Most are relatively short. Only seven are longer than half a mile.

You should have a good opportunity to view many species of North Woods fauna, including moose, mink, beaver, bear and bald eagles. Having abundant wildlife, varied terrain, spectacular scenery and a good blend of large and small lakes with tiny streams, this is truly one of the most interesting routes in all of the Boundary Waters Canoe Area.

DAY 1: **Poplar Lake,** p. 220 rods, **Meeds Lake,** p. 110 rods, **Swallow Lake,** p. 93 rods, **Pillsbery Lake,** p. 58 rods, **Hensen Lake,** p. 20 rods, **Omega Lake.** (See comments for Day 1, Route #69.)

DAY 2: **Omega Lake,** p. 35 rods, **Kiskadinna Lake,** p. 185 rods, **Muskeg Lake, Muskeg Creek,** p. 4 rods, **creek,** p. 20 rods, **Long Island Lake, Long Island River,** p. 5 rods, **river,** p. 25 rods, **Gordon Lake,** p. 140 rods, **Unload Lake,** p. 40 rods, **Frost Lake.** (See comments for Day 3, Route #65.)

DAY 3: **Frost Lake,** p. 130 rods, **Frost River,** p. 10 rods, **Octopus Lake,** p. 15 rods, **Frost River,** p. 25 rods, **river,** p. 5

rods, **river,** p. 30 rods, **Chase Lake,** p. 15 rods, **Pencil Lake,** p. 60 rods, **Frost River,** p. 10 rods, **river,** p. 4 rods, **river,** p. 10 rods, **river,** p. 12 rods, **river, Afton Lake,** p. 20 rods, **Frost River,** rapids, **Fente Lake,** p. 300 rods, **Hub Lake.** (See comments for Day 3, Route #56, for the route as far as Fente Lake.) Your last portage is hard to face after an already long day. The trail gains nearly 140 feet in elevation during the first 100 rods, then levels off, and finally slopes gently down to Hub Lake. Only four canoe rests exist along the way.

DAY 4: **Hub Lake,** p. 105 rods, **Mesaba Lake,** p. 20 rods, **Chaser Lake,** p. 7 rods, **pond,** p. 130 rods, **Dent Lake,** p. 45 rods, **Bug Lake,** p. 115 rods, **Louse River,** p. 50 rods, **river,** p. 130 rods, **Trail Lake.** Several of the portages this day are challenging, but most are downhill. The only steep uphill climb is the short carry from Chaser to a small pond. It can be treacherous, so watch your step! The 45-rod portage connecting Dent and Bug lakes follows a marshy path that can be tricky to negotiate. After Bug Lake you'll be traveling downhill, dropping a total of 117 feet to Trail Lake. The final carry is difficult—steep at times, and challenging to even an experienced tripper.

Bug Lake is slowly dying. You'll find the buildup of mud and aquatic plants a retarding force during periods of low water, when the lake is barely deep enough for the passage of a loaded canoe.

You may encounter a beaver dam or two and occasional rocky shoals along the Louse River to further slow your progress. Two nice campsites await you on Trail Lake, but neither has room enough for more than two tents. Anglers may find hungry northern pike nearby.

DAY 5: **Trail Lake,** p. 21 rods, **Louse River,** p. 56 rods, **river,** p. 41 rods, **river,** p. 20 rods, **river,** p. 59 rods, **river,** p. 36 rods, **river, Boze Lake,** p. 11 rods, **Louse River,** p. 21 rods, **river,** p. 6 rods, **Frond Lake, Louse River,** p. 15 rods, **Malberg Lake,** p. 24 rods, **Koma Lake.** You'll continue traveling downhill this day, descending a total of 69 feet from Trail to Malberg Lake. Large boulders obstruct passage frequently on the lower Louse River during low-water periods. The 6-rod carry to Frond Lake will probably not be necessary, but if the water is so low as to necessitate a portage there, you will be in for numerous liftovers all along the river. None of the portages is difficult.

If blueberries are in season, you'll find them in abundance throughout the Louse River region. Fishing is also usually very good for walleye, northern pike and bluegill in Malberg and Koma lakes.

Watch for moose! There is a dense population in the area south of Malberg Lake. During my last two visits I have seen them browsing on the shores of Malberg, once at dawn and once at dusk, including a splendid display by a large bull.

After a solitary day of paddling on the Louse River, you may be joined by an influx of paddlers on Malberg and Koma lakes, who entered the BWCA at Kawishiwi Lake, the 11th most popular entry point.

DAY 6: **Koma Lake,** p. 127 rods, **Kawishiwi River,** p. 48 rods, **river,** p. 19 rods, **Lake Polly,** p. 97 rods, **Phoebe River,** p. 15 rods, **river,** p. 92 rods, **river,** p. 24 rods, **river,** p. 59 rods, **Hazel Lake,** p. 140 rods, **Phoebe River, Knight Lake, Phoebe River, Phoebe Lake.** This day, all of your portages are uphill, as you climb a total of 175 feet from Koma to Phoebe Lake. Rest assured, however, that none is very difficult.

This is a very scenic part of the route, where moose, beaver and mink abound. You are likely to encounter few people along the Phoebe River. On Phoebe Lake, however, you may be joined by those who entered the Boundary Waters at Sawbill Lake, the BWCA's 3rd most popular entry point.

As on the Louse River, liftovers may be required along the Phoebe River during low water where boulders have obstructed passage.

There are several good campsites near the west end of Phoebe Lake. Since many people visit there, it would be wise to find a site as early as possible. Then cast your line for the walleye and northern pike lurking around you.

DAY 7: **Phoebe Lake,** p. 85 rods, **Grace River,** p. 5 rods, **river,** p. 15 rods, **river,** p. 15 rods, **Grace Lake,** p. 285 rods, **Beth Lake,** p. 140 rods, **Alton Lake,** p. 30 rods, **Sawbill Lake,** p. 100 rods, **Smoke Lake.** The long portage connecting Grace and Beth lakes ascends 68 feet, but follows a good, fairly smooth path with seven canoe rests along the way.

In addition to the three short carries along the Grace

River, a beaver dam may be another obstruction near the 5-rod portage.

Even during the less active periods of summer, you will surely encounter a good deal of canoe traffic on Alton and Sawbill lakes. Motors are no longer permitted on Sawbill and Smoke lakes, but a busy canoe-trip outfitter is still located at the southern tip of Sawbill Lake.

DAY 8: **Smoke Lake,** p. 90 rods, **Burnt Lake,** p. 230 rods, **Kelly Lake,** p. 65 rods, **Jack Lake,** p. 12 rods, **Weird Lake,** p. 80 rods, **Temperance River,** p. 240 rods, **South Temperance Lake.** Your first long portage climbs to 70 feet above Burnt Lake before leveling off and then dropping 100 feet to Kelly Lake. About midway across the trail, you'll cross an abandoned logging road immediately before entering a swampy area. There are 4 canoe rests along the way. The long final portage also climbs more than 60 feet along the Temperance River to South Temperance Lake, with 5 canoe rests along the way.

This is another one of the more scenic regions in the BWCA, as you paddle up the Temperance River flowage, where shallow, narrow lakes are surrounded by towering hills and connected by lovely rapids.

DAY 9: **South Temperance Lake,** p. 10 rods, **Brule Lake,** p. 15 rods, **South Cone Lake,** p. 25 rods, **Middle Cone Lake,** p. 2 rods, **North Cone Lake,** p. 160 rods, **Cliff Lake,** p. 14 rods, **Wanihigan Lake,** p. 14 rods, **Winchell Lake.** If the water level is high enough, you may be able to eliminate the short passage out of Brule Lake by paddling through the shallow creek that leads north to South Cone Lake. The only challenging carry of the day is the half-mile path to Cliff Lake, which climbs more than 80 feet above North Cone Lake.

The scenery is splendid as you penetrate the region northeast of the Cone lakes. The Misquah Hills extend east from Wanihigan Lake parallel to the south shore of Winchell Lake. From your campsite on the north shore you will view peaks rising nearly 350 feet above this popular lake. Enjoy the view as you troll for one of the northern pike or lake trout silently submerged nearby.

DAY 10: **Winchell Lake,** p. 60 rods, **Gaskin Lake,** p. 102 rods, **Horseshoe Lake,** p. 20 rods, **Caribou Lake,** p. 73 rods, **Lizz Lake,** p. 51 rods, **Poplar Lake.**

This is an easy last day for a rugged expedition. All the portage trails are well-traveled and follow good paths. The first two, however, do surmount steep hills. During the busier late-summer period, you are likely to encounter numerous visitors in this part of the BWCA—but no motors until you return to Poplar Lake.

Entry Point 65—Portage Lake

Permits: 24

Popularity Rank: 61

Daily Quota: 2 (including Skipper Lake)

Location: From US Highway 61 in Grand Marais, follow the Gunflint Trail northwest for 38 miles to its junction with County Road 92, where a sign points left to Iron Lake. Turn left and follow this narrow gravel road one mile southeast to the Iron Lake Campground. Turn right there, on Forest Route 150, and you will find the public landing for Iron Lake less than ¼ mile south. Portage Lake is 40 rods south from the east end of Iron Lake.

Description: The National Forest Campground at Iron Lake offers you a good place to spend the night before your trip. There are seven campsites, and a fee is charged.

Portage Lake is the least used of the 25 entry points in this guide. And it serves what is probably the least visited part of the BWCA's Eastern Region. Seldom do canoeists penetrate the area between Poplar and Long Island lakes, south of Portage Lake. Consequently, you're in for a high-quality wilderness experience as you quickly enter into a sense of true wilderness solitude and North Woods isolation.

Your peace does not come easy, however. The long portage from Portage Lake into the BWCA rates as one of the toughest entries in the Eastern Region. The USFS portage sign reads "136 rods," but that is a gross error. The trail is much, much longer, with seven canoe rests along the way, I measure it as close to 240 rods. The trail begins abruptly uphill and continues to climb steadily, often steeply, to the fifth canoe rest. It then descends to One Island Lake.

Two thirds of the way across the portage, you'll cross a logging road that is still in use. This primitive dirt road begins near the east end of County Road 92. Using a 4-wheel drive vehicle, it is possible to begin your trip here and thus eliminate the worst part of the long portage to One Island Lake. But there is no designated parking space at the portage and it isn't marked. Even if you are lucky enough to find it, you may never leave, if heavy rains occur during your trip. I recommend starting your trip at the Iron Lake Campground.

The Skipper Lake Entry Point (#49) also serves the same isolated chain of pristine lakes. For that reason, Skipper and Portage lakes are grouped together under one quota. Skipper Lake requires an even longer, though easier, portage from Poplar Lake: a one-mile trek over gently-rolling-to-level terrain. Neither is in great demand. Only 16% of the quota for Portage Lake and 9% of the quota for Skipper Lake were used during the 5-month canoeing season in 1989. These are usually among the last entry points to fill up on busy weekends.

Route #71: The Portage Route

4 Days, 31 Miles, 19 Lakes, 1 Creek, 23 Portages

Difficulty: Rugged

Fisher Maps: F-13

Travel Zone: 45

Introduction: This difficult route is recommended for the experienced tripper who values isolation more than spectacular scenery. From Iron Lake you will portage your way south to Rush Lake and then paddle west through a chain of seldom visited lakes, around which moose live in abundance. At Long Island Lake you'll turn east and follow a chain of small, riverlike lakes to Meeds Lake. You'll exit the Boundary Waters briefly to busy Poplar Lake, but will then turn west and re-enter the isolated part of the BWCA at Skipper Lake. After going westward to Rush Lake, you'll turn north and return to your origin at Iron Lake.

En route you will spend most of your time on lakes that receive very light use, with short intermissions on two of the busiest lakes in this part of the BWCA: Long Island and Poplar. All of the route will be in Travel Zone #45, which ranks in the top half of the popularity scale. But most of the visits to this region may be attributed to the popularity of Long Island Lake, where anglers seek the northern pike and lake trout inhabiting its depths.

Only 10% of the groups entering this zone come from the Portage Lake, Skipper Lake or Meeds Lake entry points (less than 1% from Portage Lake), which serve the region through which most of this route passes. Conclusion: You are in for a high-quality, often isolated wilderness experience.

DAY 1: **Iron Lake,** p. 32 rods, **Portage Lake,** p. 240 rods, **One Island Lake,** p. 60 rods, **Rush Lake,** p. 10 rods, **Banadad Lake.** Except for the long carry to One Island Lake, this is not a particularly hard day. Banadad is so long and very narrow that it more resembles a river than a lake. Even if you arrive here early in the day, go no farther. You'll find no other campsites until you reach Long Island Lake, several long portages away. You probably won't see other trippers this day. But on a quiet night, it's not unusual to hear truck traffic on the Gunflint Trail. This is an area with a high moose population, so keep a watchful eye during late afternoon and early morning hours.

DAY 2: **Banadad Lake,** p. 95 rods, **Sebeka Lake,** p. 180 rods, **Ross Lake,** p. 195 rods, **Cave Lake,** p. 109 rods, **Long Island Lake,** p. 20 rods, **Muskeg Creek,** p. 4 rods, **creek, Muskeg Lake,** p. 185 rods, **Kiskadinna Lake.** With nearly 2½ miles of portaging, this day is mighty tough. Fortunately, the four portages between Banadad and Long Island lakes are mostly downhill. But they follow rough paths that are very slippery when wet, are marshy in places, and have very few portage rests along them. Unfortunately, the final portage of the day is the worst one of all, with a climb of 170 feet en route to Kiskadinna Lake. Sleep well tonight!

Your solitude will likely be lost on Long Island Lake, which receives a great deal of traffic from the entry points at Ham, Brule and Sawbill lakes. During a busy week in August, it's not unusual for *all* of the 14 campsites here to be occupied. But you'll be paddling on the fringe of the congestion and quickly leave it when you portage to Muskeg Lake.

DAY 3: **Kiskadinna Lake,** p. 35 rods, **Omega Lake,** p. 20 rods, **Hensen Lake,** p. 58 rods, **Pillsbery Lake,** p. 93 rods, **Swallow Lake,** p. 110 rods, **Meeds Lake.** A big contrast from the previous day, this will be your easiest day! Having long, narrow lakes with shorelines forested by cedar and spruce, this area receives moderate use by visitors entering the BWCA at the Lizz Lake Entry Point (#47). Portages are not tough, but they usually go over hills, each with one or two canoe rests along the way.

DAY 4: **Meeds Lake,** p. 220 rods, **Poplar Lake,** p. 320 rods, **Skipper Lake,** p. 21 rods, **Little Rush Lake,** p. 50 rods, **Rush Lake,** p. 60 rods, **One Island Lake,** p. 240 rods, **Portage Lake,** p. 32 rods, **Iron Lake.** If you're not in shape by now, look out! Nearly 3 miles of portaging make your last day the toughest one of the trip. The first carry follows the worst path, through dense foliage and occasional marshy spots, over several small hills, but mostly downhill. This takes you outside the BWCA to Poplar Lake, where resorts, private cabins and motorboats offer you a brief but shocking reminder of the civilization to which you are soon to return. The next, mile-long portage leads you across a good, nearly level path back to the seldom visited part of the BWCA where you began. During high water periods, you can eliminate the 21-rod portage by paddling through the shallow creek connecting Skipper and Little Rush lakes. You've already experienced the Portage Lake carry, but you'll find it considerably easier this time—mostly downhill. Each of the three long portages has seven canoe rests.

Route #72: The Banadad-Mesaba-Brule Loop

8 Days, 63 Miles, 46 Lakes, 3 Rivers, 3 Creeks, 58 Portages
Difficulty: Rugged
Fisher Maps: F-13, F-12, F-5
Travel Zones: 45, 36, 41, 42, 44, 46

Introduction: This high-quality wilderness route will take you from one of the least-used entry points to one of the most isolated interior parts of the BWCA. From Iron Lake you will first head south to Rush Lake, and then steer southwest to Long Island. At Gordon Lake you will turn west and paddle down the meandering Frost River to Fente Lake. You'll then portage and paddle your way south to Sawbill Lake. From that busy lake, you will steer northeast and paddle through Cherokee Lake to big Brule Lake. Continuing northeast you'll take the Cone chain of lakes to Winchell and Poplar lakes. Then going westward to Rush Lake and north to Iron Lake, you will return to your origin at the Iron Lake access.

Much of this interesting route will be through parts of the BWCA that receive very light use—even during the busiest summer periods! Only in the vicinities of Long Island, Sawbill and Brule lakes, in fact, are you likely to encounter wilderness "crowds."

Big-game hunters (with a camera, that is) will be delighted with the opportunites. Moose, in particular, are plentiful in the region northeast of Long Island Lake and adjacent to the Frost River.

For those who seek a variety of canoeing terrain, who derive satisfaction from good hard work, and who prefer to travel where few others dare to go, this rugged loop has got it all.

DAY 1: **Iron Lake,** p. 32 rods, **Portage Lake,** p. 240 rods, **One Island Lake,** p. 60 rods, **Rush Lake,** p. 10 rods, **Banadad Lake.** (See comments for Day 1, Route #71.)

DAY 2: **Banadad Lake,** p. 95 rods, **Sebeka Lake,** p. 180 rods, **Ross Lake,** p. 195 rods, **Cave Lake,** p. 109 rods, **Long Island Lake, Long Island River,** p. 5 rods, **river,** p. 25 rods, **Gordon Lake,** p. 140 rods, **Unload Lake,** p. 40 rods, **Frost Lake.** The four portages between Banadad and Long Island lakes are mostly downhill, but they follow rough paths that are marshy in places, are very slippery when wet, and have few portage rests along the way. (See comments for Day 2, Route #56.)

DAY 3: **Frost Lake,** p. 130 rods, **Frost River,** p. 10 rods, **Octopus Lake,** p. 15 rods, **Frost River,** p. 25 rods, **river,** p. 5 rods, **river,** p. 30 rods, **Chase Lake,** p. 15 rods, **Pencil Lake,** p. 60 rods, **Frost River,** p. 10 rods, **river,** p. 4 rods, **river,** p. 10 rods, **river,** p. 12 rods, **river, Afton Lake,** p. 20 rods, **Frost River,** rapids, **Fente Lake,** p. 300 rods, **Hub Lake.** (See comments for Day 3, Route #56.) The final portage is almost unbearable at the end of an exhausting day. The trail climbs steeply for the first 100 rods, gaining nearly 140 feet in elevation, then levels off, and finally slopes gently down to Hub Lake. Only four canoe rests are located along the trail.

DAY 4: **Hub Lake,** p. 105 rods, **Mesaba Lake,** p. 80 rods, **Hug Lake,** p. 3 rods, **Duck Lake,** p. 80 rods, **Zenith Lake,** p. 480 rods, **Lujenida Lake, Kelso River, Kelso Lake,** p. 13 rods, **Sawbill Lake**. (See comments for Day 5, Route #53.) There are several nice campsites at the north end of Sawbill Lake. Canoe traffic is heavy there, however, as Sawbill is the third-most-popular entry point in the BWCA. A busy canoe outfitter is located at the southern tip of the lake.

DAY 5: **Sawbill Lake,** p. 80 rods, **Ada Creek,** p. 80 rods, **Ada Lake, Skoop Creek,** p. 12 rods, **Skoop Lake,** p. 180 rods, **Cherokee Creek, Cherokee Lake,** p. 140 rods, **Sitka Lake,** p. 105 rods, **North Temperance Lake,** p. 55 rods, **South Temperance Lake**. (See comments for Day 6, Route #65.)

DAY 6: **South Temperance Lake,** p. 10 rods, **Brule Lake,** p. 15 rods, **South Cone Lake,** p. 25 rods, **Middle Cone Lake,** p. 2 rods, **North Cone Lake,** p. 160 rods, **Cliff Lake,** p. 14 rods, **Wanihigan Lake,** p. 14 rods, **Winchell Lake**. (See comments for Day 9, Route #70.)

DAY 7: **Winchell Lake,** p. 45 rods, **Omega Lake,** p. 20 rods, **Hensen Lake,** p. 58 rods, **Pillsbery Lake,** p. 93 rods, **Swallow Lake,** p. 110 rods, **Meeds Lake**. This will be by far your easiest day of the trip. To continue onward would involve portaging over 600 rods to the next cluster of designated campsites (at Rush Lake). So, instead of pushing yourself, take it easy and enjoy your last night in the BWCA.

DAY 8: **Meeds Lake,** p. 220 rods, **Poplar Lake,** p. 320 rods, **Skipper Lake,** p. 21 rods, **Little Rush Lake,** p. 50 rods, **Rush Lake,** p. 60 rods, **One Island Lake,** p. 240 rods, **Portage Lake,** p. 32 rods, **Iron Lake**. (See comments for Day 4, Route #71.)

Entry Point 50—Cross Bay Lake

Permits: 340

Popularity Rank: 22

Daily Quota: 3

Location: From US Highway 61 in Grand Marais, follow the Gunflint Trail northwest 48 miles to County Road 47, marked by a sign pointing left to Tuscarora Lodge. Turn left and drive 0.7 mile south on this good gravel road to a parking lot and boat landing on the left side of the road, serving the Cross River. Cross Bay Lake is three portages southeast of the access, via the Cross River and Ham Lake.

Description: A much-needed new parking lot was constructed in 1993 just past the point at which the road skirts the bank of the Cross River. It easily accommodates at least a dozen vehicles. From the north end of the lot, there is a 5-rod trail that leads down some steps to a fine boat dock on the river.

There are no public campgrounds in the immediate vicinity of the access. Trail's End Campground, 11 miles north on the Gunflint Trail, is the closest place to camp the night before your trip. There is a fee charged to camp there.

Tuscarora Lodge, on Round Lake, ½ mile southwest of the landing, also offers canoeists bunkhouse accommodations and breakfast on the morning of the trip. You may also acquire complete or partial outfitting there.

Quite a bit of canoe traffic uses the Cross Bay Lake Entry Point, much of which is headed for Long Island Lake. It's a good idea to make a reservation, since Cross Bay Lake ranks high among entry points with the highest percent of quotas used, and it's one of the most frequently reserved entry points in the BWCA (5th in 1989). Motorized craft are allowed from the boat landing through Ham Lake, but they are not permitted to enter the BWCA from there. Nearly one third of the visitors to Travel Zone #45 come through the Cross Bay Lake point of entry, where the portages are easy and scenery is pleasant.

Route #73: The Snipe-Tuscarora Loop

2 Days, 14 Miles, 8 Lakes, 1 River, 9 Portages

Difficulty: Challenging

Fisher Maps: F-12

Travel Zones: 45, 37

Introduction: This good weekend route actually has two phases of difficulty: the first half is easy, but the last half is rugged. From the boat landing, you'll paddle southeast up the Cross River to Ham Lake and south to Cross Bay Lake. There you will turn west and negotiate the narrow lakes and the portages leading to beautiful Tuscarora Lake. You will then portage more than a mile northeast to Missing Link Lake and another half mile to Round Lake, where you'll end the loop at the public access, 1 mile by road from your origin.

Most of the route receives moderate use by canoeists; you'll encounter the fewest people between Snipe and Tuscarora lakes. Until 1979 Tuscarora and Missing Link lakes were part of a designated motor route beginning at Round Lake. Because of the long portages, however, very few motorists used it. In fact, only 9% of the groups that entered the BWCA there in 1977 used boats with motors. Those who did venture this way were probably in search of lake trout for which Tuscarora Lake is noted. Federal legislation in 1978, however, closed this route to motors. Now the only lake on this loop where motors are permitted is Round. On the chain of lakes between Snipe and Tuscarora, however, you can still see the remains of old rock cribs that once supported docks along this route.

Although experienced canoeists should have no trouble completing this route in two days (strong paddlers in one), neophytes might enjoy it even more by stretching it over three days, with nights spent on Snipe and Tuscarora lakes.

DAY 1: **Cross River,** p. 68 rods, **river,** p. 40 rods, **Ham Lake,** p. 24 rods, **Cross Bay Lake,** p. 47 rods, **Snipe Lake,** p. 100 rods, **Copper Lake,** p. 69 rods, **Hubbub Lake,** p. 235 rods, **Tuscarora Lake.** Cedar and spruce characterize much of the forest along this route. It's truly a boreal forest, with few hardwoods to liven up the scene in autumn. The portages are well-used and relatively easy, as you gain less than 50 feet from the launching site to Cross Bay Lake.

Elongated Cross Bay Lake is little more than a continuation of the Cross River—long and narrow, with a marshy shoreline. Watch for moose throughout this region, which contains the densest population of these beasts in this part of the BWCA Wilderness.

The 47-rod portage to Snipe Lake descends 30 feet and follows a good trail, but it could be wet at the top. Snipe is a lovely, boreal lake, surrounded almost entirely by spruce, with occasional jack pine and only a smattering of hardwoods. But there are plenty of visible rock ledges and outcroppings to make Snipe one of the more scenic lakes in this area. A very nice

Swim time at Ogishkemuncie Lake

Eagle's nest at Brule Lake

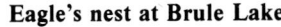

Falls near Rose Lake

From the collection of the MN Historical Society
Photo by Leland J. Prater for the USFS

Portaging the Phoebe River

Cypress Lake

Landing a smallmouth bass

On Vista Lake

From campsite on Seagull Lake

Portaging through a birch grove between Canoe and Pine lakes

Reflections at Gotter Lake

Alder Lake narrows

Skipper Lake

On Mountain Lake

Pine Lake

Fishing on Seagull Lake

On Royal Lake looking west

A quiet moment at Swamp Lake

Entrance to the Gunflint Trail in Grand Marais

From campsite on Seagull Lake

On Seagull Lake

Portage between Flying and Green lakes

Author elevating food pack at Bingshick Lake

On Kelso Lake

Mountain Lake and bluffs *From the Collection of the MN Historical Society*

campsite sits on a pine-covered, rocky point facing the northwest end of the lake.

The 100-rod portage climbs gradually up from the shore of Snipe Lake, then drops steeply down a small hill to cross a creek on a log bridge. After passing through a lovely stand of large spruce, the trail skirts the grassy shore of the creek draining the northeast end of Copper Lake.

The 69-rod portage climbs abruptly during the first 15 rods, then descends gradually the rest of the way to Hubbub Lake.

The 255-rod portage between Hubbub and Tuscarora lakes is not the challenge that it might appear to be on the map! Indeed, it just may be the highest, driest, levelest and smoothest portage on this entire route; it's simply a bit long. It has a few ups and downs at each end, but most of the trail is level to gently rolling. There are seven canoe rests along the route. Just beyond the third, you'll drop down to cross Howl Lake. Don't worry; you won't need hip boots! Howl is in the final stages of glacial-lake evolution, now nothing more than a grassy bog with a small creek flowing through the middle. A long boardwalk transports portagers from one side to the other.

Tuscarora is a pretty lake, with an abundance of exposed rock along the shoreline. There are some steep ledges, as well as sloping outcrops. In late summer, you'll find lake trout in the deepest hole (130 feet), at the southwest corner of the lake. A campsite atop a lovely rock outcropping is nearby, on a point protruding from the west shore of the lake. There are several other nice campsites on the lake.

DAY 2: **Tuscarora Lake,** p. 366 rods, **Missing Link Lake,** p. 142 rods, **Round Lake,** Forest Route 1495. Your first portage is a tough one—especially going this way! It begins immediately with a rather steep climb and continues gradually ascending for the first 100 rods, eventually gaining more than 150 feet in elevation. But it levels out after awhile, and there are 11 canoe rests along the way to help out. The path is narrow and rocky much of the way. Fortunately the next portage is downhill nearly all the way, descending nearly 100 feet en route.

Unless you have left a car at the Round Lake access, you must walk down Forest Route 1495 for nearly a mile to County Road 47 and your origin.

Route #74: The Sawbill-Tuscarora Route

7 Days, 70 Miles, 37 Lakes, 6 Rivers, 3 Creeks, 58 Portages
Difficulty: Challenging
Fisher Maps: F-12, F-5, F-11
Travel Zones: 45, 36, 41, 35, 34, 37

Introductions: This delightful loop will take you all the way to the southern edge of the BWCA and return you via some of the loveliest riverways in the central part of the Boundary Waters. From Ham Lake you will paddle south through Long Island and Cherokee lakes to Sawbill Lake. From that busy lake, you'll steer west through Alton and Grace lakes, and follow the Grace and Phoebe rivers to Lake Polly. The Kawishiwi River will lead you north to Malberg Lake. Then you will paddle east, up the Louse River to Dent and Mesaba lakes. Your final day will find you heading northeast through Mora, Crooked and Tuscarora lakes to the public landing on Round Lake. A 1¼-mile hike down Forest Route 1495 will return you to your origin on County Road 47.

The only lakes on the entire route where motors are permitted are the first and last—Ham and Round. Other parts that were formerly designated motor routes were closed to motors beginning in 1979.

You may encounter moderately heavy canoe traffic during your southward journey to Alton Lake, but you are certain to see far fewer people on your northbound return, particularly along the scenic Phoebe and Louse rivers. In that area, watch for moose, mink, beaver and bear. Why not? They are watching you!

Anglers will find walleye and northern pike in many of the lakes on this route. Lake trout are also known to inhabit Cherokee, Alton, Mesaba and Tuscarora lakes. If the fish aren't biting, you won't starve in midsummer, as blueberries grow abundantly along the midsection of the route.

DAY 1: **Cross River,** p. 68 rods, **river,** p. 40 rods, **Ham Lake,** p. 24 rods, **Cross Bay Lake,** p. 56 rods, **Rib Lake,** p. 37 rods, **Lower George Lake,** p. 28 rods, **Karl Lake,** p. 35 rods, **Long Island Lake.** This is an easy day of travel over well-worn portage trails. It is a very popular route, and during the busiest periods of late summer it is not unusual for all of the 14 campsites to be occupied. Rather than portage to the northwest end of Long Island Lake, you may paddle south from Karl to the central part of the lake. This way involves more paddling, and the campsites at the ends of this long lake are normally the last to be occupied. You should be able to arrive early enough in the day to find a campsite, regardless of which way you go.

DAY 2: **Long Island Lake, Long Island River,** p. 5 rods, **river,** p. 25 rods, **Gordon Lake,** p. 13 rods, **Cherokee Lake, Cherokee Creek,** p. 180 rods, **Skoop Lake,** p. 12 rods, **Skoop Creek, Ada Lake,** p. 80 rods, **Ada Creek,** p. 80 rods, **Sawbill Lake.** This continues along a busy canoe route served by the BWCA's third-most-popular entry point, Sawbill Lake. Portages are uphill to Skoop Lake, then mostly downhill to Sawbill. The only challenge is the long carry south from Cherokee Creek which surmounts the Laurentian Divide en route to Skoop Lake. Four canoe rests afford assistance along the ½-mile trail.

Until 1979 the waterway from Cherokee to Sawbill Lake was a designated motor route. Federal legislation in 1978, however, closed the area to motorists.

DAY 3: **Sawbill Lake,** p. 30 rods, **Alton Lake,** p. 140 rods, **Beth Lake,** p. 285 rods, **Grace Lake,** p. 15 rods, **Grace River,** p. 15 rods, **river,** p. 5 rods, **river,** p. 85 rods, **Phoebe Lake.** (See comments for Day 1, Route #53.)

DAY 4: **Phoebe Lake, Phoebe River, Knight Lake, Phoebe River,** p. 140 rods, **Hazel Lake,** p. 59 rods, **Phoebe River,** p. 24 rods, **river,** p. 92 rods, **river,** p. 15 rods, **river,** p. 97 rods, **Lake Polly.** (See comments for Day 2, Route #53.)

DAY 5: **Lake Polly,** p. 19 rods, **Kawishiwi River,** p. 48 rods, **river,** p. 127 rods, **river, Koma Lake,** p. 24 rods, **Malberg Lake,** p. 15 rods, **Louse River, Frond Lake,** p. 6 rods, **Louse River,** p. 21 rods, **river,** p. 11 rods, **Boze Lake,** p. 36 rods, **Louse River,** p. 59 rods, **river,** p. 20 rods, **river,** p. 41 rods, **river,** p. 56 rods, **river,** p. 21 rods, **Trail Lake.** (See comments for Day 3, Route #53.)

DAY 6: **Trail Lake,** p. 130 rods, **Louse River,** p. 50 rods, **river,** p. 115 rods, **Bug Lake,** p. 45 rods, **Dent Lake,** p. 130 rods, **pond,** p. 7 rods, **Chaser Lake,** p. 20 rods, **Mesaba Lake,** p. 105 rods, **Hub Lake.** (See comments for Day 4, Route #53.)

DAY 7: **Hub Lake,** p. 300 rods, **Fente Lake,** p. 15 rods, **Whipped Lake,** p. 100 rods, **Mora Lake,** p. 10 rods, **Tarry Lake,** p. 50 rods, **Crooked Lake,** p. 55 rods, **Owl Lake,** p. 63 rods, **Tuscarora Lake,** p. 366 rods, **Missing Link Lake,** p. 142 rods, **Round Lake**. Arise early this day; you have a lot of work ahead! You'll cross more than three miles of portages and cover a lot of territory en route to Round Lake. By now you should be in shape for it, but you may wish to take it easy and allow two days to complete the route.

The first long portage is on a nearly level trail for the first 200 rods, but then drops steeply down to Fente Lake. Only four canoe rests have been constructed beside the trail. The toughest carry of the day, as would be expected, is the 366-rod trail. That rugged path climbs abruptly for the first 100 rods, but then levels off most of the way. Eleven canoe rests are there to relieve you.

The day's final portage is downhill, over a rocky path that can be slippery when wet. Watch your step! Tuscarora Lake is known for its fine lake trout. Try your luck while you take a well-deserved mid-day "breather."

Entry Point 51—Missing Link Lake

Permits: 419

Popularity Rank: 18

Daily Quota: 5

Location: From US Highway 61 in Grand Marais, follow the Gunflint Trail northwest for 48 miles to County Road 47, marked by a sign pointing left to Tuscarora Lodge. Turn left and drive south on this good gravel road ¾ mile to Forest Route 1495. Turn right and follow this narrow road another ¾ mile to its end. There you'll find a parking lot large enough to accommodate about 40–50 vehicles. Access to Round Lake is 5 rods downhill from the end of the parking lot.

Description: Trail's End Campground, 12 miles north at the end of the Gunflint Trail, is the closest public campground at which to spend the night before your trip. A camping fee is charged there, and you may reserve a site in advance by calling (218) 388-2212.

This access serves the Brant Lake Entry Point #52 too, so don't be upset if you see a nearly full parking lot: the traffic is fairly evenly split between the two entry points.

As of 1979 motorboats are no longer permitted past Round to Missing Link and Tuscarora lakes. Because of the two long portages en route, however, not many motorists ever did head this way. In fact, only 9% of the groups that entered here in 1977 used motors.

The area does receive moderate use by canoeists, however. And although the Brant Lake and Missing Link Lake entry points channel traffic initially in different directions, much of that traffic converges on Gillis and/or Little Saganaga Lake.

Regardless of which route you take through Tuscarora Lake, bear in mind that Day 1 will always be *rugged*. With 508 rods of portaging in less than a two-mile span from Round Lake to Tuscarora, there is no other way to describe it than *tough*. The beauty of Tuscarora Lake, however, should make the work seem worthwhile; and to the west is some of the most lovely scenery in all the Boundary Waters Canoe Area.

NOTE: Either of the routes suggested below may be reversed by entering the BWCA through Entry Point 52—Brant Lake.

Route #75: The Gillis Lake Loop

2 Days, 12 Miles, 13 Lakes, 13 Portages

Difficulty: Rugged

Fisher Maps: F-12

Travel Zone: 37

Introduction: This weekend outing will take you across several lovely lakes and long, steep portages. From Round Lake you'll portage southwest through Missing Link Lake to Tuscarora Lake. With the roughest part of the route behind you, you will continue west through Owl Lake to Crooked Lake, and then portage north to Gillis Lake. From the northeast corner of Gillis you will paddle through a chain of pretty little lakes east to your origin at Round Lake.

Avid fishermen may want to schedule three days for this loop and go no further than Tuscarora Lake on the first day.

All of the loop is within Travel Zone #37, which receives moderately heavy use throughout most of the summer. Normally, though, there are ample campsites to accommodate the traffic. Motors are allowed only on the last three lakes of the route, which are outside the BWCA.

DAY 1: **Round Lake,** p. 142 rods, **Missing Link Lake,** p. 366 rods, **Tuscarora Lake,** p. 63 rods, **Owl Lake,** p. 55 rods, **Crooked Lake,** p. 90 rods, **Gillis Lake.** You start right out with an uphill portage from Round Lake, over a rocky path that gains nearly 100 feet in elevation. The long carry to Tuscarora Lake follows another narrow, rocky trail much of the way, but it is seldom steep. You'll hike over low hills with gradual slopes or fairly level terrain for the first ½ mile. Then you'll confront the steepest part of the path, first down and then back up. But the last 100 rods is all downhill, and you'll find a nice sandy beach at the end. Eleven canoe rests are distributed along the portage.

Tuscarora is a pretty lake, with lots of exposed rock on the shoreline. There are some steep ledges, as well as sloping outcrops. While you rest after the long portage, troll slowly for one of the luscious lake trout inhabiting the depths of that scenic lake. In late summer, you'll find them in the deepest hole (130 feet), at the southwest corner of the lake. A campsite atop a beautiful rock outcropping is nearby, on a point protruding from the west shore of the lake.

The 63-rod portage climbs over a low rise and then drops 40 feet and on a log bridge crosses a small creek draining into Owl Lake. The 55-rod portage gently descends 40 feet to Crooked Lake. Cedar is predominate in the forest bordering both Owl and Crooked lakes. For those who prefer two short carries to a longer one, the 90-rod portage to Gillis Lake may be substituted for by portages of 10 and 50 rods, joined by a 40-rod paddle on a small pond between two sets of rapids. It is probably quicker to simply portage the entire 90 rods, but the middle stretch skirts close to the pond and may be quite wet when the water level is high. An old, dilapidated log cabin sits next to the rapids at the 10-rod portage.

Gillis is a very nice, clear lake with many scenic rock outcroppings along the shoreline. There are several excellent campsites, all on rocky ledges or sloping rock outcroppings.

During much of the summer, plan on sharing this lake with several other groups. You will quickly see why it is so popular.

DAY 2: **Gillis Lake,** p. 25 rods, **Bat Lake,** p. 20 rods, **Green Lake,** p. 100 rods, **Flying Lake,** p. 10 rods, **Gotter Lake,** p. 100 rods, **Brant Lake,** p. 36 rods, **Edith Lake,** p. 50 rods, **West Round Lake,** p. 85 rods, **Round Lake.** The portages between Gillis and Brant lakes are well-traveled and not very long—but they are not easy. The carries from Gillis to Bat, from Green to Flying, and from Gotter to Brant, in particular, are steeply uphill. The 25-rod trail starts in a cedar grove and climbs abruptly more than 50 feet to the shore of Bat Lake. The 100-rod carry to Flying Lake surmounts a 100-foot hill. The first third of the trail is all uphill, and the last third is downhill. A canoe rest sits at the top. Just beyond the rest, the old portage trail (which once led straight downhill to Flying Lake) has been closed and blocked off, and the new route veers toward the southeast to "switch back" on a more gentle slope down to the lake. Before loading up with gear, make certain that you *are* on the 70-rod trail to Flying Lake, and *not* on the 75-rod portage to Crag Lake, nearby to the southeast. There is another option on the next portage. The path leads 50 rods, but many people put in after 10 rods and paddle through a shallow part of Gotter Lake that could be too low in very dry periods.

From Brant Lake on to Round Lake, the portage trails are level, smooth and very well-traveled.

Route #76: The Fraser-Kekekabic Loop

7 Days, 62 Miles, 46 Lakes, 1 River, 3 Creeks, 58 Portages

Difficulty: Challenging

Fisher Maps: F-12, F-11

Travel Zones: 37, 33, 29, 32

Introduction: This route will lead you through some of the most scenic terrain in the central part of the BWCA. Each part of the route offers a unique form of beauty, from island-studded Little Saganaga and Ogishkemuncie lakes to the large, open expanses on Kekekabic and Gabimichigami lakes to the scenic series of serene, little pools and rapids between "Gabi" and Ogishkemuncie lakes.

From Round Lake, you'll first head southwest through Tuscarora to Little Saganaga Lake. You will continue paddling southwest through a series of smaller and less-traveled lakes to the Kawishiwi River. Then you'll steer north through an isolated interior part of the BWCA en route to Fraser and Kekekabic lakes. From the east end of "Kek" you'll begin your eastward journey back to Round via Ogishkemuncie, Gabimichigami and Peter lakes.

Anglers will have an opportunity to catch lake trout, northern pike and walleye throughout the route.

Parts of the route receive fairly heavy use, particularly in the vicinities of Tuscarora to Little Saganaga Lakes and Kekekabic Lake to Ogishkemuncie. Other parts, however, are very lightly traveled, including your swing through the isolated interior of Travel Zone 33.

DAY 1: **Round Lake,** p. 142 rods, **Missing Link Lake,** p. 366 rods, **Tuscarora Lake,** p. 63 rods, **Owl Lake,** p. 55 rods, **Crooked Lake,** p. 50 rods, **Tarry Lake,** p. 10 rods, **Mora Lake.** (See comments for Day 1, Route #75.) The 50-rod trail connecting Crooked and Tarry lakes is steep, rocky and treacherous, passing over a small hill. Watch your step when the ground is wet!

DAY 2: **Mora Lake,** p. 45 rods, **Little Saganaga Lake,** p. 19 rods, **pond,** p. 19 rods, **Elton Lake,** p. 45 rods, **Makwa Lake,** p. 65 rods, **pond,** p. 89 rods, **Panhandle Lake,** p. 55 rods, **Pan Lake,** p. 19 rods, **pond,** p. 25 rods, **Anit Lake,** p. 14–35 rods, **Kivaniva Lake,** p. 40 rods, **Kawishiwi River.** You'll be traveling downhill all day, descending a total of 74 feet from Mora Lake to the Kawishiwi River. None of the portages is difficult, but their frequency will slow your progress somewhat. The part of the route southwest of Little Saganaga receives much less use than that of the previous day.

If campsites along the Kawishiwi River are occupied, portage south to Malberg Lake, where a dozen campsites are located. Fishing for walleye and northern pike is excellent in Malberg Lake.

DAY 3: **Kawishiwi River,** p. 20 rods, **river,** p. 15 rods, **Trapline Lake,** p. 30 rods, **Beaver Lake,** p. 90 rods, **Adams**

Lake, Boulder Creek, p. 15 rods, **creek, Boulder Lake,** p. 220 rods, **Cap Lake.** You will see few if any other people after you veer north from the Kawishiwi River, and your night will be spent on one of the most isolated lakes in the Boundary Waters. Between Adams and Boulder lakes, there may be a couple of liftovers along Boulder Creek, in addition to the 15-rod carry. That last long portage to Cap Lake will split after 135 rods of hiking. The right trail leads to Ledge Lake, so bear left for 85 more rods to Cap.

DAY 4: **Cap Lake,** p. 60 rods, **Roe Lake,** p. 42 rods, **Sagas Lake,** p. 65 rods, **Fraser Lake,** p. 15 rods, **Gerund Lake,** p. 30 rods, **Ahmakose Lake,** p. 90 rods, **Wisini Lake,** p. 10 rods, **Strup Lake,** p. 85 rods, **Kekekabic Lake.** None of these portages is long, but several are steep and rather exhausting. The trail from Cap to Roe climbs 40 feet. Ahmakose Lake is 48 feet higher than Gerund. And even though Wisini is a mere 10 feet higher than Ahmakose, the connecting path gains 64 feet in elevation before dropping back down to Wisini. The final two portages are also steep, but downhill. The last one climbs to its intersection with the Kekekabic Trail and then descends over 100 feet to Kekekabic Lake.

Kekekabic is a magnificent lake, with hills rising as high as 400 feet above its south shore. It receives many visitors too, so don't lose time finding a campsite. Anglers will find lake trout in its depths.

DAY 5: **Kekekabic Lake,** 5 portages through **"Kekekabic Ponds," Eddy Lake,** p. 15 rods, **Jean Lake,** p. 15 rods, **Annie Lake,** p. 15 rods, **Ogishkemuncie Lake,** p. 80 rods, **Mueller Lake,** 3 portages, **Agamok Lake,** p. 15 rods, **Gabimichigami Lake.** Those first eight, short portages are quite easy, providing more of a nuisance than a challenge. Ogishkemuncie is a pretty, island-studded lake that is very popular among canoeists beginning their trips from both the Gunflint Trail and the Fernberg Road.

The 80-rod portage south from Ogishkemuncie Lake is a challenging one; it surmounts a steep hill en route to Mueller Lake. Three portage rests along the way provide a welcome relief for the weary tripper.

At the east end of Mueller you have a choice of portages:

either three short carries around three sets of rapids, or one continuous portage of about 100 rods (bearing right) from Mueller directly to Agamok Lake. If time is of the essence, choose the latter. The other alternative, however, is worth a little extra time. All three portages are rocky and somewhat steep in places, but none exceeds 25 rods. The second portage crosses the Kekekabic Trail, which utilizes a wooden bridge to pass over a picturesque waterfall flowing parallel to the portage. Between the portages is a scenic series of serene little pools. Those who bypass the area via the longer portage are missing a real treat.

Most of the campsites at the east side of "Gabi" are outstanding for any size of group, and the view is breathtaking from those that border the main body of the lake.

DAY 6: **Gabimichigami Lake,** p. 39 rods, **Peter Lake,** p. 130 rods, **French Lake,** p. 25 rods, **Seahorse Lake,** p. 13 rods, **War Club Lake,** p. 45 rods, **Fay Lake,** p. 27 rods, **Glee Lake,** p. 53 rods, **Bingshick Lake.** You may see more backpackers than canoeists this day, as you cross the famed Kekekabic Trail four times and camp at a site used more by hikers than paddlers. Portage trails are not well-marked and are very lightly traveled. Nor is the Kekekabic Trail marked, so when you intersect it, watch carefully to see that your path leads to the next lake, not parallel to it.

All the portages are basically uphill, but none is too difficult. The only dramatic increase in elevation occurs during the 130-rod trail from the east end of Peter Lake, which climbs nearly 100 feet before dropping to French Lake. There are 3 portage rests along the way.

War Club is a very shallow lake throughout. During a dry spell, you could have problems navigating a heavily loaded canoe across it.

In addition to the designated USFS campsites on Bingshick Lake, which are quite spacious but obviously cater more to hikers than canoeists, you'll see several other sites along the north shore where hikers have settled down for the night.

DAY 7: **Bingshick Lake,** p. 13 rods, **Bingshick Creek,** p. 15 rods, **Flying Creek, Flying Lake,** p. 10 rods, **Gotter Lake,** p. 100 rods, **Brant Lake,** p. 36 rods, **Edith Lake,** p. 50

rods, **West Round Lake,** p. 85 rods, **Round Lake**. On this day you will pass quickly from the remote solitude of Bingshick Lake back into the mainstream of canoe routes originating or terminating at Round Lake.

When you join Flying Creek, only a few rods south of Bingshick Lake, be sure to follow it south. The next short portage is only a few rods away and within sight of the 13-rod carry. If you mistakenly followed the creek west, you would be steering a course back to Fay Lake—an obstacle course, that is.

Although there is a 50-rod portage trail between Flying and Gotter lakes, you should have to follow only ⅕ of it if the water level is not extremely low. Usually, a 10-rod carry will suffice, beginning with a steep climb up a log stairway.

The 100-rod portage to Brant Lake demands an exhausting climb over a steep hill. From that point on, however, the trails are wide, smooth and level all the way back to Round Lake.

Entry Point 52—Brant Lake

Permits: 360

Popularity Rank: 21

Daily Quota: 4

Location: Brant Lake is one mile, two lakes, and three portages west of Round Lake—49 miles northwest of Grand Marais. (See Entry Point 51—Missing Link Lake.)

Description: As at its neighboring entry point, motorboats and motorized canoes are not permitted into the Boundary Waters from Brant Lake. Portage trails are very easy and heavily used from Round to Brant, but not all that easy west of Brant, though heavily used. This entry offers the canoeist an easier way into the BWCA than from Round through Tuscarora. The two routes receive nearly the same amount of traffic. Since Entry Point 51 has a larger quota (5), however, it may be easier to get a permit for that entry point. More of the available permits have been used at Brant Lake (40%) than at Missing Link Lake (26%) in recent years.

In addition to the routes suggested below, you may also reverse either of the routes suggested for Entry Point 51.

Route #77: The Bingshick-Crooked Loop

3 Days, 20 Miles, 17 Lakes, 2 Creeks, 18 Portages
Difficulty: Challenging
Fisher Maps: F-12
Travel Zone: 37

Introduction: This interesting little route will take you off the beaten path to an area visited perhaps more by hikers than canoeists. You will portage across the famed Kekekabic Trail four times and camp alongside it your first night out. From Round Lake you'll paddle west through Brant to Flying Lake and then north to Bingshick. From there you'll paddle west beside the Kekekabic Trail, through a chain of shallow, peacefully secluded lakes to Seahorse Lake. After portaging south to French Lake, you will continue southeastward through Gillis to Crooked Lake. On your third day you'll head east to beautiful Tuscarora Lake and then negotiate the two roughest portages of the trip en route to Round Lake.

All the route is in Travel Zone 37, which receives moderately heavy use throughout much of the summer. A good deal of the traffic from both the Round Lake and Brant Lake entry points is channeled through Gillis or Crooked Lake. Very little of it wanders north into the chain of lakes between Bingshick and Seahorse, and that is where you'll find the most seclusion and tranquility. But the rest of the loop is quite lovely, and all but the first 3 lakes are exclusively for paddlers.

DAY 1: **Round Lake,** p. 85 rods, **West Round Lake,** p. 50 rods, **Edith Lake,** p. 36 rods, **Brant Lake,** p. 100 rods, **Gotter Lake,** p. 10 rods, **Flying Lake, Flying Creek,** p. 15 rods, **Bingshick Creek,** p. 13 rods, **Bingshick Lake.** The first three portages are fairly flat and a bit rocky, and may be muddy in a few spots after rains or early in the season. A 4-rod boardwalk crosses a boggy area near the end of the 85-rod portage, which skirts the south side of a swampy area—a good place to watch for moose browsing.

If you get a late start, there are two lovely campsites on Brant Lake. A site at the lake's northeast corner sits on a high rock outcropping slightly off the beaten path—the best spot for privacy. The central site is also elevated on a rock ledge with several "shelves" rising above the lakeshore, across from a high, wooded rock bluff, only fifty yards away, at one of the narrowest parts of the lake.

The only tough portage of the day is the 100-rod climb over a steep hill separating Brant and Gotter lakes. It's a rocky and rooty trail that drops most steeply at the west end.

Gotter Lake is unique—little more than a shallow pond in which there are many standing dead trees. When the lake is too shallow or obstructed by logs to paddle into the southwest end, where the 10-rod portage begins, canoeists must use a 50-rod trail. It follows along a low ridge bordering the north shore, joins the shorter (10-rod) portage and then steeply descends a wood stairway (28 steps) to Flying Lake.

Fifty-foot rock cliffs along the southwest shore of Flying Lake help create a lovely scene. After the 15-rod portage on Flying Creek, bear right when the creek joins Bingshick Creek. The start of the 13-rod carry to Bingshick Lake is but a few rods to the northeast. You'll find that the campsites along the north shore of Bingshick are situated more for the convenience of hikers using the Kekekabic Trail than for canoe campers.

DAY 2: **Bingshick Lake,** p. 53 rods, **Glee Lake,** p. 27 rods, **Fay Lake,** p. 45 rods, **War Club Lake,** p. 13 rods, **Seahorse Lake,** p. 25 rods, **French Lake,** p. 27 rods, **Gillis Lake,** p. 90 rods, **Crooked Lake.** This is the day when you cross the Kekekabic Trail four times. Watch carefully to make certain that you don't stray off on the hikers' trail (which would make for a long portage between lakes!). The portage trails are lightly traveled and not marked, but common sense should guide you appropriately. You'll encounter much more traffic after French Lake. Get your campsite early!

DAY 3: **Crooked Lake,** p. 55 rods, **Owl Lake,** p. 63 rods, **Tuscarora Lake,** p. 366 rods, **Missing Link Lake,** p. 142 rods, **Round Lake.** Drag your line for lake trout in Tuscarora Lake while you rest up for the portage ahead. That rugged trail climbs rather steeply for 100 rods, eventually gaining more than 150 feet in elevation, but then levels off for most of the rest of the way. Eleven canoe rests help somewhat. Your final portage is downhill, dropping nearly 100 feet on a rocky path that can be slippery when wet. Watch your step.

Route #78: The Polly-Beth-Gordon Lakes Loop

7 Days, 62 Miles, 40 Lakes, 5 Rivers, 3 Creeks, 55 Portages
Difficulty: Challenging
Fisher Maps: F-12, F-11, F-5
Travel Zones: 37, 33, 34, 35, 41, 36, 45

Introduction: On this varied route, you will begin by paddling and portaging west from Round Lake through Brant, Gillis and a chain of smaller lakes leading to the north end of lovely Little Saganaga Lake. From the south end of this island-studded gem, you will steer southwest through another series of small, lightly traveled lakes and ponds to Malberg Lake. Then you'll follow the Kawishiwi River system south to Lake Polly. Veering southeast, you'll paddle up the Phoebe River to Phoebe Lake, up the Grace River to Grace Lake, and across Beth and Alton lakes to Sawbill Lake. From busy Sawbill, you will steer your course in a northeastward direction to Cherokee and Long Island lakes. One last day of northbound travel will take you through Rib, Cross Bay and Ham lakes to County Road 47, just over a mile by road from your origin at Round Lake.

It is a good route for those who prefer small lakes and tiny rivers, connected mostly by short (but frequent) portages. Most of the loop receives moderate canoe traffic. Perhaps the least amount of traffic will be encountered south of Little Saganaga to Phoebe Lake, although Malberg, Koma and Polly attract many anglers from the Kawishiwi Lake Entry Point. The busiest part of the route is in the vicinity of Sawbill Lake and north from there all the way to the end.

At dawn and dusk, watch for moose in the areas south of Malberg Lake and north of Cherokee Lake. Large populations of that awesome beast are known to live there. Beaver and mink are also common along parts of the route.

Anglers will find the fishing to be excellent for northern and walleyed pike in many of the lakes. Lake trout inhabit Little Saganaga, Alton and Cherokee lakes. Bluegills and smallmouth bass may also be found along the way.

DAY 1: **Round Lake,** p. 85 rods, **West Round Lake,** p. 50 rods, **Edith Lake,** p. 36 rods, **Brant Lake,** p. 100 rods, **Gotter Lake,** p.10 rods, **Flying Lake,** p. 100 rods, **Green**

Lake, p. 20 rods, **Bat Lake,** p. 25 rods, **Gillis Lake.** (See comments for Day 1, Route #77). The 100-rod portage from Flying Lake to Green Lake also climbs so steeply that an alternate path is sometimes used. It veers to the left from the landing on Flying Lake and follows a "switchback" pattern to the summit of the 90-foot ridge. It offers a longer but more gradual and safer route to the top. From that point on, it is all downhill to Gillis Lake.

DAY 2: **Gillis Lake,** p. 27 rods, **French Lake,** p. 33 rods, **Powell Lake,** p. 20 rods, **West Fern Lake,** p. 30 rods, **Virgin Lake,** p. 90 rods, **Little Saganaga Lake,** p. 19 rods, **pond,** p. 19 rods, **Elton Lake,** p. 45 rods, **Makwa Lake,** p. 65 rods, **pond,** p. 89 rods, **Panhandle Lake,** p. 55 rods, **Pan Lake.** All these portage trails are used much less than those of the previous day, but they should pose no problem. The only real challenge, perhaps, is the 90-rod carry from Virgin Lake, which climbs for 27 rods and then descends nearly 100 feet to Little Saganaga Lake. Little Saganaga is a very popular lake, but the region south of it receives light traffic.

DAY 3: **Pan Lake,** p. 19 rods, **pond,** p. 25 rods, **Anit Lake,** p. 14–35 rods, **Kivaniva Lake,** p. 40 rods, **Kawishiwi River,** p. 48 rods, **Malberg Lake,** p. 24 rods, **Koma Lake, Kawishiwi River,** p. 127 rods, **river,** p. 48 rods, **river,** p. 19 rods, **Lake Polly.** From Malberg south to Lake Polly you are likely to be joined by an influx of paddlers who have entered the BWCA at Kawishiwi Lake, the 11th most popular entry point. Anglers, in particular, are lured to these lakes by their reputations for yielding good "crops" of walleye, northern pike and bluegill.

Watch for moose at dawn and dusk. They abound in this area. And so do bears! Hang your food pack well this evening.

DAY 4: **Lake Polly,** p. 97 rods, **Phoebe River,** p. 15 rods, **river,** p. 92 rods, **river,** p. 24 rods, **river,** p. 59 rods, **Hazel Lake,** p. 140 rods, **Phoebe River, Knight Lake, Phoebe River, Phoebe Lake.** All six of these portages are basically uphill, but gaining a total of only 144 feet from Polly to Phoebe. None of the carries is difficult.

This is a very scenic part of the route, where moose, beaver and mink are plentiful. You will probably encounter few other people along the Phoebe River. Phoebe Lake, however, receives a good deal of traffic from Sawbill Lake. Try to make camp early. Then cast your line for one of the walleye or northern pike that inhabits the lake.

DAY 5: **Phoebe Lake,** p. 85 rods, **Grace River,** p. 5 rods, **river,** p. 15 rods, **river,** p. 15 rods, **Grace Lake,** p. 285 rods, **Beth Lake,** p. 140 rods, **Alton Lake,** p. 30 rods, **Sawbill Lake.** In addition to the three short carries along the Grace River, a beaver dam may provide another obstruction near the 5-rod portage. The 285-rod portage from Grace Lake is not difficult, though it does gain 68 feet in elevation. It has a good, well-defined path with seven canoe rests along the way. The northern route through Ella Lake would seem easier, with two shorter carries of 130 and 80 rods. Both, however, are quite rocky and the landings at both ends of the longer one are poor for put-ins.

Most of the canoe traffic that you encounter this day (and the next) stems from Sawbill Lake, the third most popular entry point for the BWCA. Find your campsite early at the north end of the lake.

DAY 6: **Sawbill Lake,** p. 80 rods, **Ada Creek,** p. 80 rods, **Ada Lake, Skoop Creek,** p. 12 rods, **Skoop Lake,** p. 180 rods, **Cherokee Creek, Cherokee Lake,** p. 13 rods, **Gordon Lake,** p. 25 rods,. **Long Island River,** p. 5 rods, **river, Long Island Lake.** A quick lift-over may be necessary at Ada Lake, before the 12-rod portage to Skoop Lake. With 4 canoe rests along the way, the 180-rod portage trail climbs over the Laurentian Divide en route to Cherokee Creek, a rather marshy stream that leads to one of the more popular lakes in this part of the BWCA. Long Island is an equally popular lake. It is not uncommon during peak periods of the summer to find all 14 campsites there occupied.

If you prefer a more solitary campsite, stop on Gordon Lake, where only two campsites are located, at opposite ends of the long, narrow lake.

DAY 7: **Long Island Lake,** p. 35 rods, **Karl Lake,** p. 28 rods, **Lower George Lake,** p. 37 rods, **Rib Lake,** p. 56 rods, **Cross Bay Lake,** p. 24 rods, **Ham Lake,** p. 40 rods, **Cross River,** p. 68 rods, **river.** Your last day is by far the easiest of the entire trip. If you prefer a little extra paddling to a short portage, you may wish to paddle directly into the south end of Karl Lake, instead of portaging into the north end.

Watch for moose along the way. A large population dwells in this region.

Unless you have left a car at the Cross River landing, you will have to conclude your trip by hiking over a mile southwest to Round Lake, via County Road 47 and Forest Route 1495.

Entry Point 54—Seagull Lake

Permits: 1482

Popularity Rank: 5

Daily Quota: 13

Location: There are two good public accesses to Seagull Lake. The first is 54 miles up the Gunflint Trail from US Highway 61 in Grand Marais. The public landing is at the end of a short access road leading west (left) ¼ mile from the Gunflint Trail. There are outhouses, a telephone and picnic area adjacent to the large parking area.

Continue on the Gunflint Trail past this turnoff 3 miles to Trail's End Campground. A large parking lot serves public accesses to both Gull Lake (north of the parking lot) and Seagull Lake (south of the parking lot). A map and directory at the entrance will show you the way.

Description: Trail's End is a nice, large National Forest campground that provides an excellent place for you to camp the night before your trip. There is a campsite fee. You may reserve a site in advance by calling (218) 388-2212.

Seagull is the third most popular entry point in the Eastern Region of the BWCA, but it receives nearly as many visitors as its northern neighbor, Saganaga Lake (ranked 2nd in the Eastern Region). In spite of its high daily quota, don't expect to just drop by and pick up a permit during the busiest parts of the summer. Permits may be hard to come by, because Seagull ranks 8th among all entry points for quotas filled the highest percentage of the time. It's a good idea to make a reservation in advance of your arrival.

Motors of 10 H.P. or less are allowed on Seagull Lake. Federal legislation in 1978, however, prohibited motorboats on the northbound route through Alpine and Red Rock lakes to Saganaga.

Much of the area immediately north of Seagull Lake was scarred by the Roy Lake Fire of 1976. West of Trail's End Campground, across the Seagull River, one sees a solemn reminder of that destructive blaze. Very little of that natural catastrophe, however, is visible from the lakes and streams on which you will be paddling. To the contrary, Seagull grants easy access to one of the loveliest parts of the Boundary Waters Canoe Area, and the entry lake itself is an island-studded spectacle to behold.

Route #79: The Thunder Point Route

4 Days, 45 Miles, 14 Lakes, 1 River, 11 Portages

Difficulty: Easy

Fisher Maps F-19, F-11

Travel Zones: 29, 30, 32, 38, 39

Introduction: This popular, scenic loop is highlighted by a climb up the Thunder Point Trail, overlooking beautiful Knife Lake and the Canadian wilderness to the north. From the public access at Trail's End Campground, you'll paddle Southwest across beautiful Knife Lake and the Canadian borderlands. From the public access at Trail's End Campground, paddle southwest across Seagull and through Alpine and Jasper lakes to ever-popular Ogishkemuncie Lake. From there you'll swing northwest to the South Arm of Knife Lake and follow it west to Thunder Point, the midpoint of this route. Then you will follow the Canadian boundary northeast through Little Knife, Ottertrack and Swamp lakes to big Saganaga Lake. Then you'll return to Trail's End Campground via the Seagull River and Gull Lake.

If your #1 goal is to escape from other canoeists and seek isolation from all reminders of civilization, don't take this route. All the zones through which you'll be traveling rank among the 14 most popular (of 49) in the BWCA. But if scenic lakes with crystal-clear water, panoramic vistas, a spectacular waterfall and easy portages appeal to you, you're sure to love this easy loop.

DAY 1: **Seagull Lake,** p. 105 rods, **Alpine Lake,** p. 45 rods, **Jasper Lake,** p. 25 rods, **Kingfisher Lake,** p. 38 rods,

Ogishkemuncie Lake. If you prefer getting your feet wet to portaging 105 rods, you can avoid the first carry by paddling up the channel connecting Seagull and Alpine lakes. You'll encounter three short sets of rapids, up which you can easily walk your canoe (in normal or low water levels). You would find it quicker to take the 105-rod portage, however. The shallow rapids connecting Kingfisher and Ogishkemuncie lakes may also be walked up without much difficulty, eliminating another 38 rods of aching carries. Ogishkemuncie is a lovely lake with many fine campsites, but it is often filled to capacity. In fact, the travel zone in which it lies boasts the highest campsite occupancy rate in all of the Boundary Waters. It is a popular destination not only for those beginning their trip from the Gunflint Trail, but also for those who start at Moose Lake, from the Fernberg Road in the Western Region. Find a campsite early!

DAY 2: **Ogishkemuncie Lake,** p. 15 rods, **Annie Lake,** p. 15 rods, **Lake Jean,** p. 15 rods, **Eddy Lake,** p. 25 rods, **South Arm of Knife Lake**. At the end of your final portage, take time to enjoy the scenic waterfall on the creek connecting Eddy and Knife lakes. The best view of the lower falls can be found by loading up your canoe after the portage, paddling to the creek's outlet, and then hiking up the trail on the *east* side of the creek. Knife is another very popular lake—the destination for many, and the "way" for many, many more. Find a campsite in the vicinity of Thunder Point (where the South Arm joins the main part of Knife Lake). Take the time to climb ¼ mile up the Thunder Point Trail to the scenic overlook. There you'll be treated to a fabulous panorama of the international boundary from over 150 feet above the lake.

Then cast your line for one of the lake trout, walleye or northern pike that live in this crystalline border lake.

DAY 3: **Knife Lake, Little Knife Lake,** p. 12 rods, **Ottertrack Lake,** p. 80 rods, **Swamp Lake,** p. 5 rods, **Saganaga Lake**. Ottertrack Lake—long, narrow and lined with high bluffs and a rocky shoreline—is one of my favorites. Along the north shore of the lake, you may see a clearing where once stood the cabins of Benny Ambrose. Benny was a prospector who sought gold for more than 60 years, until his death in 1982 at the age of 84. On the opposite (Canadian) shoreline, there is now a commemorative plaque cemented into the base of a cliff about ½ mile before the lake splits into two arms.

At the summit of the 80-rod carry between Ottertrack and Swamp lakes, you will see a large steel marker denoting the international boundary—hence the name "Monument Portage."

Saganaga is a big, beautiful lake that is heavily traveled because of its easy access from the Gunflint Trail. Large motorboats are permitted east of American Point, where several good campsites are located. Bears have been reported on American Point, so don't leave your food on the ground while you are away from camp.

DAY 4: **Saganaga Lake, Seagull River, Gull Lake,** Trails End Campground. Your trip will end at a public access ¼ mile north of the landing from which you started. The parking lot for both accesses is between them.

Route #80: The Knife-Kawishiwi Rivers Loop

8 Days, 77 Miles, 36 Lakes, 2 Rivers, 1 Creek, 54 Portages

Difficulty: Easy

Fisher Maps: F-19, F-11, F-12

Travel Zones: 38, 32, 29, 30, 19, 20, 21, 28, 33

Introduction: This interesting loop will take you across the central part of the BWCA nearly all the way to the Fernberg Road. From Seagull Lake you will first follow the same path as for Route #79, through Ogishkemuncie to Knife Lake. Then, instead of heading northeast along the border, you will continue to paddle west to Birch Lake. From that busy border lake, you'll steer southeast through Ensign and several smaller lakes to Ima and Thomas lakes. After traveling straight south to Lake Insula, you will begin your trip back by following the Kawishiwi River northeast to Kivaniva and a series of small lakes that lead to Little Saganaga Lake. Then you'll paddle north, through a very scenic part of the BWCA, en route to Ogishkemuncie Lake. Your final day will be on the same lakes that originally carried you away from Seagull Lake.

It may seem that a route with 54 portages could not possibly be rated "easy." Indeed, if you detest portaging of any type, then you most likely will not consider this route easy. Only four of these carries, however, are over 100 rods long, and even fewer offer much challenge. Spread over eight days, they should not pose much of a problem to even a poorly conditioned rookie crew.

This loop is a good introductory trip for the first-time BWCA visitor. You'll experience both large and small lakes, tiny creeks, lovely rivers, beautiful waterfalls, Indian pictographs, large beaver homes, a good chance of seeing moose and deer, and an excellent opportunity to "run" some easy rapids.

Nearly all of the loop is well-traveled. Some parts receive heavy use, mainly from Knife Lake south to Lake Insula. Motors are no longer permitted on any part of the route.

DAY 1: **Seagull Lake,** p. 105 rods, **Alpine Lake,** p. 45 rods, **Jasper Lake,** p. 25 rods, **Kingfisher Lake,** p. 38 rods, **Ogishkemuncie Lake.** (See comments for Day 1, Route #79.)

DAY 2: **Ogishkemuncie Lake,** p. 15 rods, **Annie Lake,** p. 15 rods, **Lake Jean,** p. 15 rods, **Eddy Lake,** p. 25 rods, **South Arm of Knife Lake, Knife Lake.** (See comments for Day 2, Route #79.)

DAY 3: **Knife Lake,** p. 75 rods, **Knife River,** p. 15 rods, **Seed Lake,** p. 15 rods, **Knife River,** p. 16 rods, **Carp Lake,** p. 48 rods, **Birch Lake,** p. 100 rods, **Frog Lake,** p. 70 rods, **Trident Lake,** p. 120 rods, **Ensign Lake,** p. 53 rods, **Ashigan Lake.** During the summer of 1987 high water caused the old logging dam at the southwest end of Knife Lake, built in the early 1900's, to wash out. Consequently, the water on Knife Lake has returned to its natural level, about three feet lower than it had been during this century. For the next few years, the exposed rocky shoreline may look strange to returning visitors.

Not far from the old dam, in a cluster of three small islands in Knife Lake, is the homesite of the BWCA's last permanent resident. Dorothy Molter, who sold home-made root beer to canoeing passersby for nearly half a century, passed away in December 1986. Two of her log cabins were then moved, log by log, to Ely and reconstructed as a memroial to her.

If the water level is high enough, you may be able to eliminate all the portages along the Knife River by shooting, lining or walking your canoe down the rapids around which the portages pass. Only on two occasions will you have to lift your canoe and gear—over a small dam at the head of the river, and around a low falls at the third portage.

This is a very well-traveled part of the Boundary Waters, served by Moose Lake, the most popular entry point in all of the BWCA. The last portage is the toughest, climbing 56 feet in 53 rods.

DAY 4: **Ashigan Lake,** p. 105 rods, **Gibson Lake,** p. 25 rods, **Cattyman Lake,** p. 55 rods, **Jordan Lake,** p. 5 rods, **Ima Lake,** p. 50 rods, **Hatchet Lake,** p. 10 rods, **Thomas Creek,** p. 10 rods, **creek,** p. 10 rods, **pond,** p. 5 rods, **Thomas Lake.** You'll be climbing all day, but none of the portages is difficult as you gain 129 feet in elevation from Ashigan to Thomas Lake. Under normal water conditions, you can probably pull your canoe up through the first two rapids on Thomas Creek, eliminating two 10-rod carries. The third short portage intersects the famed Kekekabic Trail. Motors are no longer allowed in this part of the Boundary Waters. In Thomas Lake, lake trout, walleye and northern pike await your shiny lure.

DAY 5: **Thomas Lake,** p. 25 rods, **Kiana Lake,** p. 179 rods, **Lake Insula,** p. 18 rods, **Kawishiwi River, Alice Lake,** p. 20 rods, **Kawishiwi River,** p. 90 rods, **river.** The 179-rod carry—the longest portage for the entire route—is mostly downhill and not difficult. You will find a display of Indian rock paintings (pictographs) south of your final portage, on the west shore of the Kawishiwi River. Several good campsites are nearby. Map #F-11 includes all of the route *except* one short bend in the Kawishiwi River. Don't be alarmed when you find yourself "off the map" about a mile west of Alice Lake. Simply follow the river, and it's impossible (?) to get lost. (Or, if you prefer, buy map #F-4.)

DAY 6: **Kawishiwi River,** p. 15 rods, **river,** p. 20 rods, **river,** p. 40 rods, **Kivaniva Lake,** p. 14–35 rods, **Anit Lake,** p. 25 rods, **pond,** p. 19 rods, **Pan Lake,** p. 55 rods, **Panhandle**

Lake, p. 89 rods, **pond,** p. 65 rods, **Makwa Lake,** p. 45 rods, **Elton Lake**. None of these portages is difficult, but their frequency may slow your progress somewhat. This area is the most lightly traveled part of the route, though it does receive moderate use at times.

DAY 7: **Elton Lake,** p. 19 rods, **pond,** p. 19 rods, **Little Saganaga Lake,** p. 30 rods, **Rattle Lake,** p. 25 rods, **Gabimichigami Lake,** p. 15 rods, **Agamok Lake,** 3 Portages, **Mueller Lake,** p. 80 rods, **Ogishkemuncie Lake**. On this day you'll find yourself canoeing through some of the loveliest scenery in the central BWCA. At the northwest end of Agamok Lake you will have a choice of portages: either three short portages around three sets of rapids, or one continuous carry of about 100 rods from Agamok directly to Mueller Lake. I prefer the three short ones. All are rocky and somewhat steep in places, but none exceeds 25 rods. The second portage crosses the Kekekabic Trail, which utilizes a wooden bridge to pass over a picturesque waterfall flowing parallel to the portage. Those who bypass the area via the longer portage are missing a real treat!

The 80-rod carry from Mueller to Ogishkemuncie looks innocent on the map, but it's not. It begins with a steep uphill climb, before descending to lower Ogishkemuncie Lake.

DAY 8: **Ogishkemuncie Lake,** p. 38 rods, **Kingfisher Lake,** p. 25 rods, **Jasper Lake,** p. 45 rods, **Alpine Lake,** p. 105 rods, **Seagull Lake**. This is a reverse of your first day.

Entry Point 55—Saganaga Lake

Permits: 1740

Popularity Rank: 4

Daily Quota: 20

Location: From US Highway 61 in Grand Marais follow the Gunflint Trail 56 miles northwest to its intersection with Cook County Road 11. Turn right and follow this rough, winding, hilly gravel road north one mile to the public landing. There you'll find outhouses, a pay phone, and a store nearby. A fee is charged for parking next to the boat access.

Description: An excellent place to spend the night before your trip is Trail's End Campground, located at the end of the

Gunflint Trail, just beyond (west of) the Saganaga Lake turn-off. There is a campsite fee, and there are many campsites to accommodate the heavy traffic in this area. On the west side of the Seagull River, bordering the campground, is a vivid reminder of the Roy Lake Fire, which ravaged this part of the BWCA in 1976.

Saganaga Lake, part of the international boundary, is the busiest entry point in the eastern region of the Boundary Waters. It's a motor-designated lake, and many of the permits issued here are to groups using motorized craft. In spite of the large quota, a reservation is advisable during the peak periods of summer.

Since there's a Canadian Customs station in the east-central part of the lake and an entrance to Quetico Provincial Park at its west end, many canoeists who use this point of entry paddle north to the Land of the Maple Leaf. Yet many others use the lake only during the day, spending their nights at one of the many lodges and campgrounds along the Gunflint Trail.

Several private cabins, lodges and canoe outfitters are located along the southernmost part of Saganaga. You'll see the outfitter's high-powered towboats race past you on their way to Customs and Quetico Provincial Park with canoeists who prefer to save time and not to paddle across big Saganaga. These towing services do much to relieve the congestion that would otherwise occur on Saganaga Lake. But the rest of this mammoth lake is contained within the BWCA and there are no other monuments to civilization on the US side.

Route #81: The Red Rock-Seagull Loop

2 Days, 23 Miles, 5 Lakes, 1 River, 4 Portages

Difficulty: Easy

Fisher Maps: F-19

Travel Zones: 38, 39

Introduction: This is an excellent weekend route for those who don't like to portage, with only 201 rods of walking during the entire loop.

From the public landing you'll first paddle north into the main part of Saganaga Lake. Then you'll follow its shoreline southwest through Red Rock Bay to Red Rock and Alpine lakes. From Alpine you will portage east to Seagull and paddle to the north end of this beautiful, island-studded lake. After floating down the Seagull River to Gull Lake, you will return to the narrow channel of Saganaga Lake where the route began.

This loop circumnavigates the vast area destroyed by the Roy Lake Fire of 1976. Only in a few spots, however, will you witness the scarred countryside. All five lakes on the route are quite pretty, with countless islands, bays and peninsulas scattered throughout them which may confuse the inexperienced navigator.

The wildlife in this area may seldom be seen, but a bald eagle may be seen soaring overhead, and I've seen bear on American Point. Anglers will find walleye, northern pike and lake trout along most of the route. You will paddle through Travel Zones 39 and 38, two of the more heavily visited zones in the BWCA (rank third and eighth respectively). Find your campsite early!

DAY 1: **Saganaga Lake, Red Rock Bay,** p. 10 rods, **Red Rock Lake,** p. 48 rods, **Alpine Lake.** Beware of motor traffic and potentially strong winds on big Saganaga Lake. If the water level is not too low, the 10-rod portage may be avoided by paddling through the short, shallow creek connecting Red Rock Bay to Red Rock Lake. The 48-rod path goes over a small hill, but it is not difficult.

DAY 2: **Alpine Lake,** p. 105 rods, **Seagull Lake, Seagull River,** p. 38 rods, **river,** rapids, **Gull Lake, Seagull River, Saganaga Lake.** If you prefer to bypass the 105-rod carry, paddle into the channel leading north from the east end of Alpine Lake. It will loop around toward the southeast and then constrict into three short sets of shallow rapids draining into Seagull Lake. A 20-rod portage goes around the first rapids on the right (west side), but there are no paths around the last two. If the water level is not too low, you can easily run them. Otherwise walk or line your canoe between the boulders.

The 38-rod portage bypasses Seagull Falls, a small but scenic cascade next to Trail's End Campground. The trail is quite rocky, steep in places, and somewhat difficult to follow, as there are many intersecting paths from the campground. Some branches of the trail lead through campsites. The easiest route branches off to the right soon after the start and follows a gravel road for nine rods. Just past a water faucet it reenters the forest and climbs a small hill before descending steeply to the base of the falls and rapids.

You can eliminate about four miles of paddling and the 38-rod portage by ending your trip at the Seagull Lake public landing at the south end of Trail's End Campground, just east of the falls. But you will have to walk two miles to your car if you haven't made arrangements to be picked up there.

Route #82: The Knife-Fraser Route

7 Days, 75 Miles, 33 Lakes, 2 Rivers, 1 Creek, 39 Portages

Difficulty: Easy

Fisher Maps: F-19, F-11

Travel Zones: 39, 30, 19, 20, 21, 28, 29, 32, 38

Introduction: This route first follows the international boundary southwest from Saganaga all the way through Knife Lake to Birch Lake. Then you'll leave the border lakes and steer southeast through Ensign, Ima and a chain of much smaller lakes to Thomas Lake. From the east end of Thomas you will follow a northeast bearing through Kekekabic and Ogishkemuncie Lakes and return to the south end of Saganaga Lake by way of the Seagull River.

With 39 portages, the route may seem more difficult than the "easy" rating suggests. Indeed, the route could well be labeled "rugged" if covered in fewer days. Spread over 7 days, however, these 39 portages should pose no problems to even a rookie crew of overweight desk jockeys. None of the carries is long enough to worry about, and only a few follow steep gradients. If the water level is high enough, you should be able to eliminate several of the portages by shooting down some rapids and walking up some others.

It's a fun route, with plenty of variety—big lakes, tiny ponds, narrow streams, and attractive scenery everywhere you look.

Most of the loop receives moderate-to-heavy canoe traffic much of the summer. The southwest part of the route, in particular, accommodates many visitors from the nearby Fernberg Road. Accordingly, bears are often a nuisance in this part of the Boundary Waters. Take care to hang your food properly.

Anglers will have plenty of opportunities to catch all of the common canoe-country species.

DAY 1: **Saganaga Lake, Swamp Bay**. The BWCA Wilderness Act of 1978 prohibits motorists from the US part of Saganaga Lake west of American Point. The closer your campsite is to Swamp Portage, the more peaceful your night will be. Beware of wind and high waves while crossing the more open expanses of this huge lake.

DAY 2: **Saganaga Lake,** p. 5 rods, **Swamp Lake,** p. 80 rods, **Ottertrack Lake,** p. 12 rods, **Little Knife Lake, Knife Lake**. Ottertrack Lake (Cypress Lake on some maps) is long, narrow and lined with high bluffs and a rocky shoreline. It is one of my favorites. Along the north shore of the lake, you may see a clearing where once stood the cabins of Benny Ambrose. Benny was a prospector who sought gold for more than 60 years, until his death in 1982 at age 84. On the opposite (Canadian) shoreline, there is now a commemorative plaque cemented into the base of a cliff about ½ mile before the lake splits into two arms.

The farther southwest you paddle on Knife Lake, the more crowded you'll find the lake to be. Select a campsite in the vicinity of Thunder Point. Then take time to climb up the Thunder Point Trail to the scenic overlook, over 150 feet above Knife Lake. The panorama is breathtaking, especially at sunset.

If you're an angler, you'll find lake trout, walleye and northern pike inhabiting the sparkling waters in front of your campsite. Go ahead—test your luck.

DAY 3: **Knife Lake,** p. 75 rods, **Knife River,** p. 15 rods, **Seed Lake,** p. 15 rods, **Knife River,** p. 16 rods, **Carp Lake,** p. 48 rods, **Birch Lake,** p. 100 rods, **Frog Lake,** p. 70 rods, **Trident Lake,** p. 120 rods, **Ensign Lake,** p. 53 rods, **Ashigan Lake**. (See comments for Day 3, Route #80.)

DAY 4: **Ashigan Lake,** p. 105 rods, **Gibson Lake,** p. 25 rods, **Cattyman Lake,** p. 55 rods, **Jordan Lake,** p. 5 rods, **Ima Lake,** p. 50 rods, **Hatchet Lake,** p. 10 rods, **Thomas Creek,** p. 10 rods, **creek,** p. 10 rods, **pond,** p. 5 rods, **Thomas Lake**. (See comments for Day 4, Route #80.)

DAY 5: **Thomas Lake, Fraser Lake,** p. 15 rods, **Gerund Lake,** p. 30 rods, **Ahmakose Lake,** p. 90 rods, **Wisini Lake,** p. 10 rods, **Strup Lake,** p. 85 rods, **Kekekabic Lake.** Your portages this day will have their ups and downs—uphill from Fraser to Ahmakose and downhill from Wisini to Kekekabic. The two worst for northbound travelers both touch Ahmakose Lake. The 30-rod trail gains 48 feet in elevation, and the 90-rod path climbs over a 60-foot hill. But the last two descend over 100 feet to Kekekabic Lake. You're lucky to be headed north.

Kekekabic is an awesome lake, encircled with high-rising bluffs and bordered on the south by hills rising as high as 400 feet above the lake.

DAY 6: **Kekekabic Lake,** 5 Portages through **Kekekabic Ponds, Eddy Lake,** p. 15 rods, **Lake Jean,** p. 15 rods, **Annie Lake,** p. 15 rods, **Ogishkemuncie Lake,** p. 38 rods, **Kingfisher Lake,** p. 25 rods, **Jasper Lake.** All these portages are short and easy, providing more of a nuisance than a challenge.

DAY 7: **Jasper Lake,** p. 45 rods, **Alpine Lake,** p. 105 rods, **Seagull Lake, Seagull River,** p. 38 rods, **river,** rapids, **Gull Lake, Seagull River, Saganaga Lake.** (See comments for Day 2, Route #81.)

Ch. 5: Entry from the Gunflint Trail (East)

Tip of the Arrowhead Area

The far eastern region of the Boundary Waters Canoe Area contains, in my opinion, the most scenic terrain in all of the north country. It includes seven entry points that are accessible from, and to the *east* of, the Gunflint Trail (Cook County Road 12) and three entry points that are accessible from the Arrowhead Trail (Cook County Road 16). Those accessible from the Gunflint Trail are described in this chapter. The other three are described in Chapter 6.

Since 18 of the 25 entry points that are included in this guide are accessible from the Gunflint Trail, it stands to reason that traffic is rather heavy on that road during the summer months. (See comments at the start of Ch. 4 for more information about the Gunflint Trail.)

Entry Point 80—Larch Creek

Permits: 43

Popularity Rank: 53

Daily Quota: 1

Location: From Highway 61 in Grand Marais, drive 51 miles north and west on County Road 12 to a turnoff on the right side of the road just past the Seagull Guard Station, on the *north* side of unmarked Larch Creek.

Description: There is a small parking space, large enough for only a couple of vehicles, in a clearing next to the road. Access to the creek is at the bottom of the hill, just below an old beaver dam.

The closest public campground to this access is at the end of County Road 12, six miles beyond Larch Creek. Trail's End Campground is a good place to spend the night before your trip. A fee is charged. You may reserve a site in advance by calling (218) 388-2212.

Larch Creek is a delightful entry point for paddlers who like to "sneak" into the BWCA Wilderness. At the access, the creek is barely wide enough for one canoe and, in places, it winds so sharply that you may have difficulty negotiating some of the turns in a canoe longer than 17 feet. Near the end of its mile-and-a-half course to Larch Lake, however, the stream expands to nearly two rods in width.

Although there are no bonafide portages along Larch Creek, there are likely to be half a dozen obstructions (beaver dams or logs) that will necessitate "lift-overs." The creek is usually navigable, but during dry periods, you may find yourself dragging the bottom at times. Be prepared for wet feet. People who go to great lengths to avoid getting their feet wet will probably not enjoy this lovely Wilderness entry.

Larch Creek provides a tranquil access to the popular Granite River route between Gunflint and Saganaga lakes. Both of the routes described below employ parts of that route, one leading south and one leading north. Since neither is a complete loop, be prepared to either shuttle cars between entry and exit points, or to hike a few miles back to your origin.

Route #83: The Larch-Pine River Route

2 Days, 8 Miles, 4 Lakes, 1 River, 1 Creek, 5 Portages

Difficulty: Easy

Fisher Maps: F19, F-20, F-12

Travel Zone: 40

Introduction: This short and lovely route is an excellent, easy introduction to the best of what the Boundary Waters has to offer. From the landing, you'll first paddle east on tiny Larch Creek to Larch and Clove lakes. Then you'll veer south and follow the Pine River upstream to Magnetic lake and on to the southwest corner of big Gunflint Lake. En route, you'll be able to view several small rapids and a scenic waterfall. The portages are easy, the longest only ⅓ mile.

Motors are not allowed in this part of the BWCA, but they are permitted on Magnetic and Gunflint lakes, which are outside the Wilderness. The part of the route from Clove Lake to Gunflint Lake, which follows the US-Canadian boundary, was part of an extensive fur-trade route used by Indians and Voyageurs for centuries. This area is as rich in human history as it is in natural splendor.

Anglers will find small northern pike and perch in Larch Lake. Good-sized walleyes, smallmouth bass and northern pike inhabit Clove, Magnetic and Gunflint lakes. And the deep waters of Magnetic and Gunflint lakes also harbor lake trout.

While anglers will need two full days to fully avail themselves of the good fishing opportunities along this route, most paddlers could easily complete the entire route in just one day. Regardless of how long you take, be sure to have a vehicle waiting at the Gunflint Lake landing. Otherwise, you'll have to walk 6½ miles back to your origin at Larch Creek.

DAY 1: **Larch Creek, Larch Lake,** p. 25 rods, **Larch Creek, Clove Lake.** Allow plenty of time for that first 1½ miles to Larch Lake, to thoroughly appreciate an intimacy with Mother Nature that can only be enjoyed on small creeks like Larch. Don't let the small obstacles, like recurring beaver dams, be an annoyance. Consider them an integral part of a unique wilderness environment that makes this type of Wilderness entry far more appealing than entries on most large rivers and lakes.

Larch is a lovely lake, with some low rock outcroppings along its shoreline and hills beyond. If you get a late start, or if you prefer a less traveled lake for your only campsite, you may want to stop at one of the three campsites located here. Clove is also a pretty lake with three campsites, but it entertains more canoe traffic, as part of the popular Granite River route between Gunflint and Saganaga lakes. During the busiest parts of the summer, you would probably have more privacy on Larch Lake.

DAY 2: **Clove Lake,** p. 110 rods, **Pine River,** p. 35 rods, **river,** p. 13 rods, **river,** p. 15 rods, **Magnetic Lake, Gunflint Lake.** The 110-rod "Pine Portage" climbs over a low hill to bypass a section of the Pine River where there are three sets of rapids. You'll be paddling upstream on the scenic river, which splits into three channels at the next (35-rod) portage. The trail is on the Canadian side of the river. The 13-rod portage bypasses a beautiful 15-foot cascade called Little Rock Falls (the site of an old Hamms Beer commercial—look familiar?). You may be able to eliminate the final, short portage by walking or lining your canoe through the whitewater. A narrow, shallow channel separates Gunflint and Magnetic lakes, and you should have no trouble paddling through it.

Route #84: The Larch-Granite River Loop

3 Days, 24 Miles, 6 Lakes, 1 River, 1 Creek, 7 Portages

Difficulty: Easy

Fisher Maps: F-19, F-20

Travel Zones: 39, 40

Introducion: This interesting route is a variation of the popular Granite River Route that uses the Magnetic Lake entry point (see introduction to Route #85). The only difference is the first day, but that difference is significant. Rather than putting in at big Gunflint Lake, which is outside the BWCA, you'll start your expedition on tiny Larch Creek and enjoy your first day in complete wilderness solitude. After paddling east through Larch Lake to Clove Lake, you'll turn to the north and follow the Granite River flowage through Gneiss, Devil's Elbow and Maraboeuf lakes to Saganaga Lake. From near the east end of that gigantic lake, you'll then navigate carefully through a maze of islands, bays and peninsulas to the public landing at the lake's south end. Be sure to have a vehicle waiting at the landing, or you may have to walk six miles back to the Larch Creek access.

You'll be following the US-Canadian boundary from Clove Lake to Saganaga Lake. Keep that in mind when searching for campsites. Those on the east shoreline rest on Canadian soil and are, therefore, off limits to campers who have not passed through Canada Customs. The sites on the *west* side of the route lie in the BWCA Wilderness, on US soil.

Anglers should find walleyes, smallmouth bass and northern pike in most of the water along this route. Lake trout also inhabit the depths of Gneiss and Saganaga lakes. With only 24 miles to cover in three days, you should have plenty of time to cast you line.

DAY 1: **Larch creek, Larch Lake,** p. 25 rods, **Larch Creek, Clove Lake**. (See comments for Day 1, Route #83).

DAY 2: **Clove Lake,** p. 48 rods, **Granite River,** p. 72 rods, **river,** p. 25 rods, **river,** rapids, **river,** rapids, **river,** p. 25 rods, **Gneiss Lake, Devil's Elbow Lake,** rapids, **Maraboef Lake**. (See comments for Day 2, Route #85.)

DAY 3: **Maraboef Lake,** p. 27 rods, **Granite River,** p. 5–36 rods, **Saganaga Lake**. (See comments for Day 3, Route #85.)

Entry Point 57—Magnetic Lake

Permits: 612

Popularity Rank: 12

Daily Quota: 3

Location: From US Highway 61 in Grand Marais, drive 45 miles northwest on the Gunflint Trail to County Road 50. Turn right and follow this hilly gravel road ½ mile to the public landing (left side of the road) for Gunflint Lake. Magnetic Lake is straight across Gunflint Lake, 1½ miles north of the landing.

Description: A small parking area at the access will accommodate half a dozen cars. The Iron Lake Campground, 8 miles toward Grand Marais via the Gunflint Trail and County Road 92, offers a good place to spend the night before your trip. There are seven campsites there, and a fee is charged. You may reserve a site in advance by calling (218) 388-2212.

Magnetic Lake got its name from a special geologic phenomenon. Magnetic Rock, a glacially deposited block of iron located less than a mile west of the lake, is attractive to magnets. Hence your compass needle may be deflected from magnetic north as you pass through this region.

Magnetic Lake offers canoeists access to one of the most varied and interesting parts of the international boundary—a series of lovely lakes, roaring rapids, beautiful waterfalls and peaceful parts of a river system that stretches from the north end of Magnetic Lake 14 miles north to Saganaga Lake. The Granite River is picturesque, adorned with irregular shorelines of fascinating rock outcroppings, forested with mature stands of jack pine, black spruce and occasional patches of paper birch, and sprinkled with evidence of a long-gone era in our history, when Voyageurs passed this way en route to the northwestern hinterlands.

Until 1979, motorboats were allowed to travel in this part of the BWCA. Nevertheless, since only 9% of the travel permits issued in 1977 went to groups using motors, the ban on motors adversely affected very few people. In fact, this entry point jumped from 20th in popularity in 1977 to 12th in 1984, with a 16% increase in permits issued—one of only 4 entry points in the eastern region that increased in use during that period.

During July and August, use of this area is frequently heavy and reservations are advisable. Whitewater enthusiasts, in particular, are attracted to it because of the many fine rapids it offers, ranging in difficulty from easy to dangerous. For the beginning canoeist, portages are found next to most of the rapids.

So, whether you're a beginner or an advanced canoeist, the routes originating at Magnetic Lake are bound to please.

Route #85: The Granite River Route

3 Days, 26 Miles, 7 Lakes, 2 Rivers, 7–10 Portages

Difficulty: Easy

Fisher Maps: F-12, F-20, F-19

Travel Zones: 39, 40

Introduction: This fascinating route is one of the most popular short outings in this part of the BWCA. From the public landing on Gunflint Lake, you'll paddle north through Magnetic Lake and down the Pine River to Clove Lake. You'll continue winding your way north via the Granite River to Maraboef Lake. Then you'll portage into Saganaga, steer west, and then steer south to the public access at the southern tip of this enormous lake.

Since this is *not* a complete round trip, you will have to return by road to your origin at Gunflint Lake. If you don't have two cars for your group, make arrangements with one of the outfitters near the Saganaga landing to drop you off at Gunflint Lake. This way, you can leave your car at Saganaga Lake and not have to worry about meeting a pick-up deadline to return you to Gunflint Lake.

This is one of the prettiest routes in all of the Boundary Waters, with two lovely waterfalls and many rapids along the way. It may also be one of the most exciting routes, if you wish to test your canoeing skills on some of the whitewater.

Anglers should find walleyes, smallmouth bass and northern pike in most of the water along this route. Lake trout also inhabit the depths of Gunflint, Magnetic, Gneiss and Saganaga lakes. With only 24 miles to cover in three days, you should have plenty of time to cast your line.

The Granite River system was part of the extensive fur-trade route used by Indians and Voyageurs alike. Where 18th Century Voyageurs swamped their canoes, trying to avoid portages around rapids, relics have been found by modern voyagers. Flint chips from old Indian camps and gun flints from muskets have also been found at campsites adjacent to portages.

Motors are not allowed in the 14-mile stretch between Magnetic and Saganaga lakes. On a crisp, still night, however, you may hear the distant rumble from trucks driving on the Gunflint Trail. The road parallels the river system, a mere two-to-four miles west of it.

Beginning paddlers should avoid shooting most of the rapids. Inexperience often leads to poor judgment and can be dangerous. Nearly all of the portages are easy, so why take chances?

The experienced whitewater canoeist, on the other hand, may eliminate many of the portages. But always stop to check out the rapids before you plunge into them. Their difficulties vary considerably with the water level. If there is any doubt at *all,* portage!

DAY 1: **Gunflint Lake, Magnetic Lake,** p. 15 rods, **Pine River,** p. 13 rods, **river,** p. 35 rods, **river,** p. 110 rods, **Clove Lake.** A narrow, shallow channel separates Gunflint and Magnetic lakes. It should pose no problem to canoeists. The first portage bypasses a rapids that can easily be run by all but the beginning canoeist. The next short portage goes around a beautiful 15-foot drop in the river, called Little Rock Falls—a fine spot for lunch. At the third carry (Blueberry Portage) the Pine River splits into three channels, none of which is navigable. The unmarked portage is on a large rock outcropping on the Canadian shore, difficult to see from the river. Most travelers enter Clove Lake via the 110-rod carry across Pine Island, called Pine Portage. If you wish, however, you may follow a very scenic part of the river to Clove Lake, substituting three sets of rapids that involve two portages—sometimes three. The first rapids is fairly easy to run in high water, but a portage is necessary during low water periods. The next two rapids are very difficult and should not be run. Each is bypassed by a 45-rod carry.

DAY 2: **Clove Lake,** p. 48 rods, **Granite River,** p. 72 rods, **river,** p. 25 rods, **river,** rapids, **river,** rapids, **river,** p. 25 rods, **Gneiss Lake, Devil's Elbow Lake,** rapids, **Maraboef Lake.** An expert canoeist can eliminate all these portages by negotiating the rapids around which the portages pass. Even a canoeist with only intermediate skills may run all but two of them. The beginner, however, should portage. The first rapids out of Clove Lake requires skill. Swamp Portage (the next, a 72-rod carry) may be avoided by following the Granite River north to an easy rapids, followed by a very treacherous rapids that requires a 25-rod carry for all but the experts, followed in turn by a third rapids of moderate difficulty. Beginners should take the 72-rod Swamp Portage, which is level. The rest of the portages can be avoided (by all but beginners) by running all the rapids when the water level is not too low. There are several campsites in the southern end of Maraboef Lake.

DAY 3: **Maraboef Lake,** p. 27 rods, **Granite River,** p. 5–36 rods, **Saganaga Lake.** The 27-rod portage is around Horsetail Rapids, which is quite difficult to negotiate and should not be run by anyone but an expert. Old relics of the 18th Century Voyageurs have been found at the base of these rapids. Don't let your own gear add to the debris! The last portage is necessary for all, including experts. It flanks Saganaga Falls, a picturesque 5-foot cascade that attracts many picnickers and fishermen from popular Saganaga Lake. An eagle's nest was seen nearby in 1975.

The portage may be as long as 36 rods in low water. From that point on, you'll be sharing Saganaga Lake with motorists and many canoeists. Return to Gunflint Lake by driving 1 mile south on County Road 11 and 11 more miles via the Gunflint Trail back to County Road 50.

Route #86: The Granite-Kawishiwi Rivers Route

7 Days, 98 Miles, 37 Lakes, 3 Rivers, 46 Portages

Difficulty: Challenging

Fisher Maps: F-12, F-20, F-19, F-11

Travel Zones: 40, 39, 30, 29, 28, 33, 37

Introduction: This exciting loop will lead you down two of the best whitewater rivers and across several of the most scenic lakes in the BWCA. First you'll follow the Pine and Granite rivers north from Gunflint Lake to Saganaga. Then you'll veer toward the southwest and paddle along the Canadian border to the South Arm of Knife Lake. At that point, you'll turn south and portage your way to Kekekabic, Fraser and Insula lakes. Then the lovely Kawishiwi River will carry you northeast to Kivaniva Lake and several more small lakes that lead to ever-popular Little Saganaga Lake. Your final day will demand the longest and roughest portage of the whole route, en route to the trip's end at Round Lake.

With scenic vistas, picturesque waterfalls, exciting rapids and points of historic interest, this is a route that everyone will enjoy. Except for the first and last lakes, the only part of the route where motors are permitted is Saganaga Lake. Most of the loop is "paddle only."

Most of the route is actually quite easy. There are a couple of days that rate close to rugged, but by the time they arrive, you should be in pretty good shape.

DAY 1: **Gunflint Lake, Magnetic Lake,** p. 15 rods, **Pine River,** p. 13 rods, **river,** p. 35 rods, **river,** p. 110 rods, **Clove Lake,** p. 48 rods, **Granite River,** p. 72 rods, **river,** p. 25 rods, **river,** rapids, **river,** rapids, **river,** p. 25 rods, **Gneiss Lake.** (See comments for Days 1 and 2, Route #85.)

DAY 2: **Gneiss Lake, Devil's Elbow Lake,** rapids, **Maraboef Lake,** p. 27 rods, **Granite River,** p. 5–36 rods, **Saganaga Lake.** (See comments for Days 2 and 3, Route

#85.) Set American Point as your goal for the night. Motors are allowed on all of Saganaga Lake except west of that point.

DAY 3: **Saganaga Lake,** p. 5 rods, **Swamp Lake,** p. 80 rods, **Ottertrack Lake,** p. 12 rods, **Little Knife Lake, Knife Lake.** (See comments for Day 2, Route #82.)

DAY 4: **Knife Lake,** p. 33 rods, **Bonnie Lake,** p. 25 rods, **Spoon Lake,** p. 25 rods, **Pickle Lake,** p. 80 rods, **Kekekabic Lake,** p. 85 rods, **Strup Lake,** p. 10 rods, **Wisini Lake,** p. 90 rods, **Ahmakose Lake,** p. 30 rods, **Gerund Lake,** p. 15 rods, **Fraser Lake.** All but the last two of these portages will be uphill climbs—a total gain in elevation of 214 feet from Knife to Wisini Lake. The worst is the 85-rod trail connecting Kekekabic and Strup lakes. It climbs over 100 feet, intersects the Kekekabic Trail at the summit, and then drops 20 feet to Strup. The last 2½ portages are steeply downhill.

Kekekabic is an impressive lake, encircled with high-rising bluffs and bordered on the south by hills rising as high as 400 feet above the lake.

Sleep well after your roughest day so far.

DAY 5: **Fraser Lake, Thomas Lake,** p. 25 rods, **Kiana Lake,** p. 179 rods, **Lake Insula,** p. 18 rods, **Kawishiwi River, Alice Lake,** p. 20 rods, **Kawishiwi River,** p. 90 rods, **river,** p. 15 rods, **river.** (See comments for Day 5, Route #80.)

DAY 6: **Kawishiwi River,** p. 20 rods, **river,** p. 40 rods, **Kivaniva Lake,** p. 14–35 rods, **Anit Lake,** p. 25 rods, **pond,** p. 19 rods, **Pan Lake,** p. 55 rods, **Panhandle Lake,** p. 89 rods, **pond,** p. 65 rods, **Makwa Lake,** p. 45 rods, **Elton Lake,** p. 19 rods, **pond,** p. 19 rods, **Little Saganaga Lake.** (See comments for Day 6, Route #80.)

DAY 7: **Little Saganaga Lake,** p. 45 rods, **Mora Lake,** p. 10 rods, **Tarry Lake,** p. 50 rods, **Crooked Lake,** p. 55 rods, **Owl Lake,** p. 63 rods, **Tuscarora Lake,** p. 366 rods, **Missing Link Lake,** p. 142 rods, **Round Lake.** Fortunately, you should be in good shape by now for a long, tough portage. That 366-rod portage starts out with an uphill trek—steep in places—for almost 100 rods, but the rest of the trail is on mostly level to gently rolling terrain. There are 11 canoe rests for your convenience. Your origin at Gunflint Lake is 4½ miles east, via County Road 47, the Gunflint Trail and County Road 50.

Entry Point 58—South Lake

Permits: 81
Popularity Rank: 45
Daily Quota: 3

Location: South Lake is most easily accessible from Gunflint Lake. From US Highway 61 in Grand Marais, follow the Gunflint Trail 45 miles northwest to County Road 50. Turn right and drive ½ mile east to the public landing (left side of the road). South Lake is four lakes and two portages east of Gunflint Lake (2 airline miles).

Description: A small parking area at the access will accommodate half a dozen cars. The Iron Lake Campground, 8 miles closer to Grand Marias (one mile off the Gunflint Trail on County Road 92), is a good place to spend the night before your trip. There are seven campsites there, and a fee is charged.

It will take you a full day of paddling to reach South Lake from Gunflint, following the international boundary for 12 miles across two large, open lakes and two smaller ones. Motorboats are permitted throughout these border lakes, but they cannot enter the BWCA from South Lake.

Strong winds are a constant threat to the canoeist on Gunflint, North and South lakes. But a gentle west wind will enhance your progress, and only two easy portages obstruct your passage from Gunflint to South Lake.

Historic reminders of the 18th and 19th Centuries lurk along this part of the international boundary. On the north shore of Gunflint Lake, where the town of La Blaine once stood, the ovens used for baking bread may still be seen. Some abandoned remains of the Canadian Northern railroad follow the Canadian side of the border from the west end of Gunflint Lake to the east end of North Lake, a result of the mining boom that struck northeastern Minnesota in the 1880's. The remnants of an old railroad town (North Lake, Ontario) may also be found on the north shore of North Lake. A sign atop the Height of Land portage, joining North and South lakes, commemorates the French-Canadian Voyageurs, who used that spot to initiate "rookies" into their "fraternity."

Lakes are long around this part of the Canadian border. Portages are few and far between. Paddling may approach tedium. But the scenery is outstanding. Beginning canoe trippers will be sufficiently challenged, and photographers will be duly rewarded on either of the routes entering the BWCA from South Lake.

Reservations for permits are seldom necessary. Only about 15% of the available permits are used each summer.

Route #87: The Historic Border Route

2 Days, 21 Miles, 9 Lakes, 6 Portages

Difficulty: Easy

Fisher Maps: F-13

Travel Zone: 49

Introduction: This easy route will take you along part of the historic Voyageur's Highway. From the public landing, you will paddle 7 miles east across giant Gunflint Lake to Little Gunflint Lake, and continue along the Canadian border to beautiful Rose Lake. You will then portage south to Duncan Lake and again to Bearskin Lake, where you'll end this scenic route.

Have a car waiting at one of the public accesses along the south shore of Bearskin, or arrange with an outfitter in the area to pick you up and return you to Gunflint Lake. A fee will be charged for this service.

Motors are not permitted east of South Lake, but many penetrate the area west of North Lake. Your first day will be entirely outside the Boundary Waters. The second will be in Zone 49 of the BWCA, which ranks high in popularity. Only 3% of the groups who visit the area, however, come from South Lake.

Anglers will find smallmouth bass and lake trout along much of the route. Northern pike and walleye also inhabit some of the lakes.

DAY 1: **Gunflint Lake, Little Gunflint Lake,** p. 20 rods, **Little North Lake, North Lake,** p. 80 rods, **South Lake.** At the first portage you'll see railroad tracks and a small rail car used to haul heavy motorboats from Gunflint to North Lake. It is maintained for public use by the resort operators and summer residents living on Gunflint Lake. You may also use it, if you wish, to haul your loaded canoe from Little Gunflint to Little North Lake. But please respect this property of others. The 80-rod carry between North and South lakes has long been known as the Height of Land Portage. There, you will cross the Laurentian Divide. North of this continental divide, waters flow north to Hudson Bay and the Arctic Ocean. Waters on the south side flow southeast to Lake Superior and eventually to the Atlantic Ocean. It was a point of great significance to the Voyageurs: up to that point, they had been paddling against the current and portaging mainly uphill. West of South Lake, they paddled with the current in their journey to the Great Northwest.

DAY 2: **South Lake,** p. 57 rods, **Rat Lake,** p. 4 rods, **Rose Lake,** p. 80 rods, **Duncan Lake,** p. 75 rods, **Bearskin Lake.** You'll have an opportunity today to lunch at one of the most scenic places overlooking one of the most photographed lakes in the North Woods. The 80-rod carry from Rose to Duncan Lake is called the Stairway Portage. The uphill gradient from Rose Lake is so steep that a wooden stairway was built to make it safer and easier. About midway across the portage, at the top of the stairs, is a scenic overlook facing the north shore of Rose Lake, a postcard picture. Nearby is a lovely waterfall along the creek draining Duncan Lake. A bridge across the creek is part of the Border Route Trail. If time permits, you may wish to hike ¼ mile east from the portage to some spectacular high cliffs overlooking Rose Lake and the Canadian wilderness beyond. The portage levels off at the end, but it is still the roughest part of the entire trip.

You may end this route at either the east end of Bearskin Lake (County Road 66) or the portage connecting it to Hungry Jack Lake, near the southwest end of the lake (County Road 65). Regardless of which, you will have to drive back to your origin at Gunflint Lake.

Regardless of the point at which you end this route, you're in for one final scenic treat before you journey homeward. If your trip ends at the *east* end of Bearskin Lake, pack up your gear and canoes and drive just over a mile southwest on County Road 66. On the north side of the road, about six rods east of the entrance to the Flour Lake Campground, a foot trail leads north and winds its way to the top of **Honeymoon Bluff.** There you'll find a breathtaking view of Hungry Jack Lake below the bluff and Bearskin Lake in the distance. Near the top of your climb, you'll also enjoy a panoramic view overlooking Wampus Lake, south of County Road 66. The views are particularly outstanding in the fall when the leaves are turning color.

If you end your trip at the Hungry Jack Lake portage, you won't be near Honeymoon Bluff. But you are near another lovely vista. Drive ½ mile west of the portage, via County Road 65, and you will find a foot trail leading north from the road, about four rods west of the entrance to Gateway Hungry Jack Lodge. A short hike will take you to a beautiful overlook of Bearskin Lake from **Caribou Rock.**

Regardless of which bluff you assault, don't forget your camera. Each jaunt takes about 15 minutes, round trip.

Route #88: The South-Mountain-Pine Route

5 Days, 60 Miles, 23 Lakes, 1 River, 18 Portages

Difficulty: Challenging

Fisher Maps: F-13, F-14

Travel Zones: 49, 48

Introduction: Were it not for two noteworthy portages, this challenging route would certainly be rated "easy." From the Gunflint landing, you will follow the international boundary east and southeast to South Fowl Lake. Then you'll steer west and paddle your way through Pine Lake to the public access at East Bearskin Lake.

In so doing, you will be following the perimeter of *the* most scenic part of the entire BWCA. Along the entire route are high hills, and many of the lakes are bordered by striking cliffs.

Walleye fishermen will have the times of their lives paddling across some of the best walleye lakes in the Boundary Waters. Lake trout and smallmouth bass are also plentiful in many of the lakes.

While westbound, you will be paddling in Travel Zone 49, which ranks high in popularity. Most of the traffic congestion, however, is concentrated in the area south of Rose and Mountain lakes. Your eastbound travel is through Travel Zone 48, which receives moderate traffic throughout. The eastern and western ends of the route are outside the BWCA, and motors are currently allowed. The rest of the route, however, is reserved for paddlers.

DAY 1: **Gunflint Lake, Little Gunflint Lake,** p. 20 rods, **Little North Lake, North Lake,** p. 80 rods, **South Lake.** (See comments for Day 1, Route #87.)

DAY 2: **South Lake,** p. 57 rods, **Rat Lake,** p. 4 rods, **Rose Lake,** p. 660 rods, **Rove Lake, Watap Lake,** p. 100 rods, **Mountain Lake.** (See comments for Day 2, Route #87.) The 660-rod portage isn't as bad as it sounds, but *any* portage of that distance isn't easy. The first 460 rods follow a good, wide, gently up-sloping pathway. This good trail continues south to Daniels Lake. A much more difficult trail branches off to the east (left) after 460 rods and leads 200 more rods to Rove Lake.

High bluffs adorn the beautiful hills around Rose, Rove and Watap lakes—a splendid spectacle in autumn. Try your luck for lake trout this evening in Mountain Lake.

DAY 3: **Mountain Lake,** p. 90 rods, **Upper Lily Lake,** p. 40 rods, **Lower Lily Lake,** p. 140 rods, **Moose Lake,** p. 132 rods, **North Fowl Lake, South Fowl Lake.** None of these portages is difficult. The scenery continues to be lovely. But now you are back in a more frequently visited area, only a short paddle away from the end of the Arrowhead Trail, a good gravel road that serves public accesses on McFarland Lake. Find your campsite as soon as possible.

DAY 4: **South Fowl Lake,** p. 160 rods, **Royal Lake, Royal River,** p. 78 rods, **John Lake,** p. 10 rods, **Little John Lake,** p. 16 rods, **McFarland Lake,** p. 2 rods, **Pine Lake.** The length of that first long portage can vary by as much as 20–30 rods, depending on just how shallow the river is. At high water you must paddle up into the river several rods to reach the designated portage trail. During low-water periods, however, you'll have to walk along the rocky shore until you find the trail.

Under all but extreme low-water conditions, those last three short portages can be eliminated by walking or lining your canoe up the shallow rapids that connect John, Little John, McFarland, and Pine lakes.

You'll paddle past three public boat accesses and the trail-head of the rugged Border Route Trail for backpackers at the southeast end of McFarland Lake. So you might as well expect company in this part of the route.

Pine Lake is known for its fine walleye fishing. Smallmouth bass and lake trout also live there.

DAY 5: **Pine Lake,** p. 232 rods, **Canoe Lake,** p. 22 rods, **Alder Lake,** p. 48 rods, **East Bearskin Lake**. Before leaving Pine Lake, paddle to its far western end and visit lovely Johnson Falls. On the south side of the shallow creek flowing into Pine is a foot trail that winds its way almost ½ mile uphill to the 25-foot cascade. The hike takes only 15 minutes, and I'm sure you will find the reward well worth the time.

Then get "psyched" up for one of the "meanest" portages in the north country. That 232-rod trail to Canoe Lake gains over 300 feet in elevation above Pine as it climbs over two Minnesota mountains. There are 11 canoe rests for your convenience, but it is still one of the most exhausting portage that I can remember crossing. Good luck!

Obviously, this is not a complete round trip. To return to your origin at Gunflint Lake, you must drive ½ mile north to Forest Route 146, 1 mile southwest on 146, and then 18 miles northwest on the Gunflint Trail to the Gunflint Lake road.

Entry Point 60—Duncan Lake

Permits: 460

Popularity Rank: 16

Daily Quota: 4

Location: Drive northwest on the Gunflint Trail 28 miles from US Highway 61 in Grand Marais. Turn right on County Road 66 (Clearwater Road) and drive 3¼ miles on this rough, winding, hilly gravel road. The public access to Bearskin Lake is on the left side of the road, with a good put-in area and a parking lot large enough for 15–20 vehicles. Duncan Lake is a ¼ mile portage northwest of Bearskin.

If there is a strong west wind on the day of your scheduled departure, you may want to begin at the portage from Hungry Jack. To get there, follow the Gunflint Trail 1.8 miles past the Clearwater Road to the Hungry Jack Road (County Road 65). Drive north on this gravel road 2½ miles to the 21-rod portage between Bearskin and Hungry Jack lakes. A small parking lot will accommodate seven or eight cars. The lake is 8 rods downhill from the north end of the parking area.

Description: The National Forest Campground at Flour Lake offers a good place to camp the night before your trip. It is just off of the Clearwater Road, 2 miles northeast of the Gunflint Trail. There are 34 campsites available, each with a fee.

Duncan Lake provides what is probably the most scenic entry into the BWCA and access to the Canadian border. Stairway Portage follows the creek connecting Duncan and Rose lakes. A beautiful waterfall may be seen about midway across. Nearby, the rugged Border Route Trail intersects the portage, and at that point a scenic overlook faces the Canadian shore of Rose Lake from high above its southwest shoreline. The vista here rivals any in all of the Quetico-Superior country. Below the overlook, the path descends so steeply that a stairway has been constructed.

Duncan Lake is one of seven entry points providing direct access to this part of the BWCA, adjacent to the Canadian border. But it serves ⅓ of the groups who enter that travel zone (No. 49). That means particularly *heavy* traffic on Duncan and Rose lakes. It was one of only 4 entry points in the eastern region of the BWCA to increase in use from 1977 to 1984. Since 86% of its available permits are used each summer, be sure to reserve your permit far ahead of your scheduled trip. Duncan ranks 15th among entry points for quotas filled the highest percentage of the time. If you can get past the bureaucracy, you are sure to enjoy this gorgeous part of the Boundary Waters.

Regardless of the point at which you begin your trip to Duncan Lake, you'll have an opportunity to acquire a scenic panorama of Bearskin Lake and the surrounding territory either before your trip begins or after it ends.

If you begin your route at the *east* end of West Bearskin Lake, be sure to visit **Honeymoon Bluff** before heading home. About six rods east of the entrance to the Flour Lake Campground, on the north side of County Road 66, a foot trail winds its way north to the top of the bluff. There you'll find a breathtaking view of Hungry Jack Lake below and Bearskin Lake in the distance. Near the top of your five-minute climb, you'll also enjoy a panoramic view overlooking Wampus Lake, south of County Road 66. The views are especially outstanding in the fall when the leaves are turning color.

If you begin your route at the Hungry Jack Lake portage, don't drive past the **Caribou Rock** trail without stopping to take in its splendid vista. The trail begins on the north side of County Road 65, about four rods west of the entrance to Gateway Hungry Jack Lodge. A five-minute hike will take you to a lovely overlook of Bearskin Lake. Don't forget your camera!

Route #89: The Rose Lake Loop

2 Days, 13 Miles, 4 Lakes, 4 Portages

Difficulty: Easy

Fisher Maps: F-13

Travel Zone: 49

Introduction: This short, scenic route may begin at either of the public accesses on Bearskin Lake. Two short portages (totalling less than ½ mile) will lead you north through Duncan Lake to Rose Lake on the Canadian border. From the east end of Rose you will portage over 1½ miles to Daniels Lake. Then you'll paddle back to Bearskin Lake and complete the round trip.

Anglers will find smallmouth bass along most of the route. Lake trout are also known to inhabit the depths of Daniels and Bearskin lakes.

The northbound part of the route receives very heavy use, but on the return trip through Daniels Lake you will not encounter as many other visitors.

Normally, a trip with a 524-rod portage would not receive an "easy" rating. Since the 13 miles are distributed over two days, however, even the inexperienced tripper should have no problem negotiating the obstacles. A strong crew could easily complete the loop in one long day. But don't rush—take your time and enjoy the outstanding scenery all around you.

DAY 1: **Bearskin Lake,** p. 75 rods, **Duncan Lake,** p. 80 rods, **Rose Lake.** While portaging to Rose Lake, stop at the junction with the Border Route Trail and rest while you enjoy the scenic vista from the undeveloped campsite overlooking

Rose Lake. If time permits, you may wish to hike ¼ mile east from the portage to some spectacular high cliffs overlooking Rose Lake and the Canadian wilderness beyond. Watch your step as you descend the stairway to Rose Lake.

DAY 2: **Rose Lake,** p. 524 rods, **Daniels Lake,** p. 60 rods, **Bearskin Lake.** Don't let the "Long Portage" scare you. In spite of its length, it isn't rough. It follows a wide, gently sloping path over an old railroad bed, with canoe rests scattered generously along the way.

Route #90: The Gunflint-Knife-Kekekabic Route

9 Days, 120 Miles, 45 Lakes, 3 Rivers, 51 Portages

Difficulty: Challenging

Fisher Maps: F-12, F-13, F-20, F-19, F-11

Travel Zones: 49, 40, 39, 30, 29, 28, 33, 37

Introduction: This fascinating route will first take you north to the Canadian border. Then you'll follow the boundary west and north to Gunflint Lake. The scenic Pine and Granite rivers will carry you north to big Saganaga Lake. At that point you will veer southwest and continue paddling along the international boundary to the South Arm of Knife Lake. Then you will portage your way south to Kekekabic, Fraser and Insula lakes. The lovely Kawishiwi River will carry you northeast to Kivaniva Lake and several more small lakes that lead to ever-popular Little Saganaga Lake. Your final day will demand the longest and roughest portage of the whole route, en route to the trail's end at Round Lake.

Most of the route is actually quite easy, but a couple days are very close to rugged. Except for Saganaga Lake and the earlier stretch from South Lake through Gunflint, motors are prohibited from most of the route.

All your westbound travel will be along the historic Voyageur's Highway. With scenic vistas, lovely waterfalls, exciting rapids and frequent points of historic interest, this is a route that everyone will enjoy.

DAY 1: **Bearskin Lake,** p. 75 rods, **Duncan Lake,** p. 80 rods, **Rose Lake,** p. 4 rods, **Rat Lake,** p. 57 rods, **South Lake.** This is the reverse of Day 2, Route #87 (see comments).

DAY 2: **South Lake,** p. 80 rods, **North Lake, Little North Lake,** p. 20 rods, **Little Gunflint Lake, Gunflint Lake.** This is the reverse of Day 1, Route #87 (see comments). All the campsites on Gunflint Lake are located in the east end of the lake, so you haven't far to go this day, and you'll find it to be a very easy day indeed.

DAY 3: **Gunflint Lake, Magnetic Lake,** p. 15 rods, **Pine River,** p. 13 rods, **river,** p. 35 rods, **river,** p. 110 rods, **Clove Lake,** p. 48 rods, **Granite River,** p. 72 rods, **river,** p. 25 rods, **river,** rapids, **river,** rapids, **river,** p. 25 rods, **Gneiss Lake.** (See comments for Days 1 and 2, Route #85.)

DAY 4: **Gneiss Lake, Devil's Elbow Lake,** rapids, **Maraboef Lake,** p. 27 rods, **Granite River,** p. 5–36 rods, **Saganaga Lake.** (See comments for Days 2 and 3, Route #85.) Set American Point as your target for the night. Motors are allowed on all of Saganaga Lake except west of that point.

DAY 5: **Saganaga Lake,** p. 5 rods, **Swamp Lake,** p. 80 rods, **Ottertrack Lake,** p. 12 rods, **Little Knife Lake, Knife Lake.** (See comments for Day 2, Route #82.)

DAY 6: **Knife Lake,** p. 33 rods, **Bonnie Lake,** p. 25 rods, **Spoon Lake,** p. 25 rods, **Pickle Lake,** p. 80 rods, **Kekekabic Lake,** p. 85 rods, **Strup Lake,** p. 10 rods, **Wisini Lake,** p. 90 rods, **Ahmakose Lake,** p. 30 rods, **Gerund Lake,** p. 15 rods, **Fraser Lake.** (See comments for Day 4, Route #86.)

DAY 7: **Fraser Lake, Thomas Lake,** p. 25 rods, **Kiana Lake,** p. 179 rods, **Lake Insula,** p. 18 rods, **Kawishiwi River, Alice Lake,** p. 20 rods, **Kawishiwi River,** p. 90 rods, **river,** p. 15 rods, **river.** (See comments for Day 5, Route #80.)

DAY 8: **Kawishiwi River,** p. 20 rods, **river,** p. 40 rods, **Kivaniva Lake,** p. 14–35 rods, **Anit Lake,** p. 25 rods, **pond,** p. 19 rods, **Pan Lake,** p. 55 rods, **Panhandle Lake,** p. 89 rods, **pond,** p. 65 rods, **Makwa Lake,** p. 45 rods, **Elton Lake,** p. 19 rods, **pond,** p. 19 rods, **Little Saganaga Lake.** (See comments for Day 6 and part of Day 7, Route #80.)

DAY 9: **Little Saganaga Lake,** p. 45 rods, **Mora Lake,** p. 10 rods, **Tarry Lake,** p. 50 rods, **Crooked Lake,** p. 55 rods, **Owl Lake,** p. 63 rods, **Tuscarora Lake,** p. 366 rods, **Missing Link Lake,** p. 142 rods, **Round Lake.** (See comments for Day 7, Route #86.)

Entry Point 61—Daniels Lake

Permits: 76
Popularity Rank: 46
Daily Quota: 1

Location: Daniels Lake is 60 rods north of Bearskin Lake, which is 31 miles by road northwest of Grand Marais (see Entry Point 60).

Description: The Flour Lake Campground, two miles northeast of the Gunflint Trail and just off the Clearwater Road, is a good place to spend the night before your trip. There are 34 campsites, and a fee is charged to campers.

Like Duncan Lake, Daniels is one portage away from the Canadian border and beautiful Rose Lake. Unlike the Duncan route, however, entry from Daniels Lake is not accompanied by a spectacular scenic vista. Instead, it requires one of the longest portages in the BWCA—524 rods over a gently sloping path adjacent to the international boundary. That's why most Rose Lake visitors travel through Duncan Lake and why the two suggested routes herein avoid the "Long Portage" and veer east to Rove Lake (which requires a *mere* 264-rod carry.)

Along with six other entry points, Daniels Lake serves Travel Zone 49, the part of the BWCA adjacent to the Canadian border, from South Lake east to Moose Lake. Most of the zone's use stems from Daniels' neighbors on either side—Clearwater and Duncan lakes. They accommodate ⅔ of the visitors to this part of the Boundary Waters, and it is in their vicinities where most congestion occurs. Only 9% of the groups in Zone 49 enter through Daniels Lake. Nevertheless, the Daniels Lake entry point is nearly always booked up, usually reserved ahead of time. In 1984, 93% of its available permits were used. Consequently, reservations are advisable.

Route #91: The Mountain-Caribou Loop

2 Days, 24 Miles, 12 Lakes, 12 Portages
Difficulty: Challenging
Fisher Maps: F-13, F-14
Travel Zones: 49, 48

Introduction: This beautiful round trip will take you through the Boundary Waters to the international border and south to an area not contained in the BWCA. From the Hungry Jack portage to Bearskin Lake (See Entry Point 60: **Location**), you will paddle northeast through Daniels to the Canadian border. Then you'll follow the border east to Mountain Lake. A ¼-mile portage south will take you away from the land of the Maple Leaf to Clearwater Lake. You'll continue through a series of smaller lakes to East Bearskin Lake. Then you will portage out of the BWCA to Flour Lake and paddle west through Hungry Jack to the portage to Bearskin Lake, in the middle of which is the parking lot from which this route began.

Anglers will have an opportunity to catch lake trout and smallmouth bass, as well as some northern pike along this route.

Most of the lakes on this route receive moderate to heavy use throughout much of the summer, and motors are allowed on some of them. Most of the lakes, however, are restricted to "paddle only" watercraft. Although strong paddlers will have no trouble completing this loop in just two days, less experienced canoe campers will find the route more enjoyable if spread over three full days, averaging eight miles and four portages per day.

DAY 1: p. 8 rods, **Bearskin Lake,** p. 60 rods, **Daniels Lake,** p. 264 rods, **Rove Lake, Watap Lake,** p. 100 rods, **Mountain Lake,** p. 90 rods, **Clearwater Lake.** Don't be fooled by the easy beginning of the long portage to Rove Lake. The trails to Rose Lake and Rove Lake are the same for 64 rods, following a wide, gently sloping path. The good path continues to Rose Lake. The eastbound branch to Rove Lake follows a rougher, less used trail, which is also part of the rugged Border Route Trail.

The stretch from Rove to Clearwater Lake is quite scenic, with high hills and cliffs bordering the crystalline indigo lakes. You'll find lake trout, northern pike and smallmouth bass along the way. The final portage climbs steeply to nearly 100 feet above Mountain Lake, before dropping more gradually 80 feet down to Clearwater Lake. The Border Route Trail is intersected at the summit of the hill. From there, you can hike ¼ mile east to some high cliffs overlooking the west end of Mountain Lake—a detour that's well worth the effort.

Motors are currently allowed on Clearwater Lake, though the east end is far removed from the habitation at the opposite end. If you prefer a secluded lake, continue on to Caribou, where there are several good campsites.

DAY 2: **Clearwater Lake,** p. 160 rods, **Caribou Lake,** p. 60 rods, **Deer Lake,** p. 15 rods, **Moon Lake,** p. 114 rods, **East Bearskin Lake,** p. 90 rods, **Flour Lake,** p. 162 rods, **Hungry Jack Lake,** p. 10 rods. You'll have several steep uphill portages this day, but none of the climbs is too long. The first is the worst, but it climbs for only the first 60 rods and then descends the final 100 rods. There are seven canoe rests along the way. The next portage climbs steeply from Caribou Lake for 30 rods and then follows a level dirt road south to Deer Lake. Be sure to turn left or you'll walk back to Clearwater Lake. After you leave East Bearskin Lake, you'll be paddling on lakes outside of the BWCA, with private cabins, resorts and a summer camp. The ½-mile portage from Flour to Hungry Jack Lake crosses two gravel roads and runs through the Flour Lake Campground. Be alert for traffic!

Route #92: The Mountain-Royal-Flour Loop

4 Days, 46 Miles, 20 Lakes, 1 River, 19 Portages

Difficulty: Challenging

Fisher Maps: F-13, F-14

Travel Zones: 49, 48

Introduction: This scenic route will first lead you northeast through Bearskin and Daniels lakes to the Canadian border. You'll portage to Rove Lake and then follow the international boundary east and southeast to South Fowl Lake. After a night on that shallow lake, you will steer west and paddle through Pine Lake to East Bearskin Lake. Then you'll leave the Boundary Waters and return to your origin at County Road 65 by way of Flour and Hungry Jack lakes.

The eastern and western ends of this route are outside of the BWCA, and motors are allowed on lakes there. All the route in the Boundary Waters Canoe Area, though, is reserved for paddlers.

Anglers will have opportunities to fish some of the best walleye lakes in the BWCA. Lake trout and smallmouth bass are also plentiful in many of the lakes.

DAY 1: p. 8 rods, **Bearskin Lake,** p. 60 rods, **Daniels Lake,** p. 264 rods, **Rove Lake, Watap Lake,** p. 100 rods, **Mountain Lake**. (See comments for Day 1, Route #91.) Try your luck for lake trout this evening in Mountain Lake.

DAY 2: **Mountain Lake:** p. 90 rods, **Upper Lily Lake,** p. 40 rods, **Lower Lily Lake,** p. 140 rods, **Moose Lake,** p. 132 rods, **North Fowl Lake, South Fowl Lake**. (See comments for Day 3, Route #88.)

DAY 3: **South Fowl Lake,** p. 160 rods, **Royal Lake, Royal River,** p. 78 rods, **John Lake,** p. 10 rods, **Little John Lake,** p. 16 rods, **McFarland Lake,** p. 2 rods, **Pine Lake**. (See comments for Day 4, Route #88.)

DAY 4: **Pine Lake,** p. 232 rods, **Canoe Lake,** p. 22 rods, **Alder Lake,** p. 48 rods, **East Bearskin Lake,** p. 90 rods, **Flour Lake,** p. 162 rods, **Hungry Jack Lake,** p. 10 rods. (See comments for Day 5, Route #88.) After you leave East Bearskin, you will be paddling on lakes outside of the BWCA, with private cabins, resorts and a summer camp. The ½-mile portage from Flour to Hungry Jack Lake crosses two gravel roads and runs through the Flour Lake campground. Be alert for traffic!

Entry Point 62: Clearwater Lake

Permits: 431

Popularity Rank: 17

Daily Quota: 4

Location: From US Highway 61 in Grand Marais, drive north on the Gunflint Trail 28 miles to its intersection with County Road 66 (the Clearwater Road). Turn right and follow this rough, winding, hilly gravel road 5¼ miles to its end.

Description: There you'll find a good public access to Clearwater Lake, with a small parking lot next to it, large enough for 10–12 vehicles. There are no other facilities at the landing. Private cabins are adjacent to the landing, and much of the shoreline at the southwest end of Clearwater is populated—a resort, an outfitter and many private summer homes.

No camping is allowed at the access. The Flour Lake Campground, just 3 miles southwest, however, is a fine place to spend the night before your trip. There are 34 campsites, each with a fee.

Clearwater is currently a motor-designated lake. It receives a good deal of use during the summer, but only 16% of the permits in 1984 were issued to groups using motors. Though it is only one of seven entry points providing direct access to Travel Zone 49, Clearwater Lake transports one third of the visitors to this zone. That makes for heavy traffic from Clearwater to Mountain Lake on weekends and during busy summer periods.

In spite of the crowds, you will surely find a trip from this entry point to be delightful, as it leads to an area that many consider to be the most scenic part of the Boundary Waters Canoe Area. Minnesota "mountains" tower above the dark green shores of these sparkling lakes—a sight not found in the western parts of the BWCA.

Fishing is excellent in many of the lakes in the far eastern region. Anglers may want to add to the suggested number of days, in order to avail themselves of the unlimited fishing opportunities around them.

Route #93: The Pine-Alder Loop

2 Days, 18 Miles, 9 Lakes, 10 Portages

Difficulty: Challenging

Fisher Maps: F-14

Travel Zones: 49, 48

Introduction: This short, scenic route will take you to one of the prettiest spots in the eastern region of the Boundary Waters—Johnson Falls. From the public landing you'll paddle to the southeast end of Clearwater Lake and then portage to Caribou Lake. You will continue east through Little Caribou Lake to Pine Lake. After a visit to Johnson Falls you'll begin your return trip by crossing a rugged portage to Canoe Lake. After traveling westward through Alder and East Bearskin Lake, you will turn north and negotiate a series of smaller lakes and portages that will return you to your origin on Clearwater Lake. Motors are not allowed along most of the route. Only on Clearwater and East Bearskin lakes will you hear motors.

Perhaps the most exhausting portage in all of the Boundary Waters connects Pine and Canoe lakes, and the half-mile trek from Clearwater to Caribou is not all that easy, either. If you are not in shape, find a different route! Or at least stretch this route over three full days.

Anglers will find smallmouth bass along much of the route. Lake trout and walleye also inhabit some of the waters. Pine Lake, in particular, is prized for its fine walleye fishing.

DAY 1: **Clearwater Lake,** p. 160 rods, **Caribou Lake,** p. 27 rods, **Little Caribou Lake,** p. 78 rods, **Pine Lake,** p. 232 rods, **Canoe Lake.** "Psych up" for some steep climbing this day. The first portage starts steeply uphill (for 60 rods to 150 feet above Clearwater Lake), but descends most of the way to Caribou Lake. The carry to Canoe Lake is by far the worst you'll encounter. It surmounts three steep hills en route to a net increase in elevation of 200 feet from Pine to Canoe Lake. Eleven canoe rests are located along the path, which is wide and relatively smooth most of the way. The only level part of the trail, however, is through a marshy area midway across the portage.

Before you tackle that exhausting portage, take time out for a hike to lovely Johnson Falls. The trail to it begins at the western tip of Pine Lake, on the south side of a shallow creek flowing into the lake. The well-used path winds for half a mile uphill to a narrow granite gorge through which the stream cascades for 25 picturesque feet. The hike takes only 15 minutes and is well worth it.

DAY 2: **Canoe Lake,** p. 22 rods, **Alder Lake,** p. 48 rods, **East Bearskin Lake,** p. 114 rods, **Moon Lake,** p. 15 rods, **Deer Lake,** p. 60 rods, **Caribou Lake,** p. 210 rods, **Clearwater Lake.** This is a much easier day than the first, with portages mostly level or downhill. The only uphill trek is the final one, from Caribou to Clearwater Lake, which begins uphill, with one canoe rest, then levels off and follows two dirt roads for 35 rods. The 60-rod carry from Deer to Caribou follows a dirt road for 30 level rods; then leaves the road to the right as the portage trail drops steeply to Caribou Lake. If you would rather, you may skip Caribou entirely and portage from Deer directly to Clearwater, following the dirt road most of the way. This involves less total distance and less hassle, but more walking. The road continues all of the way back to County Road 66. Watch for your trail to Clearwater Lake, which veers off to the right (north) just east of a barricade across the road (to keep vehicles out of the BWCA). (See Sketch #3)

The last half of the portage trail from Caribou Lake to Deer Lake also follows the private road. It is possible, therefore, to portage directly from Deer Lake to Clearwater Lake, bypassing Caribou Lake entirely.

Route #94: The Clearwater-Royal-Moose Loop

3 Days, 38 Miles, 10 Lakes, 1 River, 10 Portages

Difficulty: Challenging

Fisher Maps: F-14

Travel Zone: 49

Introduction: As with most of the routes in the Tip of the Arrowhead Region, this loop follows long, scenic lakes, separated by infrequent but long portages. From Clearwater Lake you'll portage to West Pike Lake and paddle eastward through East Pike and John lakes to South Fowl Lake. Then you will steer north and west along the Canadian border to the west end of Mountain Lake. From there, you'll portage south to Clearwater Lake and return to your origin at the west end of that lovely lake.

Anglers will have opportunities to catch walleye, smallmouth bass and lake trout along the route. The Fowl lakes, in particular, are known for their good walleye fishing.

All the route is in Travel Zone 49, which ranks high in the number of visitors it receives each summer. Over one third of those visitors enter from Clearwater Lake. But you'll find that the Pike chain receives the least amount of use of any of the lakes in this zone.

Wind could be a problem on most of the large lakes. With four portages in excess of ½ mile, this route should be avoided by those who detest portaging. But with the carries spread over three days, most trippers won't mind. The outstanding scenery to be found is well worth a little extra effort on portages.

DAY 1: **Clearwater Lake,** p. 214 rods, **West Pike Lake,** p. 177 rods, **East Pike Lake**. Unless the wind is against you, this should be an easy day. Both portages are downhill, descending a total of 131 feet. Most of that drop is during the last half of the first portage, which descends over 100 feet to West Pike Lake, on a path used also by hikers on the Border Route Trail. The second carry is across nearly level terrain, but the path is quite rocky. Watch for moose in this area, which is the least traveled part of the entire route. Steep hills border this beautiful chain of lakes, rising as much as 500 feet above their shores.

DAY 2: **East Pike Lake,** p. 180 rods, **John Lake,** p. 78 rods, **Royal River, Royal Lake,** p. 160 rods, **North Fowl Lake,** p. 132 rods, **Moose Lake**. You are bound to see more people in this part of the loop, as you paddle near the end of the Arrowhead Trail, where three public accesses are located. The scenery is so outstanding, however, that you can overlook the people. Again, portages are fairly easy, in spite of their lengths. After a short, steep climb, the first portage then drops gradually 116 feet to John Lake. The ½-mile carry to North Fowl Lake is virtually flat.

DAY 3: **Moose Lake,** p. 140 rods, **Lower Lily Lake,** p. 40 rods, **Upper Lily Lake,** p. 90 rods, **Mountain Lake,** p. 90 rods, **Clearwater Lake**. If the wind is not a problem, this will be your easiest day of the trip, as you paddle along the scenic Canadian border. On the final portage you will cross the rugged Border Route Trail again, at the summit of an 80-foot ridge over which you must pass. If you'd like to see Mountain Lake from a different perspective, you can hike ¼ mile east on the Border Route to some high cliffs that afford a nice view of the lake's west end. The side trip is well worth the effort!

Entry Point 64—East Bearskin Lake

Permits: 587

Popularity Rank: 14

Daily Quota: 5

Location: From US Highway 61 in Grand Marais drive north on the Gunflint Trail 26 miles to its junction with Forest

Route 146. Turn right and drive one mile northeast on this good gravel road to a sign indicating "National Forest Campground." Turn right and drive ½ mile on Forest Route 142 to the public boat landing, where there is a fairly large parking lot to accommodate up to fifteen vehicles.

Description: Next to the landing is a large National Forest Campground. There are sites for 43 "units" and a fee is charged. This provides an excellent place for you to spend the night before your trip, enabling an early start the first morning.

Because of its easy accessibility and because it leads to one of the most scenic zones in all the BWCA, East Bearskin is a popular lake. Only the east end and much of the south shore are part of the Boundary Water Canoe Area. Many private summer homes are situated along the north shore, but because they are hidden you will see only their docks from the lake. Bearskin Lodge is located at the west end of the lake.

The BWCA Wilderness Act of 1978 restricted motors to not more than 10 h.p. on Alder and Canoe and 25 h.p. on the eastern part of East Bearskin Lake that falls within the BWCA. Less than 14% of the permits issued in 1984 went to motorists, however. Though the humming of motors should not plague you, you may find it hard to elude other canoeists. The outstanding scenery in this hilly region necessitates sharing!

Route #95: The Johnson Falls Loop

2 Days, 15 Miles, 8 Lakes, 8 Portages

Difficulty: Challenging

Fisher Maps: F-13, F-14

Travel Zone: 48

Introduction: This route would actually be classified "easy," were it not for one long, bad portage in the middle.

From the public landing near the west end of East Bearskin Lake, you will paddle east through Alder and Canoe lakes, before portaging that arduous trail north to Pine Lake. There, you will leave your canoe for awhile and hike to one of nature's spectacles—Johnson Falls. Then, from Pine Lake, you'll start your return trip, first northwest through Little Caribou and Caribou lakes and then southwest through Deer and Sucker lakes to your origin at East Bearskin.

The route is short, the lakes are crystalline, the scenery is beautiful. Anglers will find smallmouth bass in these lakes, and the avid fisherman may even want to add an extra day to search the depths of Pine for the tasty walleye and elusive lake trout that inhabit this long, scenic lake.

You will be paddling entirely within Travel Zone 48 during this weekend loop. Campsites are fairly abundant, but so are visitors during peak periods in late summer and on holiday weekends.

DAY 1: **East Bearskin Lake,** p. 48 rods, **Alder Lake,** p. 22 rods, **Canoe Lake,** p. 232 rods, **Pine Lake.** This would be a very easy day were it not for the 232-rod carry into Pine. After that, you'll be ready to make camp! Fortunately, however, you'll be walking this portage in the "easy" direction. Though it begins with a steep climb and ascends another hill soon after, most of the trail is downhill, dropping a total of over 200 feet. Only a small part of it is level, through a marshy area where it can be quite muddy at times. Except for this part, the path is good—wide and relatively smooth, with 11 canoe rests along the way.

Near the end of this portage, at the far west end of Pine Lake, you'll find a shallow creek flowing into Pine. On the south side of it, a well-worn trail winds for ½ mile uphill to Johnson Falls, a lovely 25-foot cascade through a narrow granite gorge. The hike takes only 15 minutes and is well worth your time.

Make camp early and enjoy the fishing on Pine Lake. Or, if you prefer the solitude of a smaller lake, continue on to Little Caribou, where one nice campsite is located in the middle of the north shore.

DAY 2: **Pine Lake,** p. 78 rods, **Little Caribou Lake,** p. 27 rods, **Caribou Lake,** p. 60 rods, **Deer Lake,** p. 15 rods, **Moon Lake,** p. 114 rods, **East Bearskin Lake.** As you would expect, since you dropped in elevation so much to Pine Lake, you must climb back up to East Bearskin. Fortunately, though, the climb is divided into several short assaults, the toughest being the last one from Moon Lake. The last half of the 60-rod portage to Deer Lake is an old road. You'll climb steeply for 30 rods to the road, then follow the level road left to the lake.

Route #96: The Pine-Mountain Loop

4 Days, 43 Miles, 18 Lakes, 1 River, 17 Portages
Difficulty: Challenging
Fisher Maps: F-13, F-14
Travel Zones: 48, 49

Introduction: Like all the routes in this area, this loop passes through beautiful terrain, over several long lakes, and across relatively few portages. From East Bearskin Lake, you will paddle east through Pine Lake to McFarland Lake and on to John and South Fowl lakes. Then you will turn north and west and follow the Canadian border to the west end of Mountain Lake. From there, you'll portage south to Clearwater Lake and continue southwest through Caribou, Deer and Moon lakes to East Bearskin Lake.

Anglers will have opportunities to catch walleye, smallmouth bass and lake trout along the way. The Fowl lakes and Pine Lake, in particular, are known for their good walleye fishing.

The route passes east through Travel Zone 48 and returns through Zone 49. Both receive moderate use, with heavy canoe traffic in places. Perhaps the busiest spots will be near McFarland and Clearwater lakes, both of which are popular entry points.

DAY 1: **East Bearskin Lake,** p. 48 rods, **Alder Lake,** p. 22 rods, **Canoe Lake,** p. 232 rods, **Pine Lake.** (See comments for Day 1, Route #95.)

DAY 2: **Pine Lake,** p. 2 rods, **McFarland Lake,** p. 16 rods, **Little John Lake,** p. 10 rods, **John Lake,** p. 78 rods, **Royal River, Royal Lake,** p. 160 rods, **North Fowl Lake, South Fowl Lake.** This will probably be the busiest part of the route. At the southeast end of McFarland Lake are public accesses to McFarland and Little John lakes, as well as to the increasingly popular Border Route Trail.

If the water level is high enough, you can eliminate the short portages connecting Pine, McFarland, Little John and

John lakes by paddling down the shallow streams connecting them.

DAY 3: **South Fowl Lake, North Fowl Lake,** p. 132 rods, **Moose Lake,** p. 140 rods, **Lower Lily Lake,** p. 40 rods, **Upper Lily Lake,** p. 90 rods, **Mountain Lake.** Mountain Lake is another beautiful lake, surrounded by high hills rising as much as 400 feet above the water. Try your luck at catching lake trout in this deep border lake.

DAY 4: **Mountain Lake,** p. 90 rods, **Clearwater Lake,** p. 160 rods, **Caribou Lake,** p. 60 rods, **Deer Lake,** p. 15 rods, **Moon Lake,** p. 114 rods, **East Bearskin Lake.** Your final day demands the most frequent portaging, with several steep uphill climbs. The first carry climbs steeply to 100 feet above Mountain Lake, crosses the Border Route Trail, and then drops 80 feet (more gradually) down to Clearwater Lake. The ½-mile carry from Clearwater Lake then begins with an uphill climb, gaining 150 feet in elevation during the first 60 rods, but descends most of the way to lower Caribou Lake. (Also see comments for Day 2, Route #95.)

Ch. 6:
Entry from the Arrowhead Trail

Tip of the Arrowhead Area

This is the same scenic northeast corner of the BWCA Wilderness that was described in Chapter 5. A total of 10 entry points provide direct access to this rugged landscape, which is sandwiched between the Gunflint Trail and the Canadian border. The seven that are accessible from County Road 12 (the Gunflint Trail) are included in Chapter 5, while the remaining three, accessible from County Road 16 (the Arrowhead Trail), are described in this chapter.

The Arrowhead Trail begins at the tiny village of Hovland, 20 miles northeast of Grand Marais via Highway 61, and leads 18 miles north to McFarland Lake. It is a hard-surface road for the first 2½ miles, but dirt and gravel the rest of the way. Eight miles up the trail you'll pass through a stand of virgin white pines that date back to the early 1800's.

There are no national-forest campgrounds along the Arrowhead Trail, although some folks do camp next to the public landing at McFarland Lake. The closest public campground is at Judge C. R. Magney State Park, along Highway 61, 5 miles southwest of Hovland. Grand Marais is the closest town of any size for procuring groceries and other supplies (see Chapter 4 for comments).

Entry Point 68—Pine Lake

Permits: 202

Popularity Rank: 31

Daily Quota: 1

Location: Pine Lake is accessed by a short portage at the west end of McFarland Lake. Park at the public landing on the *left* side of County Road 16, which you'll see just before you arrive at the bridge crossing the creek connecting McFarland and Little John lakes. You can drive right down to the shore of the lake.

Description: Pine Lake is the most popular of the three entry points at the end of the Arrowhead Trail. Although its overnight use is only slightly greater than for neighboring John Lake, Pine probably entertains more day use (no statistical data) from the cabin dwellers and occasional campers situated at the east end of McFarland. The lake is well known for its good populations of walleyed pike, smallmouth bass and lake trout.

A reservation is advised during most of the summer season. Pine Lake ranks 6th among all entry points for quotas filled the highest percentage of the time and 9th among entry points most often reserved ahead of time.

At 7½ miles long and averaging nearly ½ mile in width, Pine is one of the largest lakes in this part of the BWCA Wilderness. Because of its east-west orientation and the fact that there is not a single island on the lake, this wide open expanse is highly susceptible to the effects of a strong wind. Be cautious and paddle close to the shore, especially if a storm is threatening.

Route #97: The Caribou-Moose Loop

3 Days, 32 Miles, 13 Lakes, 1 River, 12 Portages

Difficulty: Challenging

Fisher Maps: F-14

Travel Zones: 48, 49

Introduction: This lovely route is a challenge for paddlers with no propensity for portaging. For the most part, long lakes are followed by long and often steep portages. From McFarland Lake, you'll paddle west through Pine and Little Caribou lakes to Caribou Lake. Then you'll portage north, first to Clearwater Lake and then to the west end of Mountain Lake. After exploring some breathtaking cliffs, you'll begin the eastbound part of the route by following the Canadian border through Mountain, Moose and North Fowl lakes to the mouth of the Royal River. That river will carry you northwest to John Lake. At that point, you will exit the BWCA Wilderness and paddle south across Little John Lake back to the Arrowhead Trail. A highlight of the trip will be a visit to Johnson Falls at the west end of Pine Lake.

Like most of the Tip of the Arrowhead region, this area is characterized by steep ridges that tower from 300 to 500 feet above the lakes they border. It's a beautiful setting any time of year and absolutely stunning in autumn.

Canoe traffic is likely to be moderate throughout most of the route, a bit heavier toward the west end of the loop. Boats with no more than 10 horsepower motors are permitted in the Boundary Waters on Clearwater and North Fowl lakes. And although motors are not allowed on the U.S. side of the international boundary, there are currently no motor restrictions on the Canadian side of those lakes. (Efforts are underway, however, to make this part of the Canadian border a canoeing park similar to Quetico Provincial Park.) There is also road access to the Canadian side of North Fowl Lake. So, in spite of USFS statistics that show very light use of this Canadian border region, you may, in fact, see more boaters than you might have thought likely.

Nevertheless, if seeing outstanding scenery is high on your list of canoe trip priorities and you don't mind a few tough portages to achieve that goal, you're bound to enjoy this loop. A group of competent paddlers, without too much wind resistance, should have no trouble completing this route in three days. Dedicated anglers, beginning paddlers and those who aren't "geared" for portaging, however, might want to expand their trip itineraries to four or five days. On big, wind-susceptible lakes like these, it's always a good idea to be prepared for a windbound "layover" day.

Anglers should be delighted with the opportunities along this loop. Lake trout inhabit the depths of Pine, Mountain and Moose lakes. Walleyes, northern pike, and smallmouth bass are also found in most of the lakes.

DAY 1: **McFarland Lake,** p. 2 rods, **Pine Lake,** p. 78 rods, **Little Caribou Lake.** You can probably avoid that first 2-rod portage by paddling, walking or lining your canoe through the shallow rapids separating McFarland and Pine lakes. Before portaging to Little Caribou Lake, paddle to the western tip of Pine Lake. On the south side of a small creek is a foot trail that leads nearly half a mile up the creek to Johnson Falls. It takes about 15 minutes to get there. The side trip to this lovely 25-foot cascade is well worth the effort and extra time.

The quarter-mile portage from Pine Lake climbs 100 feet to Little Caribou Lake—just a *taste* of the steeper portages yet to come.

The only campsite on Little Caribou Lake is a fine, secluded place to spend the night. If you cannot get there until late afternoon, however, you may prefer to stay on Pine Lake, where there are several sites from which to choose. Or if you proceed and find that the Little Caribou Lake site is already taken, be prepared to continue to Caribou Lake.

DAY 2: **Little Caribou Lake,** p. 27 rods, **Caribou Lake,** p. 160 rods, **Clearwater Lake,** p. 90 rods, **Mountain Lake,** p. 90 rods, **Upper Lily Lake,** p. 40 rods, **Lower Lily Lake,** p. 140 rods, **Moose Lake**. The half-mile portage from Caribou Lake climbs nearly 250 feet in the first 100 rods, before dropping 160 feet to Clearwater Lake. The west end of Clearwater Lake lies outside the BWCA, and it is populated with summer homes and a resort and outfitter. But it's also one of the prettiest lakes in the north country, bordered by steep ridges and some cliffs along the south shore. Unfortunately, you won't see the most scenic, central part of the lake.

Nevertheless, at the next portage, you *will* have an opportunity to enjoy an incredible scene. The portage climbs about 80 feet during the first 50 rods from the shore of Clearwater Lake, intersects the Border Route Trail, and then more steeply descends nearly 100 feet during the final 40 rods to Mountain Lake. From the summit of the ridge, you can hike ¼ mile east via the Border Route Trail to some high cliffs overlooking the west end of Mountain Lake. Or if time permits, you can also walk *west* on the Border Route Trail about a mile to an even more stunning panorama from a bluff about 350 feet above the lake. Either one offers a detour that's well worth the effort.

The final three portages are not difficult. You'll *descend* a total of 160 feet on all three carries, most of the drop happening on the 140-rod "Greater Cherry" portage. These last four lakes and three portages are all part of the Voyageur lore. The 18th

Century may have seen more canoe traffic than there is today.

DAY 3: **Moose Lake,** p. 132 rods, **North Fowl Lake,** p. 160 rods, **Royal Lake, Royal River,** p. 78 rods, **John Lake,** p. 10 rods, **Little John Lake**. Your final four portages are not difficult. The first descends gradually about 50 feet to North Fowl Lake. The second is virtually flat, but the length may vary by as much as 20–30 rods, depending on how shallow the mouth of the Royal River is. During high water you must paddle up into the river several rods to reach the designated portage trail. During low water, however, you'll have to walk along the rocky shore until you find the trail. Under all but extreme low-water conditions, the final short portage can be eliminated by walking or lining your canoe up the shallow rapids that connect John and Little John lakes.

This route ends at the Little John Lake boat access, which is about a hundred yards west of the McFarland Lake landing where you started.

Entry Point 69—John Lake

Permits: 183

Popularity Rank: 33

Daily Quota: 1

Location: John Lake is one lake and a short portage northwest of the public access to Little John Lake. As you near the end of the Arrowhead Trail, drive past two public landings for McFarland Lake on the left side of the road. Proceed to a small parking lot on the right (north) side of the road, just before a small bridge over the creek connecting McFarland and Little John Lake.

Description: The parking lot, which is 10 rods east of the boat landing, holds about a dozen vehicles. Don't worry if the lot is crowded with other vehicles. It serves not only two BWCA canoeing entry points (#69 and #70), but also a trailhead for the scenic Border Route Trail, a backpacker's path to Paradise.

John Lake is the second most popular of the three canoeing entry points at the end of the Arrowhead Trail. Since 1977, overnight use has increased by 226%, and now a reservation is advised during most of the summer season. John Lake ranks 7th among all entry point for quotas filled the highest percentage of the time and 6th among entry points most often reserved ahead of time. With only two permits issued to overnight visitors each day, however, you are still assured a peaceful, high-quality visit to one of the loveliest parts of the entire BWCA Wilderness.

Route #98: The Pike-Pine Route

3 Days, 25 Miles, 9 Lakes, 8 Portages

Difficulty: Challenging

Fisher Maps: F-14

Travel Zones: 48, 49

Introduction: This route consists of big lakes, bordered by high hills and separated by long portages. Wind could be a problem on most of the lakes, and the constant paddling might approach tedium *if* it were not for the magnificent scenery of the Tip of The Arrowhead. For those who hate portages, this route rates "Rugged," with four ½-mile portages. But spread over 3 days, most trippers will find it relatively easy.

From the public landing at the south end of Little John Lake, you will paddle north to John Lake and then head west through East and West Pike lakes to Clearwater. You'll see very little of this long lake as you portage out of its east end south to Caribou Lake. Then you will return by paddling east through Little Caribou and Pine lakes to McFarland, from which you can quickly walk to your car.

Your westward travel will be in Travel Zone #49. Although statistically this area ranks high in popularity (15th), two thirds of the visitors enter it from either Entry Point 60—Duncan Lake—or Entry Point 62—Clearwater Lake—and usually head north to the Canadian border lakes.

Your eastbound return will be through Zone #48, which is served by three of the more popular entry points: Clearwater Lake (ranks 17th), East Bearskin Lake (14th) and Pine Lake (34th). Much of your paddling will be on Pine Lake, which receives a good deal of traffic from McFarland Lake.

Anglers will have good opportunities to catch some tasty meals. Lake trout inhabit the depths of West Pike, Clearwater and Pine lakes. Smallmouth bass and walleyes are found in most of the lakes. John, Little John, Caribou and Little Caribou lakes also contain all sizes of northern pike and perch.

Nowhere will you see lakes more beautiful than in this part of the Boundary Waters Canoe Area. A highlight of the trip will be a visit to Johnson Falls, near the west end of Pine Lake.

DAY 1: **Little John Lake,** p. 10 rods, **John Lake,** p. 180 rods, **East Pike Lake,** p. 177 rods, **West Pike Lake.** Normally the 10-rod carry between Little John and John lakes will not be necessary. The short, shallow rapids can easily be shot under normal water conditions or walked or lined down in low water.

The other portages aren't bad, in spite of their lengths. The first one gains 116 feet, climbing gradually over a long hill, and then makes a short, steep descent to East Pike Lake. The second is quite level, but rocky. Resist the temptation to put in at a small pond about midway across the portage. The trail veers away from the pond, so there is no place to take out at the other end.

West Pike Lake is a peaceful lake where motors are prohibited. You'll find several nice campsites along the north shore, with steep hills towering more than 500 feet above you. And under its surface live lake trout, walleye and smallmouth bass. Have a pleasant evening!

DAY 2: **West Pike Lake,** p. 214 rods, **Clearwater Lake,** p. 160 rods, **Caribou Lake,** p. 27 rods, **Little Caribou Lake,** p. 78 rods, **Pine Lake.** This will be the roughest of your three days, as you portage 479 rods from West Pike Lake to Pine Lake. The longest portage on this route shares a path used by hikers on the Border Route Trail. It ascends nearly 100 feet during the first 75 rods from the shore of West Pike Lake and then levels off the rest of the way to Clearwater Lake. After a short paddling respite, you'll assault the most exhausting of the portages. It climbs more than 150 feet above Clearwater Lake, and then descends almost 250 feet to the shore of Caribou Lake. Just be glad you're not heading in the other direction! The final carry is nearly all down hill, dropping nearly 100 feet to Pine Lake.

Set up camp near the west end of Pine, and then paddle to the far western end of this beautiful lake to the mouth of a small creek. On the south side of it, a well-worn path winds for half a mile uphill to Johnson Falls, a lovely 25-foot cascade through a narrow granite gorge. The hike takes only 15 minutes and is well worth your time.

Pine Lake is well known for its good walleye fishing and you may also find lake trout and smallmouth bass there. Accordingly, you may also see many anglers who enter this lake from McFarland Lake at its eastern end.

DAY 3: **Pine Lake,** p. 2 rods, **McFarland Lake.** This will be your easiest day of your short trip, unless the winds prevail from the east. Normally no portage is necessary between Pine and McFarland lakes if you run, line or walk your canoe down the short, shallow rapids connecting these lakes.

Rather than negotiating the portage to the Little John access, you may end your journey at the McFarland Lake public access just east of the portage. A short walk north through the woods will bring you back to your car at the Little John parking lot.

Entry Point 70—North Fowl Lake

Permits: 39

Popularity Rank: 57

Daily Quota: 2

Location: North Fowl Lake is the easternmost of all BWCA Entry points. It is located about three miles, by water, east of the Little John Lake boat landing (see Location for Entry Point 69), by way of Little John and John lakes and the Royal River.

Description: The boundary between Canada and the United States lies in the middle of North Fowl Lake. While the west half of the lake is restricted to 10 horsepower motors, along with adjoining South Fowl Lake, there are currently no motor restrictions on the Canadian side of the border lakes east of Quetico Provincial Park. (Efforts are underway, however, to make this part of the Canadian border a canoeing park similar to Quetico Provincial Park.) There is also road access to the Canadian side of North Fowl Lake. So, in spite of USFS statistics that show very light overnight use of this Canadian border region, you may, in fact, see more daytime boaters than you might have expected.

Nevertheless, North Fowl Lake is, by far, the least popular of the three canoeing entry points accessible from the Arrowhead Trail for overnight entry into the Boundary Waters. While advanced reservations are advised for the other two entry points (#68 and #69), they are seldom necessary for Entry Point 70.

In addition to the one-way route described below, you may also enjoy two excellent loops from this entry point either by reversing Route #97 (three days) or by "plugging into" Route #96 (four days).

Route #99: The Voyageurs' Highway

7 Days, 70 Miles, 23 Lakes, 3 Rivers, 23 Portages

Difficulty: Challenging

Fisher Maps: F-14, F-13, F-12, F-20, F-19

Travel Zones: 49, 39, 40

Introduction: This beautiful route follows the international boundary all the way from North Fowl Lake to Saganaga Lake. It is characterized by big, long lakes and relatively few portages (averaging only three or four carries per day.) The scenery is no less than spectacular, but strong wind is an ever-present threat.

This route is part of the famed "Voyageurs' Highway." For decades during the 18th and early 19th centuries, voyageurs paddled across these same lakes and rivers en route from Lake Superior to western Canada and back again. Relics from this period of our history may still be found at the bottom of some rapids. And reminders of our more recent history may also be found along parts of the route (see the Description for Entry Point 58—South Lake).

Strong paddlers can easily complete the route in five or six days, if a strong west wind doesn't hinder progress. But, for most groups, seven days will allow plenty of time to explore foot trails along the way that lead to some panoramic vistas—and still have time to fish.

Anglers will have opportunities to fish for lake trout in all of the larger lakes along this route. Smallmouth bass are found nearly everywhere, while northern pike and walleyes inhabit many of the lakes and rivers.

It is possible to shorten this route by leaving the Boundary Waters at one of several points along the way. If your schedule is limited to only two days, you can portage south from Mountain Lake to Clearwater Lake and end at the public landing near the west end of that beautiful lake. For a three-day trip, exit through either Daniels Lake or Duncan Lake to end at the Bearskin Lake boat landing. For four days, stop at the Gunflint Lake landing. Five days will take you to the Larch Creek entry (and exit) point. Regardless of where you plan to end this route, be sure to have a car waiting there. This is one of the few routes described in this book that is not a loop. By road, it is approximately 95 miles from McFarland Lake to Saganaga Lake.

DAY 1: **Little John Lake,** p. 10 rods, **John Lake,** p. 78 rods, **Royal River, Royal Lake,** p. 160 rods, **North Fowl Lake,** p.132 rods, **Moose Lake.** In spite of what appear to be a couple of fairly long portages, this is a rather easy day for experienced canoe trippers. You can probably eliminate that first short carry entirely by paddling, walking or lining your canoe through the shallow rapids there, depending on the water level. The half-mile portage from Royal to North Fowl Lake is virtually flat, but you may have to extend the trail a few rods when the water level is low in the mouth of the Royal River. The only uphill trek of the day is on the final portage, which gradually rises about 50 feet from North Fowl to Moose Lake.

DAY 2: **Moose Lake,** p. 140 rods, **Lower Lily Lake,** p. 40 rods, **Upper Lily Lake,** p. 90 rods, **Mountain Lake.** You'll gain 160 feet in elevation between Moose and Mountain lakes, most of it on the first "Greater Cherry" portage. This should be a very easy day, however, enabling an early arrival at your campsite. If tempted to continue on, reconsider! You'll see no more designated campsites until you reach Rose Lake, which requires a 660-rod portage.

If possible, take one of the sites toward the west end of Mountain Lake. Then, if time permits, you can enjoy a side trip to some high cliffs. The 90-rod portage from Mountain to Clearwater Lake is intersected by the Border Route Trail at the summit of a steep ridge separating the two lakes. From that point you can hike ¼ mile east to a bluff overlooking the west end of Mountain Lake. Or, if time permits, a more stunning panorama can be found by hiking about a mile *west* on the

Border Route Trail. It affords an outstanding view down the length of Mountain Lake from a vantage point more than 350 feet above the water. The climb is well worth the effort!

On the way back to your campsite, the anglers in your group might want to troll for one of the many lake trout inhabiting the depths of Mountain Lake.

DAY 3: **Mountain Lake,** p. 100 rods, **Watap Lake, Rove Lake,** p. 660 rods, **Rose Lake.** This should be another short day of paddling, through one of the prettiest parts of the route. Between the two portages, long, narrow Watap and Rove lakes are bordered on the south by a 400-foot ridge with some striking palisades.

The 660-rod "Long Portage" is challenging, but perhaps not as rugged as it might seem. The first 200 rods are the roughest. Then the narrow trail joins the much smoother and wider path of an old railroad grade and follows it the final 460 rods to Rose Lake, descending more than 100 feet in all.

After you've set up camp along the sloping south shore of Rose Lake, take time to explore Stairway Portage at the southwest corner of the lake. Midway across the steep ¼ mile portage, at the top of a long set of wooden steps, is a lovely waterfall. Just above the fall, the portage intersects the Border Route Trail. From that point you can cross the creek on a log bridge and hike about ¼ mile east to the famed Rose Lake cliffs, which afford an outstanding view across the west end of the lake. (In case of emergency, or to satisfy a strong urge for a cold drink, you can also hike about three miles south from the portage via the Split Pine Trail to intersect County Road 65 just west of a resort.)

Anglers will have an opportunity to search for smallmouth bass, lake trout and walleyes in Rose Lake. Good bass sizes are reported.

DAY 4: **Rose Lake,** p. 4 rods, **Rat Lake,** p. 57 rods, **South Lake,** p. 80 rods, **North Lake, Little North Lake,** p. 20 rods, **Little Gunflint Lake, Gunflint Lake.** The 80-rod "Height of Land" portage was a milestone for the 18th Century voyageurs, as it will be for you. It's a good trail that passes over a low hill. In fact, if there weren't a sign atop the hill, you would have no way of knowing that you were crossing the Laurentian Divide—the continental divide that determines whether water flows north to the Arctic Ocean or south to the Atlantic Ocean.

The Voyageurs knew that, from this point on, they would essentially be traveling down hill. Prior to this landmark, all of their portages (and yours) had been uphill from Lake Superior.

The landmark is also significant to you in a way that didn't affect your canoeing predecessors. For the next 15 miles, you'll be paddling outside the BWCA Wilderness on five lakes where there are no motor restrictions. There are private cabins and four resorts along the south shore of Gunflint Lake and at the lake's west end. All the campsites are located at the east end of the lake, however, where you shouldn't be bothered by too much civilization.

Anglers will find good-sized fish in big Gunflint Lake, including lake trout, walleyes, northern pike and smallmouth bass.

DAY 5: **Gunflint Lake, Magnetic Lake,** p. 15 rods, **Pine River,** p. 13 rods, **river,** p. 35 rods, **river,** p. 110 rods, **Clove Lake.** If there is any chance of a brisk west wind this day, try to get an early start, or you may have to spend the whole day at your campsite. (See Introduction to Route #85 and comments for Day 1, Route #85.)

DAY 6: **Clove Lake,** p. 48 rods, **Granite River,** p. 72 rods, **river,** p. 25 rods, **river,** rapids, **river,** rapids, **river,** p. 25 rods, **Gneiss Lake, Devil's Elbow Lake,** rapids, **Maraboef Lake.** (See comments for Day 2, Route #85.)

DAY 7: **Maraboef Lake,** p. 27 rods, **Granite River,** p. 5–36 rods, **Saganaga Lake.** (See comments for Day 3, Route #85.)

Ch. 7: Wilderness Weekends

This chapter is designed to help you quickly identify the short, overnight routes from each entry point, when all the time you can spare is just a weekend or a holiday. Each route can be completed comfortably by most canoeists in two full days, camping one night in the Wilderness. Only the "highlights" are included here:

Destination = where to aim for a campsite.

Departing Entry Point = at what point you will exit the BWCA Wilderness.

Miles = the total miles travelled.

Portages = the total number of portages encountered.

Longest = the length of the longest portage along the route.

Difficulty = the overall rating of the route: easy, moderate or rugged. A few subjective comments then follow.

That's all. Not all of the lakes and portages are mentioned, nor are all the points of interest along the way. You can find these details on the preceding pages of this book. By knowing where the route starts, where it ends and what the destination is, you should be able to "fill in the blanks."

The best and quickest way to find the details about any of these routes is to first consult the introduction to the appropriate entry point. Then read about the first day or two of the first route described for the entry point. If you desire more information about any of the lakes or rivers included in a route, consult the index. Nearly all the Wilderness Weekend routes mentioned in this chapter are parts of longer routes described elsewhere in this book. Some, in fact, are *identical* to routes described earlier. They are mentioned here simply for completeness.

Some of the short routes included in this chapter are complete loops. But, unlike most of the routes in this book, many of them do not start and end at the same place. They start at one entry point and end at another. That is because many of the entry points simply don't lend themselves to short 2-day loops. For these routes, then, you'll have to shuttle vehicles from entry point to exit point, or make arrangements with an outfitter or resort operator to drop you off at an entry point, after leaving your vehicle at your ending point. For a fee, most outfitters are willing to do that.

Of course, in addition to the suggestions found here, you can always plan a round trip, which requires only backtracking from your destination. Just paddle as far as you comfortably can in one day. Then, the following morning, pack up and return to your car by the same route that brought you to your campsite. The options are virtually unlimited.

#38 Sawbill Lake

Destination	*Departing E.P.*	*Miles*	*Portages*	*Longest*	*Difficulty*
Kelso Lake	Sawbill Lake	8	3	30 rods	Easy

You can make a short loop by paddling north on Sawbill Lake to the Kelso River, and then returning to Sawbill by way of Alton Lake. You're not likely to escape from other people, but it's an easy enough route for a group with no prior BWCA experience. Pick your campsite as early as possible and then explore the surrounding area. There is a good chance to see a moose.

#39 Baker Lake

Destination	*Departing E.P.*	*Miles*	*Portages*	*Longest*	*Difficulty*
S. Temperance L.	Brule Lake	15	7	240 rods	Moderate

This is an excellent introduction to wilderness canoe camping, travelling through some of the loveliest scenery in the Boundary Waters. It's a good blend of small and large lakes, rivers and rapids. (See Day 1 of Route #55.)

#40 Homer Lake

Destination	*Departing E.P.*	*Miles*	*Portages*	*Longest*	*Difficulty*
Juno Lake	Brule Lake	12	4	70 rods	Easy

This loop is Route #57, one of the better short loops in this part of the BWCA to escape from most other people without making a long, difficult portage.

#41 Brule Lake

Destination	*Departing E.P.*	*Miles*	*Portages*	*Longest*	*Difficulty*
Winchell L.	Brule Lake	14	11	200 rods	Moderate

This loop is Route #59. Were it not for two half-mile-plus portages, this would be rated as an easy outing. But they are not difficult carries. Winchell is a beautiful lake with several excellent campsites.

#43 Bower Trout Lake

Destination	*Departing E.P.*	*Miles*	*Portages*	*Longest*	*Difficulty*
Swan Lake	Bower Trout	11	12	90 rods	Moderate

This one-way route is described as Day 1 of Route #62. You'll have to backtrack on the second day. But the scenery is so appealing, you surely won't mind seeing it twice.

#44 Ram Lake

Destination	*Departing E.P.*	*Miles*	*Portages*	*Longest*	*Difficulty*
Vista Lake	Morgan Lake	9	9	400 rods	Rugged

This is Route #64. It's not recommended for inexperienced canoeists. In addition to the 400-rod portage, which is not too difficult, there is a gruelling 190-rod path, as well as an uphill 110-rod carry. Good luck!

#45 Morgan Lake

Destination	*Departing E.P.*	*Miles*	*Portages*	*Longest*	*Difficulty*
Vista Lake	Morgan Lake	9	8	400 rods	Moderate

This loop is Route #66. With a 400-rod portage taken twice, you might expect this to be rated "rugged." But it's not a bad trail. This is a good holiday weekend route where you can quickly escape from the crowds.

#47 Lizz Lake

Destination	*Departing E.P.*	*Miles*	*Portages*	*Longest*	*Difficulty*
Caribou L.	Swamp Lake	10	4	155 rods	Moderate

This distance is measured from the public access at the west end of Poplar Lake. It's much shorter if you start at one of the resorts near the middle or the east end of the lake. (See introductory comments for Entry Point 47.)

#48 Meeds Lake

Destination	*Departing E.P.*	*Miles*	*Portages*	*Longest*	*Difficulty*
Gaskin Lake	Lizz Lake	12	9	220 rods	Moderate

This is Route #69. After the first long (220 rods) portage, it's actually a fairly easy loop. Don't expect complete solitude on any part of the route, buy you'll likely see far fewer people on the first day than on the second.

#65 Portage Lake

Destination	*Departing E.P.*	*Miles*	*Portages*	*Longest*	*Difficulty*
Rush Lake	Skipper Lake	10	6	320 rods	Rugged

This is one of the best parts of the BWCA in which to escape from other people, because long portages discourage most potential visitors. It's also a good place to see moose browsing along the shorelines.

#50 Cross Bay Lake

Destination	*Departing E.P.*	*Miles*	*Portages*	*Longest*	*Difficulty*
Snipe Lake	Missing Link L.	14	9	366 rods	Rugged

This is Route #73, except that you'll be camping on Snipe Lake rather than Tuscarora. That enables an easy first day and a more secluded campsite, but also a more difficult second day. You can avoid that rugged part of the route by simply backtracking from Snipe Lake to your origin.

#51 Missing Link Lake

Destination	*Departing E.P.*	*Miles*	*Portages*	*Longest*	*Difficulty*
Gillis Lake	Brant Lake	12	13	366 rods	Rugged

This loop is Route #75. In addition to this loop, you can also reverse Route #73, mentioned above with the Cross Bay Lake Entry Point. Both routes are rewarding for the canoeist who likes to *work* for a worthy destination.

#52 Brant Lake

Destination	*Departing E.P.*	*Miles*	*Portages*	*Longest*	*Difficulty*
Brant Lake	Brant Lake	5	6	85 rods	Easy

This one-way route simply takes you from Round Lake to the Brant Lake entry point and back again—a very easy introduction to lake canoeing in the BWCA. There are a couple of nice campsites at the north end of Brant.

#54 Seagull Lake

Destination	*Departing E.P.*	*Miles*	*Portages*	*Longest*	*Difficulty*
Alpine Lake	Saganaga Lake	23	4	105 rods	Easy

This loop is simply the reverse of Route #81. It's an easy loop for competent paddlers, but the distance may be rather challenging to a novice. During the summer, you'll see people everywhere you turn, as well as motorboats on Seagull and Saganaga lakes.

#55 Saganaga Lake

Destination	*Departing E.P.*	*Miles*	*Portages*	*Longest*	*Difficulty*
Saganaga L.	Saganaga L.	18+	0	0	Easy

With no portages, this is the loop for people who want to carry a cooler and lawn chairs. Simply explore big, beautiful Saganaga Lake to your heart's content! Make the quiet southwest end of the lake, beyond American Point, your destination (where motorboats are prohibited). If time and energy permit, paddle across Cache Bay (after getting permission from the Quetico Park ranger on the small island inside the entrance to the bay) to catch a glimpse of magnificent Silver Falls.

#80 Larch Creek

Destination	*Departing E.P.*	*Miles*	*Portages*	*Longest*	*Difficulty*
Clove Lake	Magnetic Lake	8	5	110 rods	Easy

This is Route #83. It offers one of the most peaceful and private entries into the BWCA that you can find—anywhere—without a portage. But be prepared for wet feet. You must lift your canoe over several beaver dams.

#57 Magnetic Lake

Destination	*Departing E.P.*	*Miles*	*Portages*	*Longest*	*Difficulty*
Gneiss Lake	Saganaga Lake	26	10	110 rods	Moderate

This is Route #85, except you'll be doing it in two days insted of three, and camping on Gneiss Lake, instead of Clove and Maraboef lakes. What is an easy route over three days is a challenging two-day route.

#58 South Lake

Destination	*Departing E.P.*	*Miles*	*Portages*	*Longest*	*Difficulty*
South Lake	Duncan Lake	21	6	80 rods	Easy

This is Route #87. If you prefer extensive paddling with few portages, this is a good way to spend a weekend. With a prevailing west wind, or no wind at all, most folks should have no trouble covering 21 miles in 2 days.

#60 Duncan Lake

Destination	*Departing E.P.*	*Miles*	*Portages*	*Longest*	*Difficulty*
Rose Lake	Daniels Lake	13	4	524 rods	Easy

This loop is Route #89. Even with a 524-rod portage, this short loop is not difficult when spread over two full days. You should also have time to hike along the beautiful Border Route Trail.

#61 Daniels Lake

Destination	*Departing E.P.*	*Miles*	*Portages*	*Longest*	*Difficulty*
Clearwater L.	East Bearskin L.	24	12	160 rods	Moderate

This loop is Route #91. Although experienced trippers should have no trouble completing the loop in two days, a weekend might not be long enough for neophytes. Some of the portages are exhausting.

#62 Clearwater Lake

Destination	*Departing E.P.*	*Miles*	*Portages*	*Longest*	*Difficulty*
Canoe Lake	Clearwater	18	10	232 rods	Moderate

This loop is Route #93. With three exhausting portages along this route, it is not recommended for inexperienced or poorly conditioned trippers. Only seasoned veterans should attempt it in just two days.

#64 East Bearskin Lake

Destination	*Departing E.P.*	*Miles*	*Portages*	*Longest*	*Difficulty*
Pine Lake	East Bearskin L.	15	8	232 rods	Moderate

This loop is Route #95. With an exhausting portage at the midpoint of this loop, it is not recommended for poorly conditioned trippers. A seasoned veteran who was travelling light, however, could probably complete the loop in just one day.

#68 Pine Lake

Destination	*Departing E.P.*	*Miles*	*Portages*	*Longest*	*Difficulty*
Pine Lake	Pine Lake	20	0	0	Easy

This route simply takes you from the McFarland Lake landing to the west end of Pine Lake and back again. The highlight is a hike to Johnson Falls. Although there is a 2-rod portage between McFarland and Pine lakes, it should not be necessary if you are willing to walk, line or run your canoe through the shallow rapids joining the lakes.

#69 John Lake

Destination	*Departing E.P.*	*Miles*	*Portages*	*Longest*	*Difficulty*
East Pike L.	McFarland L.	9	4	260 rods	Moderate

This short loop requires two big portages that might discourage anyone who is not in the best physical condition. After climbing over a low hill separating John and East Pike lakes, you'll have an even tougher portage to McFarland Lake. It climbs steeply to nearly a hundred feet above East Pike before dropping more gradually over 250 feet down to McFarland Lake.

#70 North Fowl Lake

Destination	*Departing E.P.*	*Miles*	*Portages*	*Longest*	*Difficulty*
Moose Lake	North Fowl L.	16	8	160 rods	Moderate

This one-way route leads to beautiful Moose Lake on the Canadian border and then back again. Moose is usually the most peaceful of the border lakes, since there are long portages at both ends to keep motorboats off the Canadian side of the lake. (See comments for Day 1 Route #99.)

Appendix I

Routes Categorized by Difficulty and Duration

Duration	Route #	Entry Point Name (and #)
Easy Trips		
2 days	#57	Homer Lake (#40)
2 days	#83	Larch Creek (#80)
2 days	#81	Saganaga Lake (#55)
2 days	#87	South Lake (#58)
2 days	#89	Duncan Lake (#60)
3 days	#67	Lizz Lake (#47)
3 days	#84	Larch Creek (#80)
3 days	#85	Magnetic Lake (#57)
4 days	#79	Seagull Lake (#54)
7 days	#82	Saganaga Lake (#55)
8 days	#80	Seagull Lake (#54)
Challenging Routes		
2 days	#59	Brule Lake (#41)
2 days	#66	Morgan Lake (#45)
2 days	#69	Meeds Lake (#48)
2 days	#73	Cross Bay Lake (#50)
2 days	#91	Daniels Lake (#61)
2 days	#93	Clearwater Lake (#62)
2 days	#95	East Bearskin Lake (#64)
3 days	#55	Baker Lake (#39)
3 days	#60	Brule Lake (#41)
3 days	#77	Brant Lake (#52)
3 days	#94	Clearwater Lake (#62)
3 days	#97	Pine Lake (#68)
3 days	#98	John Lake (#69)
4 days	#62	Bower Trout Lake (#43)
4 days	#92	Daniels Lake (#61)
4 days	#96	East Bearskin Lake (#64)
5 days	#53	Sawbill Lake (#38)
5 days	#61	Brule Lake (#41)
5 days	#68	Lizz Lake (#47)

Appendix I (continued)

Duration	Route #	Entry Point Name (and #)
Challenging Routes (continued)		
5 days	#88	South Lake (#58)
6 days	#63	Bower Trout Lake (#43)
7 days	#74	Cross Bay Lake (#50)
7 days	#76	Missing Link Lake (#51)
7 days	#78	Brant Lake (#52)
7 days	#86	Magnetic Lake (#57)
7 days	#99	North Fowl Lake (#70)
9 days	#90	Duncan Lake (#60)
Rugged Expeditions		
2 days	#64	Ram Lake (#44)
2 days	#75	Missing Link Lake (#51)
4 days	#71	Portage Lake (#65)
6 days	#58	Homer Lake (#40)
7 days	#54	Sawbill Lake (#38)
7 days	#56	Baker Lake (#39)
8 days	#65	Ram Lake (#44)
8 days	#72	Portage Lake (#65)
10 days	#70	Meeds Lake (#48)

BWCA Travel Zone Data
(Eastern Region)

NO.	TRAVEL ZONE NAME	GROUPS ENTERING NO.	GROUPS ENTERING RANK	NO. OF CAMPSITES	CAMPSITE OCCUPANCY RATE	
20	Ensign Lake	3010	5th	53	45%	
21	Snowbank Lake	2347	11th	67	33%	
22	Lake One	2959	6th	82	37%	
23	Clearwater-Petro	371	45th	20	16% →	Second Lowest in BWCA
24	South Farm Lake	1001	31st	21	30%	
25	Gabbro Lake	1228	27th	45	29%	
26	Isabella Lake	635	39th	29	18%	
27	Perent Lake	368	46th	24	18%	
28	Insula Lake	2544	10th	91	43%	
29	Kekekabic Lake	1991	12th(T)	56	35%	
30	Knife Lake	2663	8th	70	52%	
31	Hanson Lake	967	34th	26	45%	
32	Ogishkemuncie Lake	1856	14th	30	71% →	Highest in BWCA
33	Adams Lake	1233	26th	46	32%	
34	Kawishiwi Lake	1029	30th	49	34%	
35	Alton Lake	1584	18th	44	38%	
36	Mesaba Lake	1150	28th	24	40%	
37	Little Saganaga L.	1699	17th	89	35%	
38	Seagull Lake	2699	7th	63	41%	
39	Saganaga Lake	4896	3rd	85	46%	
40	Granite River	716	38th	21	51%	
41	Cherokee Lake	2584	9th	36	37%	
42	Baker Lake	987	33rd	23	29%	
43	Homer Lake	312	47th	9	30%	
44	Brule Lake	1371	22nd	34	44%	
45	Long Island Lake	1286	23rd	57	37%	
46	Winchell Lake	959	35th	39	28%	
47	Bower Trout Lake	411	44th	19	21%	
48	Pine Lake	1284	24th	39	40%	
49	Clear Water Lake	1797	16th	44	50%	

Groups Entering: No. – The total number of groups that entered this zone in 1977. (41,857 groups entered the BWCA, in all, in 1977.)

Groups Entering: Rank – With "1" being the most visited travel zone of the 49 designated.

No. of Campsites – Designated US Forest Service sites throughout the travel zone.

Campsite Occupancy Rate – Campsites occupied ÷ sites available in the travel zone during the 105 nights of the Visitor Distribution Program.

Appendix III
BWCA Travel Permit Data*
Eastern Region

EP #	Entry Point (EP) Name	Quota	No. Permits	Rank	Motor Use	1st #	Zone Rank
The Sawbill Trail Region:							
38	Sawbill Lake	14	1888	3rd	No	41	11
39	Baker Lake	3	244	29th	No	42	34
40	Homer Lake	2	197	32nd	No	43	48
41	Brule Lake	10	1055	7th	No	44	24
West Gunflint Trail Region:							
43	Bower Trout Lake	1	100	41st	No	47	45
44	Ram Lake	2	112	39th	No	47	45
45	Morgan Lake	1	41	55th	No	47	45
47	Lizz Lake }	7	359	20th	No	46	35
48	Meeds Lake }		165	35th	No	45	23
65	Portage Lake	2	24	61st	No	45	23
50	Cross Bay Lake	3	340	22nd	No	45	23
51	Missing Link Lake	5	419	18th	No	37	17
52	Brant Lake	4	360	21st	No	37	17
54	Seagull Lake	13	1482	5th	10 h.p.	38	8
55	Saganaga Lake	20	1740	4th	25 h.p.	39	3
Tip of the Arrowhead Region:							
57	Magnetic Lake	3	538	15th	No	40	38
80	Larch Creek	1	43	53rd	No	40	38
58	South Lake	3	81	45th	No	49	15
60	Duncan Lake	4	460	16th	No	49	15
61	Daniels Lake	1	76	46th	No	49	15
62	Clearwater Lake	4	431	17th	10 h.p.	49	15
64	East Bearskin Lake	5	587	14th	25 h.p.	48	25
68	Pine Lake	1	202	31st	No	48	25
69	John Lake	1	183	33rd	No	49	15
70	North Fowl Lake	2	39	57th	No	49	15

Quota: The maximum number of overnight travel permits issued at the entry point each day.

No. Permits: For all modes of travel through each entry point, including paddle canoes, motor boats, hiking and other means.

Rank: With "1" being the most popular entry point, this is based on the total number of travel permits issued for each of 79 designated BWCA entry point categories.

Motor Use: Whether or not motors are allowed through the entry point; and, if so, what horsepower limit.

1st Zone #: The first travel zone to which the entry point leads.

1st Zone Rank: The popularity of the first travel zone to which the entry point leads (#1 being most popular): 1977 U.S.F.S. data.

*Statistics are from the 1989 Visitor Distribution period (May 1-September 30)—U.S.F.S. data.

Canoe Trip Outfitters

Canoe-trip outfitters provide a valuable service to the first-time visitor to the Boundary Waters Canoe Area. For a reasonable fee, an outfitter will provide you with EVERYTHING needed for a wilderness canoe trip. All you must do is show up with your toothbrush. The outfitter will take care of the rest.

Not all people are "cut out" for wilderness tripping. If you are not sure of yourself, it is foolish to invest hundreds of dollars in your own gear and specialized clothing. After you have tried it, if it seems likely that you will return to the BWCA at least once every year, THEN you may want to own your own gear, to save money in the long run.

To obtain current brochures from the outfitters in the Eastern Region of the BWCA, write to (or call):

Minnesota Arrowhead Association
Box 204, Duluth, MN 55801
(218) 722-0874

Lutsen-Tofte Tourism Association
Box 115, Lutsen, MN 55612

Tip of the Arrowhead Association
Box 265
Grand Marais, MN 55604
(218) 387-2524 or (800) 622-4014 (in Minnesota)

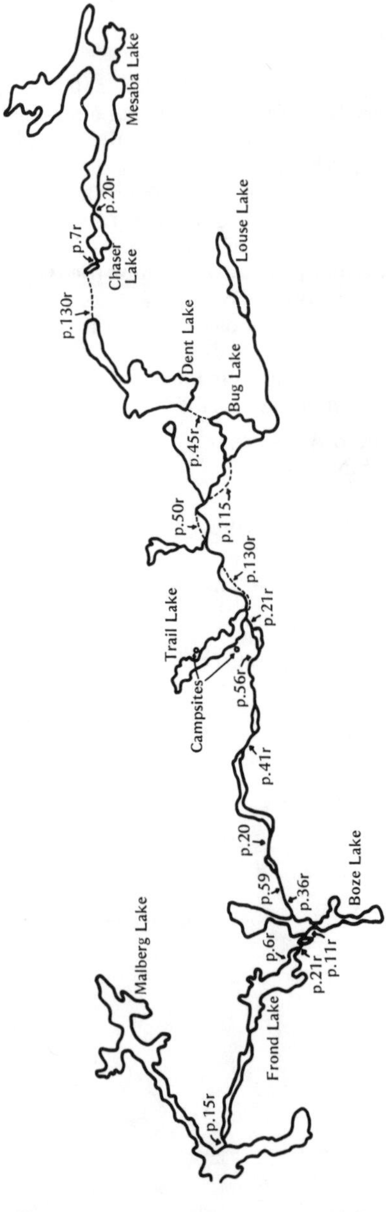

SKETCH #1: The Louse River

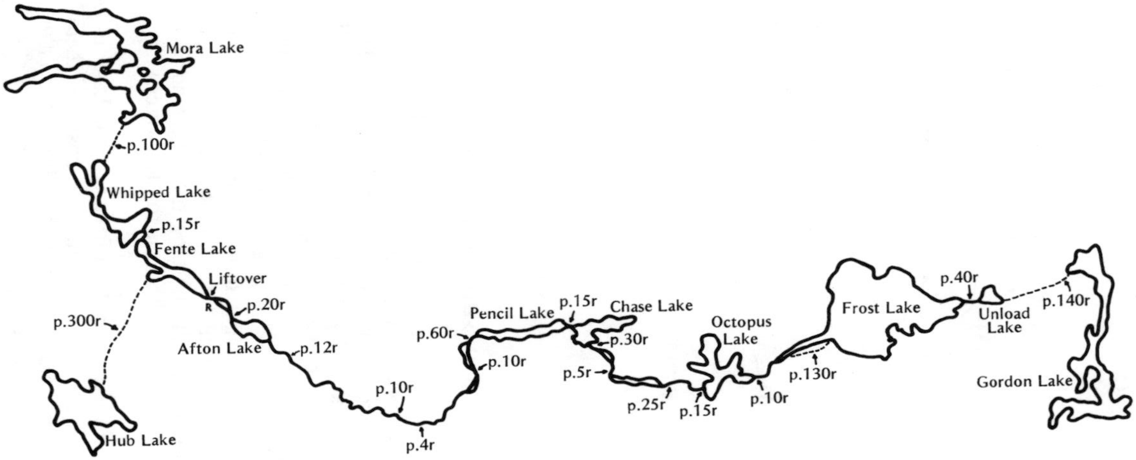

SKETCH #2: The Frost River

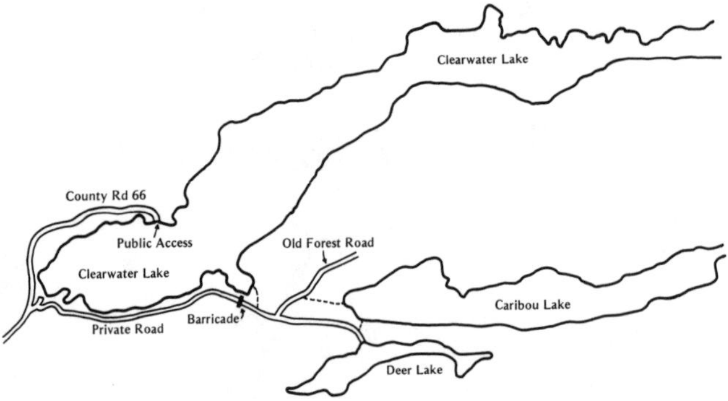

SKETCH #3: Clearwater-Caribou-Deer Lakes

Explanatory Note: The portage from Caribou Lake to Clearwater Lake is somewhat confusing, since it is not marked and it does intersect two roads. The foot trail from Caribou first climbs steadily up a gently sloping path to the summit of a ridge. At that point, it veers left and follows a narrow, old forest road (unimproved) for 20 rods to a good, private road that extends all the way from Deer Lake to County Road 66. Continue walking west (right fork) on this road for 15 rods. Just before you come to a dirt barricade across the road (to keep vehicle traffic out) the portage trail veers north (right) and continues on a good, level course to Clearwater Lake.

The last half of the portage trail from Caribou Lake to Deer Lake also follows the private road. It is possible, therefore, to portage directly from Deer Lake to Clearwater Lake, bypassing Caribou Lake entirely.

Index

Ada Creek 40, 70, 90, 95, 108
Ada Lake 40, 70, 90, 95, 108
Adams Lake 37, 101
Afton Lake 43, 49, 70, 82, 89
Agamok Lake 37, 101, 114
Ahmakose Lake 101, 120, 130, 140
Alder Lake 136, 144, 146, 150, 151
Alger Smith Lumbering Camp 62, 71
Alice Lake 114, 130
Allen Lake 57, 76, 78
Alpine Lake 111, 113, 115, 117, 120
Alton Lake 33, 36, 45, 83, 95, 108
Ambrose, Benny 111, 119
American Point 112
Anit Lake 44, 100, 107, 114, 130, 140
Annie Lake 37, 101, 111, 113, 120
Arrowhead Trail 153, 156, 161
Ashigan Lake 113–114, 119

Baker Lake 18, 38–42, 45, 166
Banadad Lake 65, 87, 89
Bat Lake 99, 107
bears 4–5
Bearskin Lake 133, 138, 139, 142
Bearskin Lodge 149
Beaver Lake 37, 101
Beth Lake 33, 36, 45, 83, 95, 108
Bingshick Creek 102, 104
Bingshick Lake 102, 104–105
Birch Lake 113, 119
Bonnie Lake 130, 140
Border Route Trail 19, 133, 142, 148, 152, 156, 162–163
Boulder Creek 37, 101
Boulder Lake 37, 101
Bower Trout Lake 18, 57–61, 64, 71, 166
Boze Lake 34, 82, 95
Brant Lake 18, 48–49, 99, 102–104, 169
Brule Bay 58, 62, 64, 166
Brule Lake 18, 50–58, 62, 64, 71, 77–78, 84, 90
Bug Lake 35, 82, 95
Burnt Lake 41, 45, 50, 84
BWCA Wilderness Act 2, 27–29

Cache Bay 112, 117
Cam Lake 49, 55
Canadian Northern Railroad 131
Canadian Shield 8
Canoe Lake 136, 144, 146, 150, 151
Cap Lake 37, 101
Carp Lake 119
Caribou Lake 65, 76–78, 80, 84, 143, 146, 150, 152, 156, 159
Caribou Rock 134, 138
Caribou Trail 46, 51
Carl Lake 74
Carp Lake 113
Cattyman Lake 114, 119
Cave Lake 65, 87, 89
Chase Lake 43, 49, 70, 82, 89
Chaser Lake 35, 82, 95
Cherokee Creek 70, 90, 95, 108
Cherokee Lake 42, 49, 54–56, 65, 70, 78, 90, 95, 108
Chippewa Indians 1
Clearwater Lake 19, 142–143, 144–148, 152, 156, 159, 170
Cliff Lake 53, 77, 84, 90
Clove Lake 123, 125, 127–128, 129, 140, 164
Cone Creek 53
Copper Lake 92
Crescent Lake Campground 46, 51
Crocodile River 19
Crooked Lake 96, 98, 100, 105, 130, 140
Cross Bay Lake 92, 94, 108
Cross River 92, 94, 108

Daniels Lake 19, 139, 141–144, 170
Deer Lake 143, 146, 150, 152
Dent Lake 35, 82, 95
Devil's Elbow Lake 125, 128, 129, 140, 164
Duck Lake 35, 38, 50, 70, 90
Dugout Lake 58, 61, 64, 71
Duncan Lake 19, 133, 136–139, 170

Eagle Mountain 19, 51

East Bearksin Lake 19, 136, 143, 144, 146, 148–153, 171
East Pike Lake 148, 159
Eddy Lake 37, 101, 111, 113, 120
Edith Lake 99, 102, 104, 106
Ella Lake 33
Elton Lake 44, 100, 107, 115, 130, 140
Ely Greenstone 8, 10
Ensign Lake 113, 119

Fay Lake 102, 105
Fente Lake 38, 43, 49, 70, 82, 89, 96
fires 3–4
Fisher, W. A. Company 22
Flour Lake 143, 144
Flour Lake Campground 141, 145
Flying Creek 102, 104
Flying Lake 99, 102, 104, 106
Fraser Lake 37, 101, 120, 130, 140
French Lake 102, 105, 107
Frog Lake 113, 119
Frond Lake 34, 82
Frost Lake 42–43, 49, 69–70, 81, 89
Frost River 43, 49, 70, 81–82, 89

Gabimichigami Lake 37–38, 101–102, 115
Gasket Lake 49, 55
Gaskin Lake 63, 69, 76, 77, 80, 84
Gateway Hungry Jack Lodge 134, 138
Gerund Lake 37, 101, 120, 130, 140
Gibson Lake 114, 119
Gillis Lake 98–99, 105, 107
Glee Lake 102, 105
Gneiss Lake 125, 128, 129, 140, 164
Gordon Lake 42, 49, 54, 56, 65, 69, 78, 81, 89, 95, 108
Gotter Lake 99, 102, 104, 106
Grace Lake 33, 36, 45, 83, 95, 108
Grace River 33, 36, 45, 83, 95, 108
Grand Marais 59
Granite River 125, 128, 129, 140, 164
Grassy Lake 53, 54, 62
Green Lake 99, 106
Gull Lake 112, 117, 120
Gunflint Lake 123–125, 127, 129, 132, 135, 140, 163–164
Gunflint Ranger Station 24
Gunflint Trail throughout

Ham Lake 18, 90–94, 108, 168
Hatchet Lake 114, 119
Hazel Lake 34, 36, 45, 83, 95, 107
Hensen Lake 57, 69, 76, 78, 80, 87, 90
Homer Lake 18, 45–49, 166
Honeymoon Bluff 133, 137
Horseshoe Lake 57, 63, 65, 69, 76–78, 80, 84
Hovland 153
Hub Lake 38, 49–50, 70, 82, 89–90, 95–96
Hubbub Lake 92
Hug Lake 35, 38, 50, 70, 90
Hungry Jack Lake 143, 144

Ice Age 9–10
Ima Lake 114, 119
Insula, Lake 114, 130, 140
Iron Lake 87–90
Iron Lake Campground 85, 131

Jack Lake 40, 42, 50, 84
Jake Lake 73–74
Jasper Lake 111, 113, 115, 120
Jean, Lake 37, 101, 111, 113, 120
John Lake 19, 135, 144, 148, 151, 157–159, 162, 171
Johnson Falls 136, 146, 150, 156, 160
Jordan Lake 114, 119
Juno Lake 47–49
Judge C. R. Magney State Park 153

Karl Lake 94, 108
Kawishiwi River 34, 36–37, 44, 83, 95, 100, 107, 114, 130, 140
Kekekabic Lake 37, 101, 120, 130, 140
Kekekabic Ponds 37, 101, 120
Kekebabic Trail 19, 38, 102, 115, 130
Kelly Lake 40–42, 45, 50, 84
Kelso Lake 35, 38, 50, 70, 90
Kelso River 35, 38, 50, 70, 90
Kiana Lake 114, 130, 140

Kingfisher Lake 111, 113, 115, 120
Kiskadinna Lake 54, 56, 69, 78, 81, 87
Kivaniva Lake 44, 100, 107, 114, 130, 140
Knife Lake 111, 113, 119, 140
Knife River 113, 119
Knight Lake 34, 36, 45, 83, 95, 107, 130
Koma Lake 34, 37, 44, 82–83, 95, 107
Kroft Lake 57, 63, 66, 68, 69

Larch Creek 19, 121–125, 169
Laurentian Divide 35, 40, 49, 55, 70, 108, 133, 163
Larch Lake 123, 125
Lily Lake 52, 54, 62
Little Caribou Lake 146, 150, 155–156, 159
Little Gunflint Lake 132, 135, 140, 163
Little John Lake 135, 144, 151, 157, 159, 162
Little Knife Lake 111, 119, 130, 140
Little North Lake 132, 135, 140, 163
Little Rock Falls 124
Little Rush Lake 65, 88, 90
Little Saganaga Lake 38, 44, 100, 107, 130, 140
Little Trout Lake 57, 63, 66, 68, 69
Lizz Lake 18, 65, 74–80, 84, 167
Long Island Lake 54, 56, 65, 69, 78, 81, 87, 89, 94–95, 108
Long Island River 54, 56, 65, 69, 78, 81, 89, 95, 108
Louse River 34–35, 82, 95
Lower George Lake 94, 108
Lower Lily Lake 135, 144, 148, 152, 156, 162
Lujenida Lake 35, 38, 50, 70, 90
Lux Lake 74

Magnetic Lake 19, 123, 125–129, 140, 164, 170
Magnetic Rock 125
Makwa Lake 44, 100, 107, 115, 130, 140
Malberg Lake 37, 44, 82, 95, 107
Maraboef Lake 125, 128, 129, 140, 164
Marshall Lake 57, 61, 64, 71
McFarland Lake 19, 135, 144, 151, 155, 160
Meeds Lake 18, 78–81, 87–88, 90, 168
Mesaba Lake 35, 38, 50, 70, 82, 90, 95
Middle Cone Lake 53, 77, 84, 90
Misquah Hills 67, 77, 84
Misquah Lake 57, 63, 66, 68, 69
Missing Link Lake 18, 93, 96, 98, 100, 105, 130, 140, 168
Molter, Dorothy 113
Moon Lake 143, 146, 150
Moose Lake 135, 144, 148, 156–157, 162
Mora Lake 38, 43–44, 96, 100, 130, 140
Morgan Lake 18, 72–74, 167
Mountain Lake 135, 142, 144, 148, 152, 156, 162–163
Mueller Lake 37, 101, 115
Mulligan, John E. 53, 62
Mulligan Lake 53, 54, 56, 62
Muskeg Creek 54, 56, 69, 78, 81, 87
Muskeg Lake 54, 69, 78, 81, 87

North Cone Lake 53, 77, 84, 90
North Fowl Lake 19, 135, 144, 148, 151, 152, 157, 160–162, 172
North Lake 132, 135, 140, 163
North Temperance Lake 40, 42, 56, 65, 70, 78, 90
Noyons, Jacques de 1

Octopus Lake 43, 49, 70, 81, 89
Ogishkemuncie Lake 37, 101, 111, 113, 115, 120
Omega Lake 54, 56–57, 69, 76, 78, 81, 87, 90
One Island Lake 87–90
Ottertrack Lake 111, 119, 130, 140
Owl Lake 96, 98, 100, 105, 130, 140

Pan Lake 44, 100, 107, 114, 130, 140
Panhandle Lake 44, 100, 107, 114, 130, 140
Pencil Lake 43, 49, 70, 82, 89
Peter Lake 102
Peterson Lake 40–42, 45
Pickle Lake 130, 140
Pigeon River 10

Pillsbery Lake 57, 76, 78, 80, 81, 87, 90
Pine Lake 135–136, 144, 146, 151, 153–155, 159–160, 171
Pine River 127, 129, 140, 164
Phoebe Lake 33, 34, 36, 45, 83, 95, 107–108
Phoebe River 34, 36, 45, 83, 95, 107
Pleistocene Epoch 7
Polly Lake 34, 36, 44–45, 83, 95, 107
Poplar Lake 65, 76–81, 84, 88, 90
Poplar Lake Lodge 74
Portage Lake 19, 85–90, 168
Powell Lake 107
Precambrian period 7–10
Primitive Management Area 26

Quetico Provincial Park 112
quotas 22

Ram Lake 18, 57, 63, 65–69, 167
Rat Lake 133, 135, 139, 163
Rattle Lake 38, 115
Red Rock Bay 117
Red Rock Lake 117
Rib Lake 94, 108
Rib Lake Trail 19
Rockwood Lodge 74
rod 21
Roe Lake 37, 101
Rose Lake 133, 135, 138, 139, 163
Ross Lake 65, 89
Round Lake 93, 96–100, 103, 104–106, 130, 140
Rove Lake 135, 142, 144, 163
Royal Lake 135, 144, 148, 151, 157, 162
Royal River 135, 144, 148, 151, 157, 162
Roy Lake Fire 110, 116
Rum Lake 57, 63, 65, 68, 69
Rush Lake 65, 87–90

Saganaga Lake 19, 111, 115–120, 125, 128–130, 140, 169
Sagus Lake 37, 101
Sawbill Lake 10, 31–33, 35–36, 38, 40–41, 45, 50, 70, 83, 90, 95, 108, 166
Sawbill Outfitters 31
Sawbill Trail 31, 51
Seagull Falls 117
Seagull Lake 18, 109–115, 117, 120, 169
Seagull River 112, 117, 120
Seahorse Lake 102, 105
Sebeka Lake 65, 87, 89
Seed Lake 113, 119
Sioux Indians 1
Sitka Lake 40, 42, 56, 65, 70, 78, 90
Skidway Lake 58, 61, 64, 71
Skipper Lake 19, 65, 88, 90
Skoop Creek 40, 70, 90, 95, 108
Skoop Lake 40, 70, 90, 95, 108
Smoke Lake 40, 45, 50, 83–84
Snipe Lake 92
South Brule River 57–58, 61, 62, 64, 71
South Cone Lake 53, 77, 84, 90
South Fowl Lake 135, 144, 151–152
South Lake 19, 131–135, 139–140, 163, 170
South Lake Trail 19
South Temperance Lake 40, 42, 50, 56, 64–65, 70–71, 78, 84, 90
Split Pine Trail 163
Spoon Lake 130, 140
Stairway Portage 163
Strup Lake 37, 101, 120, 130, 140
Superior Roadless Primitive Area 2
Swallow Lake 80, 81, 87, 90
Swamp Bay 119
Swamp Lake 19, 111, 119, 130, 140
Swan Lake 58, 61, 62, 64, 71

Tarry Lake 96, 100, 130, 140
Temperance River 40, 42, 50, 84
Thomas Creek 114, 119
Thomas Lake 114, 119–120, 130, 140
Thunder Point 111, 119
Tofte 31
Tofte Ranger Station 24
Town Lake 49, 55
Trail Lake 34–35, 82, 95
Trail's End Campground 91, 109, 115, 117
Trapline Lake 37, 100
travel zones 20–21
Trident Lake 113, 119
Tuscarora Lake 92, 93, 96, 98, 100, 105, 130, 140

Tuscarora Lodge 91

Unload Lake 49, 69, 81, 89
Upper Lily Lake 135, 144, 148, 152, 156, 162

Vern Lake 47, 49
Vern River 47, 49, 50
Vernon Lake 57, 62, 64, 71
Vesper Lake 49, 55
Virgin Lake 107
Vista Lake 57, 63, 65–66, 68, 69, 73–74
Voyageurs 1, 127, 131, 161

Wanihigan Lake 53, 54, 62, 77, 84, 90
War Club Lake 102, 105
Watap Lake 135, 143, 144, 163
Weird Lake 40, 42, 50, 84
West Fern Lake 148, 159
West Round Lake 99, 103, 104, 106
Whack Lake 47
Whipped Lake 38, 43, 96
Wilderness Act of 1964 11
Winchell Lake 53, 54, 62–63, 76, 77, 84, 90
Windigo Lodge 74
Wisini Lake 37, 101, 120, 130, 140

Zenith Lake 35, 38, 50, 70, 90

A word about canoe rests:

In the discussions of routes in this book, reference is often made to the number of canoe rests found along portages in the BWCA Wilderness. These horizontal-log resting spots were originally built and maintained throughout the Wilderness to make portaging a bit easier. Their location is included in the route descriptions to help canoeists better gauge their progress across portages. For instance, if a 320-rod portage has 9 canoe rests, you can assume that there are portage rests approximately every 32 rods along the trail (nine rests creates ten "divisions" of the portage, with the last rest at the end of the trail). It was customary for portage rests to be distributed approximately every 40–50 rods on longer portages. Shorter portages (60–100 rods long) were likely to have one portage rest near the midpoint of the trail. It has been the policy of the Forest Service in recent years, however, to not maintain these canoe rests. And, in 1993, forestry officials decided to eliminate canoe rests altogether after 1995. So you may actually find fewer rests than are mentioned in the various route descriptions, perhaps no rests at all.